Wild Kingdoms

EXPLORE AMERICA

Wild Kingdoms

THE READER'S DIGEST ASSOCIATION, INC.

Pleasantville, New York / Montreal

WILD KINGDOMS was created and produced by ST. REMY MULTIMEDIA INC.

STAFF FOR WILD KINGDOMS
Series Editor: Elizabeth Cameron
Art Director: Solange Laberge
Editors: Alfred LeMaitre, Elizabeth Warrington Lewis
Assistant Editor: Neale McDevitt
Photo Researcher: Geneviève Monette
Cartography: Hélène Dion, David Widgington
Designer: Anne-Marie Lemay
Research Editor: Robert B. Ronald
Copy Editor: Judy Yelon
Index: Christine Jacobs
System Coordinator: Éric Beaulieu
Technical Support: Mathieu Raymond-Beaubien, Jean Sirois
Scanner Operators: Martin Francoeur, Sara Grynspan

ST. REMY STAFF
PRESIDENT, CHIEF EXECUTIVE OFFICER: Fernand Lecoq
PRESIDENT, CHIEF OPERATING OFFICER: Pierre Léveillé
VICE PRESIDENT, FINANCE: Natalie Watanabe
MANAGING EDITOR: Carolyn Jackson
MANAGING ART DIRECTOR: Diane Denoncourt
PRODUCTION MANAGER: Michelle Turbide

Writers: Rita Ariyoshi—Molokai Island
Kim Heacox—The Far North
Jim Henderson—Atchafalaya Basin, Mountain Oasis
Rose Houk—The Sandhills
Steven Krolak—The Mojave Desert
Rick Marsi—The North Woods
Jeremy Schmidt—Bob Marshall Country
Scott Thybony—Cochise County
Chelle Walton—Buck Island Reef

Contributing Writers: Adriana Barton, Julie Crysler, Dolores Haggarty, Enza Micheletti

Address any comments about *Wild Kingdoms* to U.S. Editor, General Books, c/o Customer Service, Reader's Digest, Pleasantville, NY 10570

READER'S DIGEST STAFF
Editor: Kathryn Bonomi
Art Editors: Eleanor Kostyk, Nancy Mace
Assistant Production Supervisor: Mike Gallo
Editorial Assistant: Mary Jo McLean

READER'S DIGEST GENERAL BOOKS
Editor-in-Chief, Books and Home
Entertainment: Barbara J. Morgan
Editor, U.S. General Books: David Palmer
Executive Editor: Gayla Visalli
Art Director: Joel Musler

Opening photographs
Cover: Denali National Park and Preserve, Alaska
Back Cover: Monarch butterflies, Atchafalaya Basin, Louisiana
Page 2: Guadalupe Mountains National Park, Texas
Page 5: Bullfrog, Atchafalaya Basin, Louisiana

The credits and acknowledgments that appear on page 144 are hereby made a part of this copyright page.

Library of Congress Cataloging in Publication Data

Wild kingdoms.
      p.   cm.—(Explore America)
   Includes index.
      ISBN 0-89577-902-1
      1. Natural history—United States—Guidebooks.   2. United States—Guidebooks.   I. Reader's Digest Association.   II. Series.
QH104.W53   1996
508.73—dc20   96-19171

CONTENTS

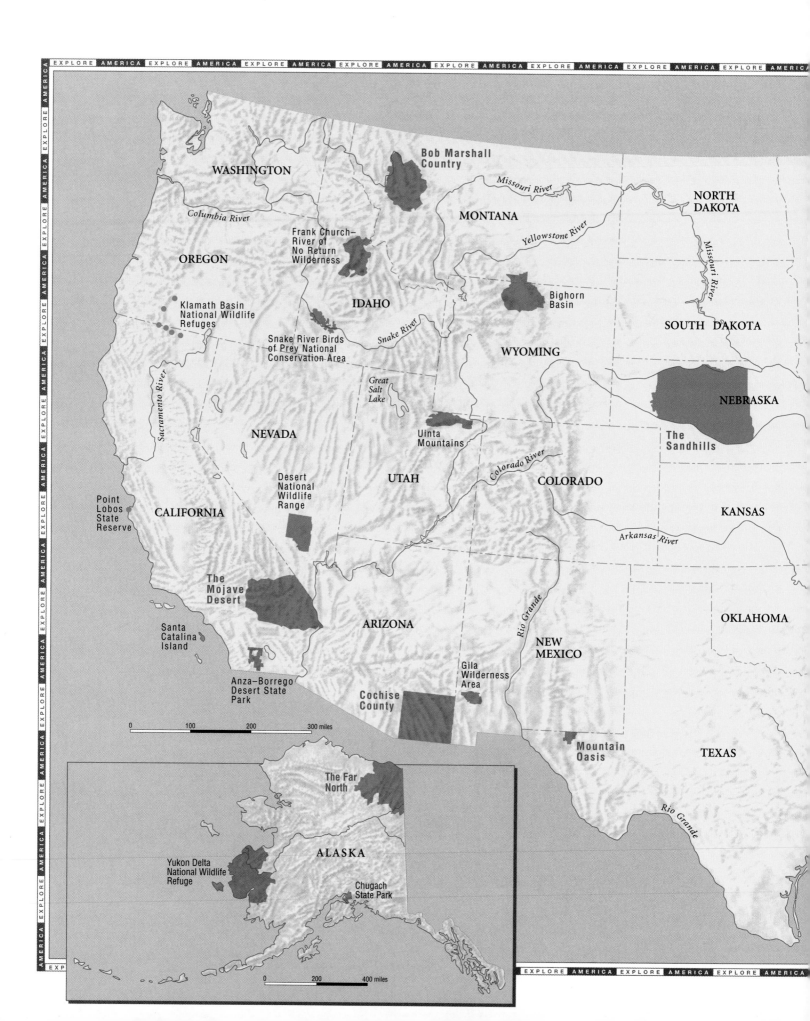

WASHINGTON

Columbia River

Bob Marshall
Country

Missouri River

MONTANA

NORTH
DAKOTA

OREGON

Frank Church–
River of
No Return
Wilderness

Yellowstone River

Missouri River

Klamath Basin
National Wildlife
Refuges

IDAHO

Bighorn
Basin

SOUTH DAKOTA

Snake River

Snake River Birds
of Prey National
Conservation Area

WYOMING

Sacramento River

*Great
Salt
Lake*

NEBRASKA

NEVADA

Uinta
Mountains

The
Sandhills

Point
Lobos
State
Reserve

Desert
National
Wildlife
Range

UTAH

Colorado River

COLORADO

CALIFORNIA

KANSAS

Arkansas River

The
Mojave
Desert

ARIZONA

OKLAHOMA

Santa
Catalina
Island

Rio Grande

NEW
MEXICO

Anza–Borrego
Desert State
Park

Gila
Wilderness
Area

Cochise
County

Mountain
Oasis

TEXAS

0   100   200   300 miles

Rio Grande

The Far
North

ALASKA

Yukon Delta
National Wildlife
Refuge

Chugach
State Park

0   200   400 miles

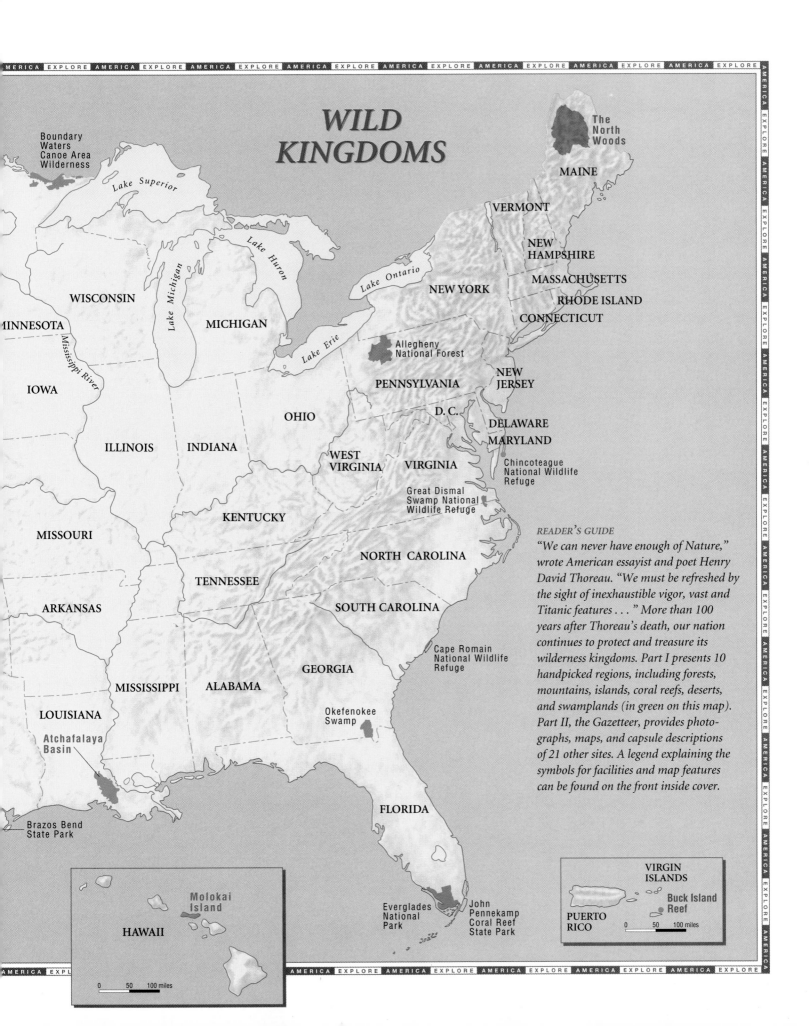

WILD KINGDOMS

Boundary
Waters
Canoe Area
Wilderness

Lake Superior

The
North
Woods

MAINE

VERMONT

NEW
HAMPSHIRE

WISCONSIN

Lake Huron

Lake Michigan

MICHIGAN

MINNESOTA

Lake Ontario

NEW YORK

MASSACHUSETTS

RHODE ISLAND

CONNECTICUT

Mississippi River

Lake Erie

IOWA

Allegheny
National Forest

PENNSYLVANIA

NEW
JERSEY

OHIO

D. C.

DELAWARE

MARYLAND

ILLINOIS

INDIANA

WEST
VIRGINIA

VIRGINIA

Chincoteague
National Wildlife
Refuge

MISSOURI

Great Dismal
Swamp National
Wildlife Refuge

KENTUCKY

NORTH CAROLINA

READER'S GUIDE

TENNESSEE

ARKANSAS

SOUTH CAROLINA

*"We can never have enough of Nature,"
wrote American essayist and poet Henry
David Thoreau. "We must be refreshed by
the sight of inexhaustible vigor, vast and
Titanic features . . ." More than 100
years after Thoreau's death, our nation
continues to protect and treasure its
wilderness kingdoms. Part I presents 10
handpicked regions, including forests,
mountains, islands, coral reefs, deserts,
and swamplands (in green on this map).
Part II, the Gazetteer, provides photographs, maps, and capsule descriptions
of 21 other sites. A legend explaining the
symbols for facilities and map features
can be found on the front inside cover.*

Cape Romain
National Wildlife
Refuge

GEORGIA

MISSISSIPPI

ALABAMA

LOUISIANA

Okefenokee
Swamp

Atchafalaya
Basin

FLORIDA

Brazos Bend
State Park

Molokai
Island

VIRGIN
ISLANDS

Buck Island
Reef

HAWAII

Everglades
National
Park

John
Pennekamp
Coral Reef
State Park

PUERTO
RICO

0   50   100 miles

0   50   100 miles

THE NORTH WOODS

The forests, lakes, and mountains of Maine's northern woods hold tight to their dark secrets.

Those who enter Maine's North Woods find themselves in the embrace of a secret world. "Far in the dark of a continent," wrote the author of *Walden*, Henry David Thoreau, describing this great dense forest where shiny black ravens soar overhead, drifting and diving as they croak out their primitive messages.

Maine's woods made a deep impression on Thoreau. He visited the state four times between 1838 and 1857 and discovered there "nature primitive—powerful gigantic aweful and beautiful, untamed forever." His essays about his wilderness experience, which were collected in a single volume published posthumously under the title *The Maine Woods*, still continue to ring true for modern-day visitors to the region.

An aerial view of Maine's great northern woods today reveals a forest that stretches out for miles. Spruce, fir, pine, and hemlock cloak the hills and valleys, the occasional brilliant white stand of birches contrasting with the deep green of the conifer boughs. Under the spreading branches,

BRAVING THE ELEMENTS
Campers pull their heavily laden sleds across the snow-covered ice of the Allagash River at sunset, above.

MIRROR IMAGE
Overleaf: Clouds hover above Mount Katahdin, meaning "highest land" in the Algonquian language of the local Abnaki Indians.

thousands of balsam fir seedlings compete for both space and light. Blue-shadowed mountains break through the thick forest in unexpected numbers. The steep granite slopes are piled here and there with worn rounded boulders. The rubble, now riddled with lichens, was ground up and left behind by melting glaciers that reshaped the watery landscape as they made their inexorable retreat.

A closer look at the terrain brings into view places where a glacier has gouged clawlike scratches into the surface of a rock ledge. The proximity also reveals glacial ponds called kettle holes that are slowly shrinking and drying throughout the woods. Created by the weight of ice blocks left behind by the glaciers, these ponds are clogged with decaying vegetation. The kettle holes attract moose, who wade up to their bellies among the water plants to escape the black flies that infest Maine from mid-May to early July.

THE WOODS AND LOGGERS

The magnificent North Woods —extending roughly 2.8 million acres from Baxter State Park and Moosehead Lake in the south to the Canadian border—are partitioned by rivers. Two of them, the Allagash and the Upper St. John, offer skilled canoeists opportunities to test their mettle. On a sunny day, the region's lakes

and ponds gleam like fragments of a shattered mirror. Moosehead, the largest lake in the area, encompasses 120 square miles. Other large lakes, such as Chamberlain and Eagle, and myriad ponds, sustain a variety of fish species, including speckled brook trout, which can be seen at twilight rising to the surface to catch flies.

The faint buzz of a chain saw in the still cool air reminds visitors of humanity's encroachment on the wilderness. Ironically it is the logging industry that has kept the woodland intact. It was initially surveyed and explored during a logging boom in

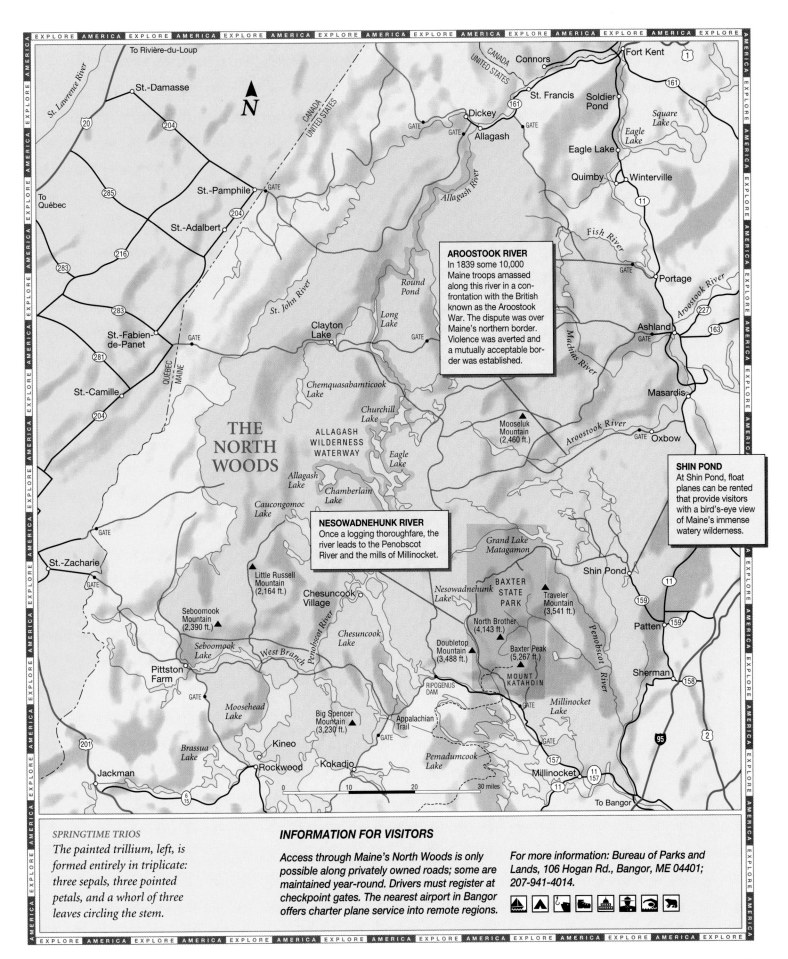

To Rivière-du-Loup

CANADA
UNITED STATES

Connors

Fort Kent

1

St.-Damasse

161

St. Francis

Soldier
Pond

Square
Lake

161

Dickey

Eagle
Lake

20

204

GATE

GATE

GATE

Allagash

Eagle Lake

St.-Pamphile

GATE

285

Quimby

Winterville

11

St.-Adalbert

204

Fish River

216

283

GATE

Portage

Round
Pond

283

Allagash River

AROOSTOOK RIVER

In 1839 some 10,000 Maine troops amassed along this river in a confrontation with the British known as the Aroostook War. The dispute was over Maine's northern border. Violence was averted and a mutually acceptable border was established.

227

Ashland

163

281

St.-Fabien-
de-Panet

GATE

St. John River

Clayton
Lake

Long
Lake

GATE

Machias River

Aroostook River

Masardis

St.-Camille

204

Chemquasabamticook
Lake

Churchill
Lake

GATE

Oxbow

Mooseluk
Mountain
(2,460 ft.)

THE NORTH WOODS

ALLAGASH
WILDERNESS
WATERWAY

Eagle
Lake

SHIN POND

At Shin Pond, float planes can be rented that provide visitors with a bird's-eye view of Maine's immense watery wilderness.

Allagash
Lake

Chamberlain
Lake

Grand Lake
Matagamon

Caucongomoc
Lake

NESOWADNEHUNK RIVER

Once a logging thoroughfare, the river leads to the Penobscot River and the mills of Millinocket.

Shin Pond

GATE

St.-Zacharie

Little Russell
Mountain
(2,164 ft.)

Nesowadnehunk
Lake

BAXTER
STATE
PARK

Traveler
Mountain
(3,541 ft.)

11

159

GATE

Chesuncook
Village

North Brother
(4,143 ft.)

159

Patten

Seboomook
Mountain
(2,390 ft.)

Penobscot River

Chesuncook
Lake

Doubletop
Mountain
(3,488 ft.)

Baxter Peak
(5,267 ft.)

Penobscot River

Sherman

Seboomook
Lake

West Branch

MOUNT
KATAHDIN

158

201

Pittston
Farm

GATE

RIPOGENUS
DAM

GATE

Millinocket
Lake

95

2

Moosehead
Lake

Big Spencer
Mountain
(3,230 ft.)

Appalachian
Trail

GATE

GATE

Brassua
Lake

Kineo

Pemadumcook
Lake

157

Jackman

Rockwood

Kokadjo

Millinocket

11
157

6
15

0   10   20   30 miles

11

To Bangor

SPRINGTIME TRIOS

The painted trillium, left, is formed entirely in triplicate: three sepals, three pointed petals, and a whorl of three leaves circling the stem.

INFORMATION FOR VISITORS

Access through Maine's North Woods is only possible along privately owned roads; some are maintained year-round. Drivers must register at checkpoint gates. The nearest airport in Bangor offers charter plane service into remote regions.

For more information: Bureau of Parks and Lands, 106 Hogan Rd., Bangor, ME 04401; 207-941-4014.

PURPLE PASSION
While opossums, raccoons, and foxes, all relish Maine's lowbush blueberries, above, no animal nurses a passion for them quite like the black bear. The berries may comprise as much as half of its summer diet.

RAW BEAUTY
The lichen-encrusted boulders of Mount Katahdin, right, are ornamented with clusters of white alpine flowers.

the 1830's, and much of the area is still owned by timber interests that produce pulp and paper, Maine's largest manufacturing industry. Were it not for the fact that logging demands vast tracts of forest, land development would have fragmented what is now the most continuous stretch of forest in the northeastern United States. Ninety percent of the Pine Tree State is wooded, including most of Aroostook County, a 6,453-square-mile chunk of Maine's North Woods that is larger than the states of Connecticut and Rhode Island combined.

Many maps of the forest fail to indicate what can be seen in the view from above—the large network of roads that spans the area. All roads are privately owned and many are permanently maintained. Fortunately for campers, hikers, and canoeists, the landowners, in partnership with Maine's natural resources agencies, have formed a consortium called North Maine Woods, Inc., that allows visitors to use the roads and to explore the land.

Visitors do face restrictions, however. Roads are controlled at checkpoints, and visitors are asked to check in and out. They are also asked to pay fees to gain access to trails, lakes, and mountains, and they need permits to use authorized sites.

Lumber trucks not only have the right-of-way on these gravel thoroughfares, they also rule the road by the roar of their great diesel engines and the weight of their cargo. When the road trembles with the weight of an enormous lumber truck bearing 25 full cords of wood, other drivers pull off to the side and allow the trucks to roar past them.

Fortunately, logging in the Maine woods is spread over such a broad area that encounters with the trucks are rare. Alone in the woods, amid fir and spruce, visitors experience the tranquillity of a world free of human presence. A carpet of duff muffles the sounds of hikers' footsteps. Mushrooms pop up everywhere. Here and there the predominant earth tones are enlivened by splashes of brilliant color. British soldier lichens grow on fallen tree trunks that rot slowly back into the soil. The lichens add a crimson relief to the muted color scheme. Where pine needles litter the ground, lady slippers, or moccasin flowers, offer up a showy display of pink, yellow, and white blooms in the dappled sunlight. Cobalt berries ripen on the stems of clintonia lilies. Old logging sites are overgrown with briar, and black bear and moose trails cut through blueberry thickets and around moss-covered boulders. Clusters of brilliant pink fireweed flowers abound.

| LAND OF CONTRASTS |

Such gentle beauty seems to belie the "universally stern and savage" world described by Thoreau. During the writer's visits to the Maine woods, his eyes were opened to their primitive power. Visitors need only ascend to the top of Mount Katahdin to see the savage face of the wilderness.

The windswept summit of Mount Katahdin rears above the surrounding landscape of Baxter State Park. Reaching 5,267 feet above sea level, Katahdin is the northern terminus of the Appalachian Trail. Thoreau himself tried to climb it but got lost in mist during the ascent. "It was, in fact, a cloud factory," he wrote later to a friend. The last three miles of the climb are especially challenging: from here to the top of Baxter Peak, the mountain's highest point, the trail rises some 4,000 feet. However, on a clear day the view from the top is spectacular and well worth the effort.

Below the mountain heights lie 202,064 acres of lakes, streams, and forest belonging to Baxter State Park. Donated to the state by Percival Baxter, a former governor, the park is for the most part a roadless wilderness, navigable only on foot. A dirt road skirts the park's perimeter, and spur roads lead to campgrounds and trailheads. The trail network consists of more than 175 miles of footpaths. Visits to Baxter State Park must be planned ahead of time. There isn't a single grocery store or gas station inside the park. Camping is allowed only at roadside campgrounds and authorized backcountry sites. Advance registration is required, since no more than 1,000 people are allowed to spend the night in the park at any one time.

Thoreau described these northern woods as obeying "no forest laws but those of nature." On his last trip, he canoed the length of Moosehead Lake as a prelude to a trip down the Allagash River. Thousands of canoeists have followed in his wake, thanks to the creation of the Allagash Wilderness Waterway. This 92-mile corridor of Allagash River, lakes, and ponds begins near the northwestern corner of Baxter State Park and ends where the north-flowing Allagash joins the St. John River at the

MIDDAY SHOWER
A cow moose, below, one of an estimated 25,000 moose in Maine, stands in gloomy contemplation of a downpour. Awkward and timid, moose reminded Thoreau of "great frightened rabbits, with their long ears and half-inquisitive, half-frightened looks."

DECEPTIVE CALM
Some portions of the Allagash River are placid, left, but the river also has some Class II whitewater sections that should be rafted only by experienced canoeists.

BERRY LOVER

The cedar waxwing, below, got its name because of its fondness for the red cedar berry and for the wax-like substance on its wingtips.

PEEKABOO

In Baxter State Park, few havens are safe from the long-tailed weasel, right. A nocturnal hunter, it darts out of its hiding places behind boulders and in hollow logs, killing small birds and mammals with a bite to the back of the neck.

northernmost point in the state. Canoeists who start at one end take a week to 10 days to emerge at the other. Established in 1966, the Allagash Wilderness Waterway was made part of the National Wild and Scenic River System in 1970. Development and logging are prohibited within 500 feet of the watery corridor.

WOODLAND CREATURES Along the waterway, beavers can be seen at dusk gnawing the saplings that grow along the edges of lakes. They grasp the small branches in their forepaws and, like picnickers eating cobs of corn, twirl them slowly as they munch on the soft outer bark. When they sense danger, the beavers duck under water and warn their neighbors of the encroaching threat by whacking their flat tails on the water's surface.

14

out during the spring and summer months. Large bulls weigh up to 1,200 pounds and measure seven feet tall at the shoulder. As comfortable in water as they are in the forest, moose plow across lakes at impressive speeds that an experienced canoeist would find hard to match.

Neither moose nor canoeist rivals the loon in swiftness. Propelled on deep dives by a pair of powerful legs, this underwater flier folds its wings flat on its back and pierces the the surface of the water like an avian spear.

Thoreau's trip on the Allagash River deepened his reverence for Maine's forested landscape. It also instilled in him a fear that the woodland might not survive the ravages of continued logging. A generation of loggers had already preceded him by the time he first tramped the Maine woods in 1846. Everywhere Thoreau walked, he encountered signs of their presence: stumps, dams, and abandoned camps littered the places where loggers had searched for and felled the gigantic white pines known as the whales of the forest. If logging continued unabated, Thoreau later wrote, the great North Woods would be depleted. The bleating of sheep would replace the loon's call, and any sizable tree would be cut down.

Thanks to the farsightedness of some conservationists and members of Maine's timber industry, Thoreau's worst fears never materialized, and the great forest has survived. "Not only for strength, but for beauty," wrote Thoreau, "the poet must, from time to time, travel the logger's path and the Indian's trail . . . far in the recesses of the wilderness." Like the poet, visitors today are likely to be changed forever by the primitive splendor of Maine's North Woods.

Elsewhere in the North Woods, hungry black bears feed on abundant patches of blueberries and raspberries. Occasionally they ratchet up the trunks of balsam firs, hunting for bugs and scarring the tender bark with their claws. In their foraging patterns, bears are creatures of habit. They walk the same trails season after season, even placing their wide, padded paws in the same footprints pressed deep in the soil by other bears.

When the sap runs in spring, moose eat the bark of a tree called the striped maple, better known as moosewood among Maine woodsmen. These massive herbivores also savor the succulent buds of alders and willows. In autumn bull moose gear up for the contests of the mating season by thrashing their antlers through thickets. Such mock battles rub the soft velvet off their huge palmate antlers— some approaching six feet in width—that branched

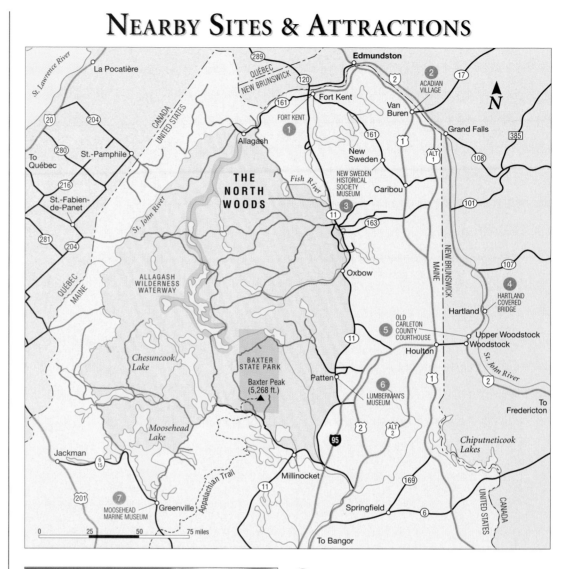

The blockhouse at Fort Kent, right, has a second-story overhang that is reminiscent of fortifications constructed in the 1700's.

1 FORT KENT, MAINE

In 1839 the state of Maine built Fort Kent in order to protect its interests in an escalating border dispute between the United States and Great Britain over the rich timberlands of northern Maine. The massive wooden fort, named for Gov. Edward Kent, was erected at the confluence of the Fish and St. John rivers. Although the fort was armed and manned, it never saw military action and was sold to private buyers in 1858; the state bought it back 31 years later for $300. The complex once included officers' quarters and a hospital, but all that remains today is the blockhouse, which was constructed of thick cedar logs hewed from the surrounding forest. Collections of paintings and antique logging tools are on exhibit inside the blockhouse. Located in Fort Kent on Hwy. 1.

2 ACADIAN VILLAGE, MAINE

Many Acadians were expelled from New Brunswick in the 1750's when they refused to pledge allegiance to the Crown of England. While some eventually made their way to Louisiana—where they were called Cajuns—a large number settled in northern

Maine. The descendants of these tenacious settlers still speak French. Acadian Village consists of a collection of replicated and relocated buildings from the 17th, 18th, and 19th centuries, including a railroad station, schoolhouse, general store, shoe shop, and church. The rustic farmhouses are appointed with antique furniture and crafts; old plows and farming equipment are on display in a simple wooden barn. The general store is stocked with merchandise of the era, and other buildings exhibit period items ranging from a barber's chair to a blacksmith's anvil. Located in Van Buren on Hwy. 1.

③ NEW SWEDEN HISTORICAL SOCIETY MUSEUM, MAINE

A small group of Scandinavian homesteaders, attracted by the gentle rolling hills and fertile farmland of Aroostook County, migrated to this region in the late 1880's and established the towns of New Sweden and Stockholm. The history of these early settlers is recorded at the New Sweden Historical Society Museum, which houses an interesting collection of their tools and hand-made furniture. The homesteaders' artifacts are on display in a replica of the original *Kapitoleum*, or town hall, and two authentic log cabins have also been decorated with family portraits and period furniture and crafts, including an elegant spinning wheel. Located in New Sweden on Hwy. 161.

④ HARTLAND COVERED BRIDGE, NEW BRUNSWICK

Legend has it that travelers who hold their breath while passing through a covered bridge will have a wish granted. But visitors who try thieir luck on the Hartland Covered Bridge may have a hard time— at 1,282 feet, it is the longest covered bridge in the world. Opened in 1901, the bridge wasn't covered over until 1922, after ice destroyed a section of it. Once the bridge had been outfitted with wooden walls and a roof, snow had to be carted onto the bridge in winter so sleds could use it. The Hartland Covered Bridge is the most famous in an area that once boasted about 400 covered bridges. As well as providing thousands of people, horses, carriages, cars, and sleds easy access to either bank of the picturesque St. John River, the bridge has also served as the site of several weddings. Located in Hartland off Hwy. 2.

⑤ OLD CARLETON COUNTY COURTHOUSE, NEW BRUNSWICK

Erected in 1833, Old Carleton County Courthouse has served as New Brunswick's first county seat, a stagecoach shop, and a site for military reviews and agricultural fairs. Now a museum, this elegant two-story clapboard building contains restored jurors' and lawyers' chambers, and a courtroom furnished with period pieces. The Carleton County Historical Society administers the courthouse and its diverse collection of historic documents, antique clothing, photographs, and 19th-century law books. One of the most unusual exhibits displays about 1,000 lead soldiers representing 18th- and 19th-century British regiments lined up with military precision. Located in Upper Woodstock on Hwy. 2.

⑥ LUMBERMAN'S MUSEUM, MAINE

The logging industry played a vital role in Maine's development, and visitors would be remiss not to make a stop at the Lumberman's Museum. Divided into a series of reconstructed logging camps, the museum houses an extensive collection of tools and equipment used by the woodsmen who logged the forests of the Pine Tree State in the 1800's and the early decades of the 1900's. One building at the site was reconstructed from the original hand-hewn logs. The various logging camps display vehicles ranging from horse-drawn logging sleds and primitive snowmobiles to steam-powered log haulers and other equipment. The blacksmith's shop exhibits a farrier, a wheelwright, and the smith's tools of the trade. There is also a replica of the camp office, where business was conducted. Evocative old photographs and paintings, as well as barrel-making demonstrations, help round out a detailed portrait of the lumberjacks who eked out a living in this isolated region. Located in Patten on Hwy. 11.

⑦ MOOSEHEAD MARINE MUSEUM, MAINE

The highlight of this museum is the *Katahdin*, a refurbished 1914 lake steamer. Built to transport the rich and famous to resorts on Moosehead Lake, the 110-foot *Katahdin* was once known as the queen of the waterways. But when the resorts closed following World War I, this resplendent boat was put to work towing log rafts up and down the lake. The *Katahdin* was retired in 1976 and is now a floating museum, preserving the history of a bygone era. From the boat's interior, which is decorated in dark mahogany, plush velvet, smooth leather, and shiny brass, visitors get a sense of the sumptuous living enjoyed by early passengers. A collection of marine artifacts is also on display. Today visitors can take short cruises aboard the *Katahdin*—the oldest steel-hulled craft built by the historic Bath Iron Works. Located in Greenville on Hwy. 15.

The covered bridge over the St. John River in Hartland, New Brunswick, above, was designated a national historic site in 1980. A commemorative stamp of the bridge was issued in 1995.

Young folk dancers, below, wear traditional Swedish costumes when they perform in the Mid-Summer Festival in New Sweden.

BUCK ISLAND REEF

*Ideals of geography and ocean current
combine to make Buck Island
one of the jewels of the Caribbean.*

At first sight, picture-perfect Buck Island teases visitors with its tropical charm. Gifted with beaches of fine white coral sand and mesmerizing water of uncounted shades of blue, the island draws daily charter boats carrying passengers eager to unravel its watery secrets and explore its onshore habitat. Yet to those who look beyond its easy grace, this tiny wind-whipped island reveals a community of plants and animals struggling to survive. Indifferent to their own beauty, island flora and fauna adapt creative strategies in order to stay alive and reproduce.

Located off the northeastern side of its lush, populated neighbor, St. Croix, Buck Island is encircled by a surface-piercing coral reef, which acts as a protective barrier. Together island and reef make up the Buck Island Reef National Monument, which has been part of the national park system for over 30 years. Through careful management, this 880-acre monument in the Virgin Islands is recapturing the natural harmony it enjoyed before Europeans settled here two centuries ago.

Just beyond the coral reef's embrace, the sea floor drops 2,000 fathoms to the depths of the Virgin Island Trough. Only experienced captains can maneuver their crafts through natural inlets to reach the nearshore reef. Here, snorkelers protected behind the barrier reef can get a closer look at the living reef, which is the watery home

ANGELIC HUES
An angelfish, below, seen in profile,
presents a golden visage. Elusive by
nature, it hides in crevices from
potential predators.

ORANGE CUP POLYPS
Overleaf: The polyps that make up
the living coral reef are tiny, hollow
cylinders of tissue crowned by wav-
ing tentacles. Equipped with sting-
ing cells, the tentacles trap and
neutralize plankton for food.

to a universe of unforgettable creatures. Brilliant
sea fans wave lazily, providing a dainty counterpoint to mammoth heads of brain coral that rise
from the briny bottom. Flame-colored elkhorn
coral thrusts out its crusty arms to reach for a passing school of graceful blue tang. A queen angelfish
makes her royal entrance, while a swaggering half-
yellow bluehead wrasse dominates his yellow
harem. The short-lived male spawns frequently

in an effort to maintain the species. When he dies,
one of his harem, in an intriguing example of gen-
der crossing, slowly metamorphoses into a male
wrasse—duo-hued colors and all.

CARIBBEAN
CARNIVAL

Fifteen feet below the ocean's
gentle swells, a Caribbean
carnival unfolds as stoplight
parrotfish, grunts, black and
white sergeant majors, French angelfish, triggerfish,
blue chromis, groupers, and trumpetfish all parade
to the coral reef to nibble and munch on their
underwater fare.

Coral reefs are living structures that are born
when millions of tiny organisms called polyps
attach themselves to a hard surface and secrete
a tough external skeleton. Over time the polyp and
its descendants build on one another, creating fantastic shapes—pillars, trees, fingers, antlers, and
bulbous brains—that rear from the sea floor. Coral
forms only under strict conditions: the right light,
temperature, salinity, motion, depth, oxygen

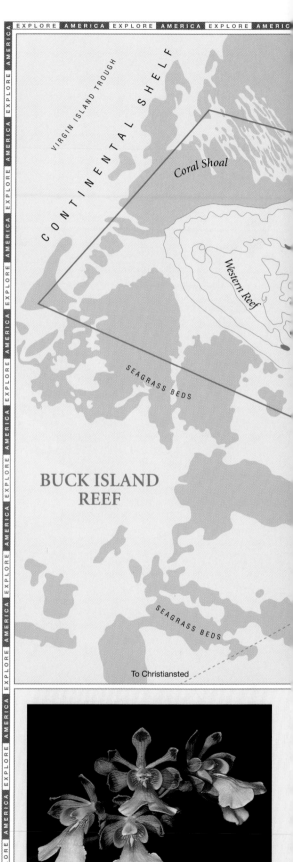

VIRGIN ISLAND TROUGH

CONTINENTAL SHELF

Coral Shoal

Western Reef

SEAGRASS BEDS

**BUCK ISLAND
REEF**

SEAGRASS BEDS

To Christiansted

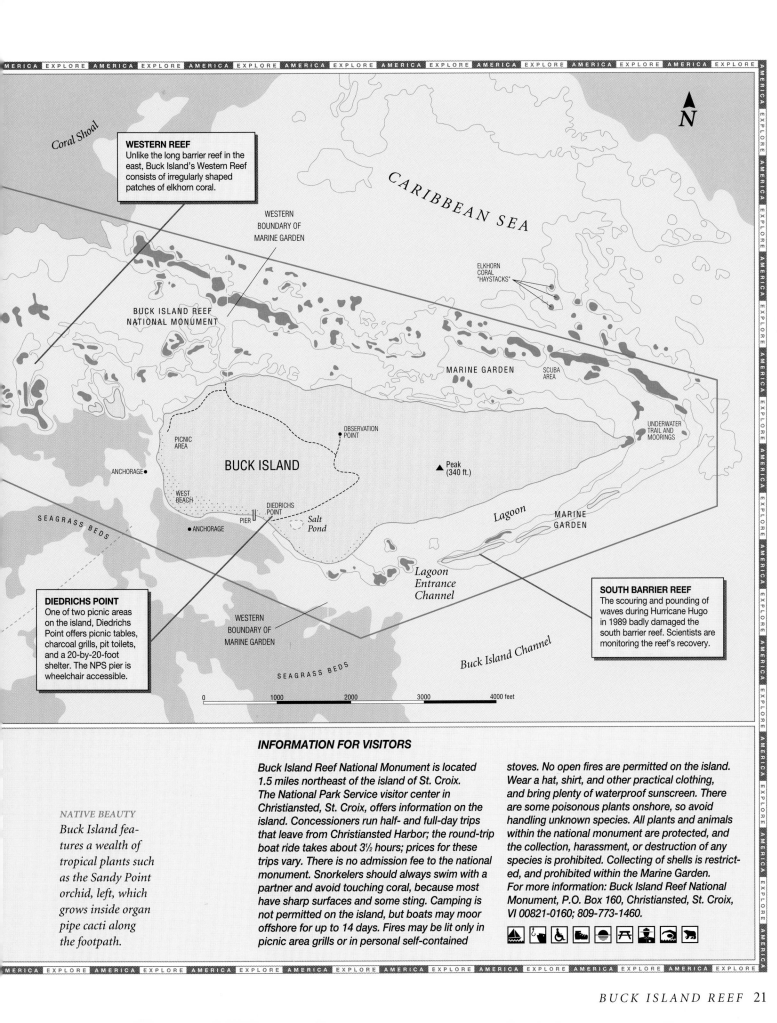

N

Coral Shoal

WESTERN REEF
Unlike the long barrier reef in the east, Buck Island's Western Reef consists of irregularly shaped patches of elkhorn coral.

WESTERN BOUNDARY OF MARINE GARDEN

CARIBBEAN SEA

ELKHORN CORAL "HAYSTACKS"

BUCK ISLAND REEF NATIONAL MONUMENT

MARINE GARDEN

SCUBA AREA

UNDERWATER TRAIL AND MOORINGS

PICNIC AREA

OBSERVATION POINT

BUCK ISLAND

▲ Peak (340 ft.)

ANCHORAGE ●

WEST BEACH

DIEDRICHS POINT

PIER

Salt Pond

● ANCHORAGE

Lagoon

MARINE GARDEN

SEAGRASS BEDS

Lagoon Entrance Channel

DIEDRICHS POINT
One of two picnic areas on the island, Diedrichs Point offers picnic tables, charcoal grills, pit toilets, and a 20-by-20-foot shelter. The NPS pier is wheelchair accessible.

WESTERN BOUNDARY OF MARINE GARDEN

SOUTH BARRIER REEF
The scouring and pounding of waves during Hurricane Hugo in 1989 badly damaged the south barrier reef. Scientists are monitoring the reef's recovery.

Buck Island Channel

SEAGRASS BEDS

0   1000   2000   3000   4000 feet

INFORMATION FOR VISITORS

NATIVE BEAUTY
Buck Island features a wealth of tropical plants such as the Sandy Point orchid, left, which grows inside organ pipe cacti along the footpath.

Buck Island Reef National Monument is located 1.5 miles northeast of the island of St. Croix. The National Park Service visitor center in Christiansted, St. Croix, offers information on the island. Concessioners run half- and full-day trips that leave from Christiansted Harbor; the round-trip boat ride takes about 3½ hours; prices for these trips vary. There is no admission fee to the national monument. Snorkelers should always swim with a partner and avoid touching coral, because most have sharp surfaces and some sting. Camping is not permitted on the island, but boats may moor offshore for up to 14 days. Fires may be lit only in picnic area grills or in personal self-contained

stoves. No open fires are permitted on the island. Wear a hat, shirt, and other practical clothing, and bring plenty of waterproof sunscreen. There are some poisonous plants onshore, so avoid handling unknown species. All plants and animals within the national monument are protected, and the collection, harassment, or destruction of any species is prohibited. Collecting of shells is restricted, and prohibited within the Marine Garden. For more information: Buck Island Reef National Monument, P.O. Box 160, Christiansted, St. Croix, VI 00821-0160; 809-773-1460.

damselfish protecting its territory against the encroachment of a blue-striped lizardfish.

Farther from shore, snorkelers might catch a glimpse of a toothy barracuda cruising through the reefs. The fierce-looking predator has an unwarranted reputation for being vicious; unless alerted to the presence of food, the great fish is unaggressive. More dangerous to humans is the scorpionfish that hides in the shallows of the shoreline reef and harms those who touch its sharp spines. It's as though the fish lies in wait, ready to punish the person who treads on the delicate coral that is so vulnerable to a careless footstep.

The reef puts up its own defense as well. Elkhorn and staghorn coral abrades the skin of those who come too close. Sea urchins, fire worms, stingrays, and barbed snails arm themselves against intruders. Mustard-colored fire coral delivers a stinging retribution to all who touch it.

Like the fire coral, much of the vegetation on land proves the foolhardiness of the notion that

SPIKY PASSENGER

A bromeliad clings to the lower branch of the fish poison tree, above. This plant's spiky rose-colored upright leaves channel rainfall into its cuplike base. Bromeliads are epiphytes, plants that take root in the branches of trees and shrubs.

supply, and global position must be present for it to grow. Thus coral develops only in the shallow waters of tropical islands, within 22° north and south of the equator. And because of prevailing winds and the rotation of the earth, it is found only off the east coasts of the world's continents.

The warm clear waters around Buck Island are an ideal reef-building environment. Some 8,000 to 10,000 years ago, colonies of polyps began to multiply as the gentle Caribbean currents brought them ample quantities of the microscopic plankton on which they feed.

MARINE GARDEN

Buck Island's principal coral reef lies within the Marine Garden that curves around the island's eastern end. The reef is closed to all fishing and collecting. A snorkel trail leads through natural passages of an elkhorn coral reef and 12-foot-deep coral grottoes. Along the trail are interpretive plaques inscribed with directional arrows and identifications.

But for many visitors the greatest thrill comes with the chance discovery of a nook or cubbyhole containing its own special microcosm. Those who take the time to observe the rhythms and patterns of the reef's sea life may be rewarded by sights such as the retractable feather duster worm, the reclusive gold-spotted eel, brilliant anemones, or a tenacious

the beautiful in nature is also always hospitable. Take, for example, the lovely hollylike Christmas bush: a lance protrudes from each point of its leaves that will puncture the skin and inflict a nasty rash. Likewise the stinging bush, also known as the touch-me-not: Its golden underleaf needlelike hairs deliver a sharp jab of pain as they lodge into the skin. Three varieties of thorny cactus—the Turk's-cap, organ-pipe, and prickly pear—are predominant on the island's arid eastern half, and maintain their defenses even when in bloom. Ground-level burgrass prohibits barefoot travel, and the thorny acacia, stinging nettle, and prickly knicker bean keep hikers to the trodden path. Most noxious of all is the manchineel, the bad boy of Caribbean botany. The plant's tiny green applelike fruit is extremely poisonous, and the sap in its leaves blisters skin on contact.

Such natural artillery is invaluable for an island more vulnerable than its name might suggest. For centuries, man imposed his will on the island, upsetting nature's delicate balance while harvesting the native hardwoods. The dark green lignum vitae tree—also called the "wood of life" for its medicinal sap—once grew in great numbers here. In a fitting tribute to this majestic tree with its fragile flowers and healing serum, 18th-century German mapmakers applied their word for lignum vitae—*Pockholz*—to the island. By the beginning of the 19th century, however, few of these remarkable trees remained on the island. European colonists found the trees' dense, self-lubricating wood, which was impervious to termites, ideally suited for everything from ship fittings and bowling balls to frames for windows and doors.

As the lignum vitae trees were being destroyed, the island became a pasture for imported goats, and parts of the land were repeatedly burned to maintain nourishing forage. A copy error on a map of the island changed its name from Pockholz to Bocken Island, which was later shortened to Bock (German for buck) possibly after the male goat.

GHOSTLY APPARITION
Rarely seen during the day, the ghost crab, above, scuttles across beaches with astonishing speed and buries itself in the sand just above the high-tide mark.

UNDERWATER FOREST
Buck Island Reef's underwater trail features sights such as the massive elkhorn coral, left, which shelters a host of smaller multicolored corals and other marine creatures, including the four-eyed butterflyfish.

Buck Island's quiet, wave-lapped beaches entice visitors to the edge of the turquoise water.

It wasn't until the late 1950's that the last of the problematic goats were removed and the island embarked on the long road to recovery.

INTRODUCED SPECIES

The goat was not the only animal whose introduction altered the island's delicate indigenous profile. In the 1880's planters brought in mongooses to eliminate the rats that were gnawing at the roots of the sugar plants. But the diurnal mongoose failed to eliminate the nocturnal rat. Instead it decimated the populations of other native creatures. Some naturalists believe the mongoose is responsible for the near-extinction of the St. Croix ground lizard, a species that survives today only on two nearby keys. Fortunately beginning in 1980 the National Park Service initiated a concerted effort to trap and remove mongooses from the island. Now only a few remain. Not so

the wily rat, whose presence in large numbers continues to plague the island.

Still, with the goats gone, the indigenous vegetation has gradually regained its hold. Along the almost mile-long nature trail that runs from beach to hilltop and back, hikers can find orchids, yellow elder (the territorial flower, known locally as ginger Thomas), the sweet smelling wild frangipani, and tiny lavender floral clusters of lantana. Waving guinea grass paints the hillsides a bright green. Sea grape trees provide cooling shade on the beach. On the island's lusher, more protected northwestern side, the reintroduced lignum vitae tree is making a comeback.

Along with the new habitat created by the restoration of plant life has come the return of such species as the endangered brown pelican—a humorous sight with its awkward dive-bomb fishing routine—and the threatened least tern, a gull-like bird.

Roosting frigatebirds, also known as man-o'-wars, await the chance to steal catch from fellow birds. Other frigatebirds float on warm air currents above the island's 340-foot peak, their distinctive W silhouettes printed against a clear blue sky. The Carribbean elaenia, (local people call it the pee whistler) and the black-whiskered vireo, or the John Phillips, also inhabit the island. Boasting an energy level rivaling that of a hummingbird, the bananaquit, or sugar bird, hunts for insects on the gumbo-limbo tree (referred to by locals as the tourist tree because its red peeling bark resembles sunburned skin).

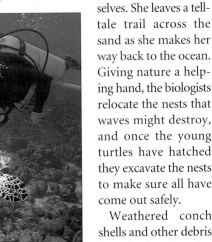

St. Croix natives once used its leaves as a salve for wounds and to reduce fever.

On the ground, hidden in the shadows from the intense tropical sun, anole lizards do their territorial push-ups. Hermit crabs overtake the discarded top shells of whelks, a local food source. Termites make trails and bulging nests on the sides of trees. Almost imperceptible but for its gleaming web, a gasteracantha spider patiently awaits dinner, as cabbage butterflies flutter by.

For a broader view of Buck Island's habitats, visitors can meander along a picturesque nature trail that follows the shore of a salt pond and leads to an observation point. From this lookout hikers can gaze at the dramatic color variations of the corals and the vast expanse of ocean. The craggy cliffs of Buck Island, like its neighbor, St. Croix, were created not by volcanic activity as for the nearby islands but by the uplifting of rock due to tectonic pressures. Locals call the claylike sedimentary layers rotten rock because it crumbles at the touch.

MIRACLE OF SURVIVAL

The seashore is a special place for the female sea turtles that nest on the island every two years or so. Three species of sea turtles are truly the island's pride. Having survived human heedlessness, they are symbolic of nature's ability to recover when given the chance. Every year endangered green, leatherback, and hawksbill turtles lumber ashore to lay their eggs, furthering one of nature's greatest miracles of survival. Two months later the hatchlings emerge, and—if they escape the attention of seabirds, mongooses, and other predators—scramble to the sea.

During the summer when hawksbill turtles nest, National Park Service biologists patrol the beaches throughout the night. Once she has laid her nest of about 140 eggs, the mother turtle abandons her offspring so that they will learn to fend for themselves. She leaves a tell-tale trail across the sand as she makes her way back to the ocean. Giving nature a helping hand, the biologists relocate the nests that waves might destroy, and once the young turtles have hatched they excavate the nests to make sure all have come out safely.

Weathered conch shells and other debris litter the shorelines festooned with algae. Not far away lies some coral rubble, broken up by surf and left stranded. The pieces of coral and the bleached trunks of fallen trees farther inland are reminders that nature can be self-destructive: over the last decade three hurricanes have temporarily tipped the island's balance.

Despite such blows to its hard-won equilibrium, Buck Island continues to astonish visitors with its resilient beauty. On the beach adjacent to the turtle sites, children picnic in the sand. At the water's edge swimmers slip into the warm, clear turquoise ocean shielded from turbulence by the barrier reef. Deeper still, masked snorkelers glide through the silent beauty of the underwater trail. As they return to St. Croix at the end of the day, a boatload of day-trippers sights a sea turtle poking its nose up like a goodwill ambassador. Each experience testifies to man's newfound role as protector and offers a splash of hope for the future.

LONG-DISTANCE NAVIGATOR
A juvenile hawksbill turtle, left, although ungainly on land, is a powerful swimmer, traveling thousands of miles every two to three years to nest on Buck Island.

LEAPING LIZARD
The anole, below, changes color from brown to green, just like its Old World cousin, the chameleon. Hooked toe pads enable the animal to cling to most surfaces.

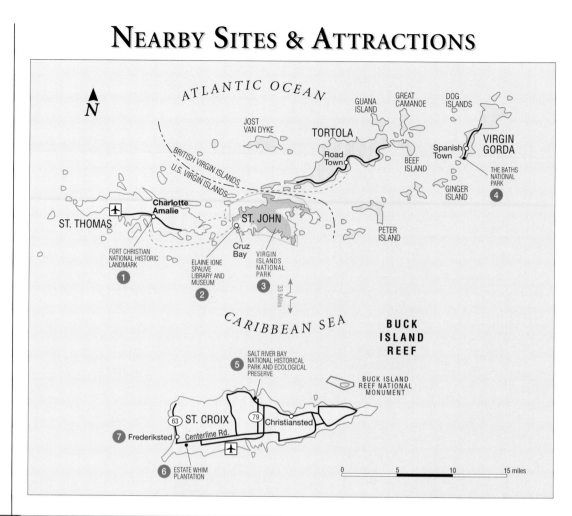

The cell doors stand wide open at picturesque Fort Christian in Charlotte Amalie, below. Named for Danish King Christian V, the fort formerly served as the town jail.

① FORT CHRISTIAN NATIONAL HISTORIC LANDMARK, ST. THOMAS

Nestled in the picturesque harbor town of Charlotte Amalie, Fort Christian is the oldest structure on St. Thomas—a distinction that hasn't been easy to achieve. Built in the mid-1600's and originally the center of the first Danish settlement on the island, the sturdy brick fort survived horrific fires and hurricanes that flattened much of the town in the 18th and 19th centuries. The rust-red fort has been used as a military outpost, church, rectory, and governor's house, and most recently as the town jail. Today the fort holds artifacts instead of prisoners in its new role as a historic landmark. Local and natural history are illustrated in exhibits that include a collection of turn-of-the-century furniture. Located in Charlotte Amalie near King's Wharf.

② ELAINE IONE SPAUVE LIBRARY AND MUSEUM, ST. JOHN

Housed in an elegant 1735 manor house, the museum is perched on a hill overlooking a tranquil bay. Its unique collection includes pre-Columbian artifacts and colonial pieces that tell the history of the West Indies and of St. John. Natural history buffs will enjoy the museum's exhibits of local marine life. The half-mile walk from the ferry dock to the museum is lined by Cruz Bay's pastel-colored houses, restaurants, and shops, which display the creations of local artisans. Located on Southside Rd. in Cruz Bay.

③ VIRGIN ISLANDS NATIONAL PARK, ST. JOHN

After buying up large tracts of land on St. John, Laurance Rockefeller donated 5,000 acres of this subtropical paradise in 1956 to the National Park

Devil's Bay Beach, left, is tucked among the tumbled boulders of The Baths National Park on the island of Virgin Gorda.

Service. Today the lush park encompasses some 7,200 acres of land and another 5,650 acres of offshore reefs. In this tropical park visitors can soak up the sun on the fine white sands of a palm-lined beach, spot a West Indian whistling-duck swimming in a pond, and meander past fragrant bay rum trees near Cinnamon Bay. The turquoise waters of the offshore living coral reef are home to spotted eagle rays, redlip blennies, stoplight parrotfish, green and hawksbill sea turtles, and schools of squid. The national park's visitor center is located a short walk from the public ferry dock in Cruz Bay.

4 THE BATHS NATIONAL PARK, VIRGIN GORDA

The huge, rounded rocks that litter the shore of Virgin Gorda—one of the largest of the British Virgin Islands—are the remnants of the volcanic upheaval that originally formed the Virgin Islands. Piled high by the water's edge, the giant stones create a series of caves and grottoes. Within the caverns, crystalline sea pools are illuminated by shafts of golden sunlight, which filter through the numerous cracks and crevices. Sheltered from the surf, these pools are ideal for swimming and snorkeling. This terrain also makes a striking backdrop for the sailboarders who ride the wind and waves. Located 1 mile southwest of Spanish Town.

5 SALT RIVER BAY NATIONAL HISTORICAL PARK AND ECOLOGICAL PRESERVE, ST. CROIX

Salt River is renowned for its coral formations, mangrove forests, varied wildlife, and historical significance. It was established in 1992 as a unit of the National Park Service. Its dedication one year later marked the 500th anniversary of the arrival of Columbus here—the only documented landing by the explorer on U.S. soil. More than 20 endangered species of plants and animals can be found at Salt River, among them hawksbill turtles, which seek shelter in the mangrove trees' half-submerged roots, and roseate terns. Beneath the water's surface, divers exploring the multicolored coral formations in the shallow depths of the bay come upon an underwater canyon that plunges to depths of 130 feet beyond the canyon wall. Within this unusual landscape coral, plants, and fish live in an ecosystem that is unique to St. Croix. Located on the northern coast of the island on Hwy. 79.

6 ESTATE WHIM PLANTATION, ST. CROIX

Several structures from this once bustling and profitable sugar plantation of the 18th century remain intact today. The largest, an oval residence built in the neo-classical style, now serves as a museum. Known as the Greathouse, the building's three-foot-thick walls are made of limestone, coral, and rubble, bonded with mortar made from molasses. Located in the corner of a sugarcane field, the Watchhouse served a dual purpose: as a lookout to spot fires and runaway slaves by night, and as a safe play area for the children of mothers who toiled in the fields during the day. The circular path made by oxen, horses, and mules in turning the mill to extract cane juice is still visible. The foundations of the laborers' village and of the sugar factory are part of this important archeological site. Located east of Frederiksted on Centerline Rd.

7 FREDERIKSTED, ST. CROIX

With its wide shady streets, Victorian houses adorned with gingerbread trim, and exquisite waterfront overlooking a blue-green sea, Frederiksted is one of the treasures of the Virgin Islands. The town was once protected from smugglers and pirates by Fort Frederick, which is located just north of the pier. Built between 1752 and 1760, the fort was recently restored to its 1820's appearance and is now a national historic site. Other attractions in the town include St. Patrick's Church, built of coral in 1843; Victoria House, constructed in 1803 and partially destroyed in the 1878 uprising of former slaves; and Bellhouse, named because its owner adorned the stairs with a multitude of bells. Located off Hwy. 63 in western St. Croix.

The windmill at Estate Whim on St. Croix, below, was used to power the grinding of sugarcane for its juice. The structure's design is based on a Dutch-style mill.

ATCHAFALAYA BASIN

The nation's largest wetland is a watery maze that shelters a staggering range of wild creatures.

The aluminum flat-bottomed boat slips its mooring on a nameless canal at the edge of the Atchafalaya Swamp, glides into Bayou Black, and begins a rambling excursion along the inky waterways that crisscross some of the most primitive, isolated, and untamed land in the United States. Here and there alligators laze on the banks of the bayous, and nutrias—fur-bearing rodents the size of bulldogs—doze on the trunks and branches of fallen willows. Eagles ride thermal updrafts toward the midday sun; great blue herons, their enormous wings outstretched, skim the opaque water in search of crawfish; and snowy egrets stand like white statues against an embankment of dark vines. The gray Spanish moss, which hangs from the towering bald cypresses like matted beards, parts now and then to show evidence of human intrusion into the region—remnants of a turn-of-the century lumber mill, a gnarled and corroded knot of pipes abandoned by oil prospectors, and a dilapidated cabin still used during the hunting season.

The navigable waterways of the Atchafalaya branch off into channels that meander into the swamp, hiding themselves under dazzling carpets of the ubiquitous purple hyacinth. This virtually indestructible water plant grows in such dense mats that it forms floating islands where other vegetation, including cattails and willow trees, take root. The hyacinth has prospered in spite of every eradication attempt using arsenals that range from threshers to chemicals and flamethrowers. The *Louisiana Conservationist* once described such a failed effort: "A full cone of fire, hot enough to melt a block of steel, was squirted on a hyacinth raft. When the fuel was exhausted, a frog emerged from the blackened mat and began sunning itself."

Though the water hyacinth is not native to the Atchafalaya River basin—a Japanese exhibitor brought the plants from South America in 1884 and distributed them as souvenirs at the New Orleans International Cotton Exposition—the plant may be the perfect metaphor for the swamp. It is delicate, fragile, and alluring in appearance but hardy, tenacious, prolific, and enduring beneath. Although humankind has invaded, plundered, and exploited the basin, it has yet to be conquered. The Atchafalaya has been assaulted and battered by tornadoes, hurricanes, and torrential rains but, like the resilient hyacinth, the swamp has always repelled the enemy and healed itself.

| DUE COURSE | Fed by the Red and Mississippi rivers, the Atchafalaya River rises from a hardwood-dotted flatland some 40 miles north- |

west of Baton Rouge. While the Mississippi snakes its way down through New Orleans to a bird's-foot delta that extends more than 100 miles into the Gulf of Mexico, the Atchafalaya (pronounced uh-chaf-uh-lie-uh) plunges due south on a more direct route to the sea. It gouges through a shifting plain of alluvial muck left by retreating glaciers at the end of the last ice age and expires in a sprawling coastal marsh below Morgan City.

The name of the river comes from the Attakapas Indian word *chafalia*, meaning "long river." Until the early 1700's the basin was the domain of the Chitamachas Indians, who hunted and fished along Grand Lake in the lower swamp. With the arrival of French explorers, the Native inhabitants retreated to more remote inner swamps. Few Europeans showed interest in the Atchafalaya, preferring to settle on drier, more open ground. Nevertheless, the late 1700's saw the arrival of French-speaking Acadians, expelled from Nova Scotia by the British. These resourceful denizens of the bayous, known as Cajuns—a corruption of the French word *Acadiens*—survived through a combination of

NESTING COUPLE

Great blue herons, above, are among the thousands of birds— belonging to more than 300 species—that can be seen in the Atchafalaya Basin.

CYPRESS SWAMP

Overleaf: Along the Atchafalaya Basin's SiBon Canal, second-growth cypress trees rise above mats of blooming water hyacinths and the stumps of giant cypresses cut down when the basin was logged during the early 1900's.

INFORMATION FOR VISITORS

I-10 is the main east–west route across the Atchafalaya Basin, and Hwy. 90 serves most of the communities on the western side and southern end of the basin. Airports at Baton Rouge and New Orleans are served by regularly scheduled flights. The climate of southern Louisiana is humid and subtropical; summer temperatures average 82°F. A state welcome center is located at State Capitol Dr. and Third St. in Baton Rouge. Local entrepreneurs offer a wide range of swamp tours and expeditions. For more information: Louisiana Office of Tourism, P.O. Box 94291, Baton Rouge, LA 70804-9291; 504-342-8119.

FESTIVE COLORS

The red needles of a dormant cypress tree, above, add a splash of color to the swamp.

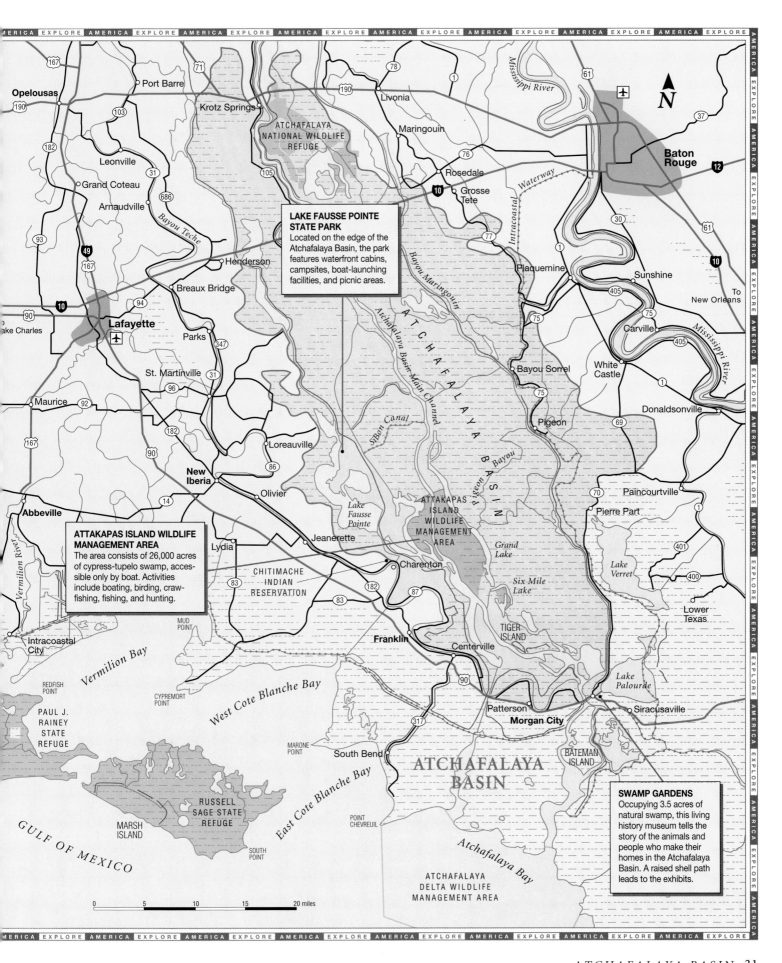

hunting, trapping, fishing, and farming. The population of southern Louisiana is a true gumbo of cultural influences, ranging from French, Spanish and Anglo-American to Caribbean and African. But the Cajuns are most closely associated with life in the Atchafalaya Basin.

A LIQUID LAND

The Atchafalaya Basin was once a 40-mile-wide swath of temperamental subtropical landscape described by the American author Harnett T. Kane in *The Bayous of Louisiana* as "liquid land . . . a place that seems often unable to make up its mind whether it will be earth or water, and so it compromises."

Then man-made flood-control channels and levees were built, shrinking the basin to an area approximately 20 miles wide and 150 miles long. Still, the Atchafalaya remains North America's largest freshwater swamp, and water still defines its history, nature, bounty, people, and its future. A liquid land discourages trespass or intrusion, imposing an isolation that has served not only to preserve an astonishing array of plant and animal life but also to protect the cultures of Chitimacha, Coushatta, and Houma Indians, and the Cajuns who later took up residence on the bayous.

As recently as 50 years ago, there were bayou towns lacking overland access. Children traveled to school by boat and commerce was also conducted that way. In the 1940's oil company workers probing the marshes near the gulf came upon villages in which secluded Houma Indians still spoke the archaic French taught to them by the earliest colonists.

LOUISIANA GATOR

The threatened American alligator, below, is found throughout the basin. Ungainly in appearance, the animal stays still for long periods of the day, but moves rapidly when aroused by the sight of food.

Lumberjacks and drilling rigs eventually penetrated the Atchafalaya Basin, not an easy feat as highway engineers discovered in the 1960's and 1970's. The swamp was so uncompromising that it took until the mid-1970's to complete Interstate 10 between New Orleans and Houston, nearly 20 years after the federal road-building program was begun. The 45-mile slab of I-10 that crosses the Atchafalaya between Baton Rouge and Lafayette is said to be, mile for mile, the most expensive piece of highway ever constructed.

To motorists who drive the elevated thoroughfare, the swamp reveals little of its true nature. However, beneath the dark canopy of willows and behind the stands of cypress, cottonwood, and red maple lies an immense wilderness whose solemn grandeur and stark beauty were described by travel author Macon Fry as being "on the scale of the Grand Canyon."

But the basin's seductions are more subtle than those of the huge canyon, whose monumentality overwhelms the eye. The Atchafalaya can be sensed, heard, and even tasted. Mountains, valleys, and great rivers evolve imperceptibly, but the swamp is like a living organism that alters its appearance under the influence of a brief rainfall or a transient wind. The canyon is breathtaking; the wet and wicked swamp is soul-stirring.

A 15-foot alligator sliding soundlessly into a cove filled with water lilies, the chatter of cicadas and hordes of tree frogs, the coo of a mourning dove, the sour odor of decaying plants and animal carcasses, the daring leap of a flying squirrel, the splash of wild irises against dense shadows—all give the swamp a tenebrous mystique, an edge of danger, a rejection of intimacy. For all that the senses absorb, it is impossible to know the swamp well.

Where it parts company from the Mississippi, the Atchafalaya River flows on an ever-rising bed of silt, past land that is really more savanna than bog, until it comes to Krotz Springs and the Atchafalaya Wildlife Refuge. From there on, signs

A curtain of Spanish moss on the branches of a venerable cypress tree, opposite page, frames the arrival of the day at Lake Fausse Pointe, in the eastern part of the basin.

of humanity are left behind and the river enters a jungle where few roads go, no townships exist, and time is virtually at a standstill.

The upland flora—red oaks, pecans, hickories, ash, ferns, wild berries, and prairie grasses—gives way to vegetation that flourishes in a wetter environment. Bald cypresses, the Louisiana state tree, stand knee-deep in the moist flats and backwaters. A century ago, cypress trees were the swamp's most coveted product. Some of them had dominated these waters for a millennium and grown to an enormous size. Then the timber companies harvested them, leaving behind waterlogged stumps that mark the merciless clear-cutting. Bald cypress, tupelo, and the fast-growing willows take root in

streams, slowing them almost to a halt. This hydrological phenomenon led the first French settlers to call the streams "sleeping water."

BAYOU BOUNTY — Like almost everything else in the swamp, the inert-looking waters are deceptive. The bayous are the lifeline of a profuse ecosystem that has sustained generations of fishermen, trappers, and hunters. Alligators, a protected species for the last 30 years, have multiplied to the point that closely regulated alligator trapping is permitted at certain times of the year.

Crawfish are a plentiful food source—for man and beast—and the basis of a major recreational sport. Fertilized in spring by an influx of silt-laden overflow from the Mississippi and Red rivers, the bayous and adjacent swamps produce a rich crop of weeds and grasses in summer. Young crawfish feed on the vegetation when the waters rise once again in spring. The ample food supply ensures spectacular volumes of crawfish. Of the 29 species of crawfish that are found in the bayous, 2 are harvested in commercial quantities. Ninety-nine percent of the nation's crawfish catch comes from Louisiana and 89 percent of that is consumed within the state. The crawfish are caught in two-foot-wide nets that are set in the water and baited with chicken. Fishermen use cane poles to haul their crawfish harvest from the water.

The swamp produces an abundance of edible delights. Frogs, crabs, white-tailed deer, wild boars, and snapping turtles that grow to a yard in width—all have been turned into table delicacies by Indians, Cajuns, and successive waves of settlers. That which is not edible has other market value. The muskrats, opossums, nutrias, otters, and raccoons hunted in the Atchafalaya Basin contribute to Louisiana's stature as the world's top fur producer. (During the 1980's more pelts were taken here than in all the Canadian provinces combined.)

BEGUILING TRAP

Dew outlines the delicate threads of a spider's web, above, disguising its deadly purpose. The Atchafalaya provides perfect breeding conditions for arachnids and insects.

fresh deposits of silt, and are today the dominant vegetation of the Atchafalaya Swamp.

Long before it reaches the coastal marsh, the river slows, feeding smaller waterways, and absorbing others. It spills its cargo of silt, dams up a canal but creates another and shares its space with sloughs, small lakes, and bayous with names like Bloody, Jakes, Sorrel, Alligator, and Pigeon. Water—on land, from the sky—is the sovereign element here. Rainfall is four to five inches a month and evaporation seems trapped as if inside a closed container, like that of a distillery.

Palmetto palms, hibiscus, and other tropical shrubs and bushes proliferate under these conditions, as do wildflowers and water plants. Besides the mettlesome purple hyacinth, American lotus and duckweed—a flowering plant so small it looks like algae—take up residence on the languid

WATCHFUL AMPHIBIAN

The cypress and tupelo forests of the Atchafalaya are home to several species of amphibians, including the gray tree frog, right.

For a long time, even the prolific Spanish moss (an epiphyte that takes root in the branches of other plants) was the basis of a minor industry. Cajuns poled skiffs through the narrow waterways to collect the generous growths that drip from the branches of live oaks and cypress trees. The moss was then sold as a stuffing for mattresses, furniture, and automobile upholstery. If they dared, the moss pickers could supplement their income by selling the skins of the copperhead and cottonmouth snakes that lurk in the branches overhanging the bayous.

Nearer to the Gulf of Mexico, the land becomes more liquid and the waterways seem to meld into one, sprawling over cordgrass flats and ridges of sediment deposited by gulf currents, inland rains, and hurricane winds. The marsh appears more fragile than the inland basin, but its sturdiness is a testament to the land's amazing resuscitative capacity. The silt ridges are called cheniers—taken from *chêne*, the French word for oak—because of the majestic live oak trees that have taken root on them. The cheniers were formed when the sediment carried west from the Mississippi Delta was blown back by storm winds onto the marshes and beaches that stretch toward Texas. Over the centuries, these ridges of alluvial deposit—some of them 20 and 30 miles long—have extended the coastline farther into the Gulf of Mexico, providing a habitat for sturdy live oaks, which in turn protect the cheniers from erosion.

High winds, though, are a constant menace, as the live oaks attest. The trees develop a permanent stoop from the constant pressure of gulf breezes and squalls. Like the other natural oddities of the Atchafalaya Basin, the tormented, misshapen oaks enhance the swamp's foreboding aspect.

Nature here is capricious and unforgiving. If the rains and winds are sufficiently forceful, they can obliterate the cheniers, but even then the marsh adapts. The silt merely disperses, scattering to form new surfaces for plant growth and for nesting waterfowl. This region is the continent's largest winter layover for migratory ducks and geese, and more than 375 species of birds—egrets, herons, brown pelicans, ospreys, great horned owls, wrens, and eagles among them—reside in the swamp.

THE HAND OF MAN

But for all its restorative abilities and survival mechanisms, the Atchafalaya is vulnerable—to both human encroachment and natural forces. Hurricanes can bring in deadly saltwater inundation, as can oil exploration crews when they cut new channels to facilitate their work. Sand and clay borne by floodwaters reshape the flat, pliable earth, destroying some habitats and

MINIATURE TRACERY
A delicate Chinese lantern vine coils around the bark of a tree trunk, below.

building new ones. Man's encroachment accelerates and magnifies the problem. Runoff from the entire Mississippi Valley, from Canada to the Gulf of Mexico, carries with it the silt and sediment gathered from half the continent.

Efforts to control the Atchafalaya's flow began in 1855 with the removal of logjams at the river's head in an attempt to open it to navigation. The elimination of the jams contributed to increased flooding and the buildup of a large delta. In the 1900's engineers began work on a system of dams and levees that would prevent flood damage to population centers such as Baton Rouge and New Orleans. Today the Atchafalaya acts as a vital floodway, receiving its ration of the Mississippi's flow (about one-third) through a man-made dam and outlet. Thus the Mississippi is prevented from changing course and joining the Atchafalaya on its shorter route to the gulf.

Overflow is deterred by dredging the Atchafalaya and building higher levees in the upper basin, protecting farms and grasslands, but significantly altering the swamp's ecological character. Deprived of

water, the cypresses wither, animals desert the area, and ponds once teeming with fish dry up.

Attempts to confine the swamp may have a more conspicuous consequence. The waters of the Mississippi dump an estimated 135 million tons of silt a year into the Atchafalaya. At one time that sediment was spread by flood waters over a much wider basin. But as the swamp has been impounded in levees to protect towns, cane fields, rice paddies, refineries, and other outgrowths of civilization, the river's silt has less room to disperse. The alluvial cargo is slowly remaking the swamp, changing the course of some streams and filling up others entirely. Many of the backwater lakes thus created provide vital habitats for fish and wildlife. In Atchafalaya Bay, sedimentation is creating wetland where there was once only water. While in the upper portion of the basin, sedimentation has filled in many former wetland areas that have since been cleared for agriculture.

In the end, the struggle may be eternal: man, the elements, the land, and the creatures all vying for a place that may ultimately be mastered by none.

If someday the Mississippi joins the Atchafalaya, the basin might well return to its beginnings. There are still remote places in the swamp where it is easy to imagine what that beginning was. Where the trees rise up against a vanishing sun and cast long shadows over a nameless bayou, the air is heavy and still, and the twilight is broken by the cry of a million creatures.

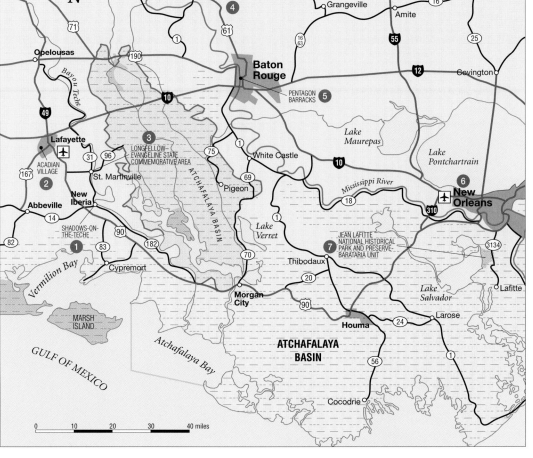

A street corner saxophonist in New Orleans, above, carries on the city's tradition as the birthplace of jazz.

① SHADOWS-ON-THE-TECHE

Surrounded by massive live oaks and overlooking Bayou Teche, the exquisitely proportioned Shadows-on-the-Teche plantation presents a fine example of Southern grace. The house was commissioned in 1831 by sugar planter David Weeks. Unfortunately Weeks died after his mansion was completed in 1834. In 1863, as Union troops occupied the main floor, Weeks' widow, Mary Clara, died peacefully in an upper bedroom. Shadows-on-the-Teche was restored to its original splendor in the 1920's by Mary Clara's great-grandson. The facade of the brick mansion features eight pearl-white columns that front full-length porches. The interior is furnished in the style of the mid-1800's and includes original family pieces. With its French doors, wide galleries, and outside staircase, the plantation house is a perfect expression of colonial charm. Located at 317 East Main St. in New Iberia on Hwy. 182 West.

② ACADIAN VILLAGE

Perched on the banks of a man-made bayou in Lafayette—Cajun Capital of the World—Acadian Village presents an authentic look at 19th-century Acadian life. From the understated dignity of the chapel to the period songbooks and old photographs on display in the quaint, simply furnished cabins, this 10-acre museum preserves and explains the culture and way of life of the early Acadians who settled in this region. Also nestled in the lush gardens is the Mississippi Valley Museum. The museum's collection includes ancient spearheads and paintings that depict the life of the missionaries who worked among the region's Native American tribes. Located in Lafayette off Hwy. 167.

③ LONGFELLOW-EVANGELINE STATE COMMEMORATIVE AREA

St. Martinville is the setting of Henry Wadsworth Longfellow's beloved poem *Evangeline*, a tale of star-crossed lovers whose tragic wanderings led them from Nova Scotia to the heart of Creole country. The poem connotes the trials of the Acadians, who eventually settled the bayous of Louisiana after they were exiled from their Canadian homeland in the early 1800's. The Longfellow-Evangeline State Commemorative Area celebrates their poignant history. The centerpiece of the 157-acre park is an Acadian cabin, a two-story adobe-and-brick edifice built about 1800. Also on the grounds is a raised plantation house in the style of the dwellings built by the first Acadian immigrants. A picnic area is located near a lagoon surrounded by trees draped with Spanish moss. Located in St. Martinville off Hwy. 31.

4 ROSEDOWN PLANTATION AND GARDENS

Sitting in regal splendor at the end of an avenue lined by 200-year-old oaks, the Rosedown mansion epitomizes 19th-century elegance. Owners Daniel and Martha Turnbull's taste for high-quality craftsmanship is evident in the two Greek Revival wings added to the small central house in 1844. The couple's style is reflected everywhere, from the stunning French wall-coverings and dazzling Italian chandeliers that grace the main house to the delicate statues and fountains sprinkled throughout the grounds. A talented amateur horticulturist, Mrs. Turnbull laid out extensive gardens and was one of the first people in the region to import azaleas. Scattered among the sweet olive trees and fragrant gardenias, 14 historic buildings, including the old milk shed and a doctor's office, give visitors a glimpse of 19th-century plantation life. Located in St. Francisville off Hwy. 61.

5 PENTAGON BARRACKS

Standing on the site of an 18th-century British fortification, the Pentagon Barracks were built over a five-year period during the early 1800's. Construction was grueling, with soldiers and slaves hauling felled cypress trees from nearby swamps and fashioning bricks from river clay and silt. Gen. Zachary Taylor was stationed here in 1848 when he received the news that he had won the presidential election. During the Civil War, the barracks were occupied at various times by troops from both sides. Today visitors can tour four of the original two-story columned buildings that enclose the parade ground. Located on State Capitol Dr. in Baton Rouge.

6 NEW ORLEANS

Using the sweat and muscle of French convicts, Jean-Baptiste Le Moyne built New Orleans on this swampy part of the Mississippi River in 1718. Rough-hewn boardwalks once spanned the muddy expanses now occupied by the ornate buildings of the city's French Quarter with their wrought-iron balconies. The lush Garden District contains the grand homes built by Americans after the Louisiana Purchase in 1803. Renowned for its Mardi Gras celebration, New Orleans offers a year-round potpourri of jazz clubs, art galleries, antique shops, and several unusual museums. Visitors can see Civil War medical equipment and an aquarium of live leeches at the New Orleans Pharmacy Museum, and trace the history of a misunderstood local religion at the New Orleans Historic Voodoo Museum. Located on Hwy. 10.

7 JEAN LAFITTE NATIONAL HISTORICAL PARK AND PRESERVE, BARATARIA UNIT

The rich natural and cultural history of the Mississippi Delta is expertly interpreted at the Barataria Preserve Unit of the Jean Lafitte National Historical Park and Preserve. The park supports a unique ecosystem that includes natural levee forests, bayous, swamps, and marshes. Along more than eight miles of hiking trails, visitors can see prehistoric Native bone and shell mounds. Keen-eyed hikers can spot drillholes used by oil exploration crews and the once-orderly rows and ditches of abandoned cotton plantations. Teeming with wildlife, the preserve is home to a host of strange creatures, including huge snapping turtles, nine-banded armadillos, and massive alligators. The park's other units, located in Thibodaux and New Orleans, are dedicated to Louisiana's Acadians, the 1815 Battle of New Orleans, and the city's French Quarter. The Barataria Unit is located 15 miles from New Orleans on Hwy. 45.

A statue of Evangeline, above, in St. Martinville, conveys the yearning of Longfellow's heroine for her lover. The town was the site of the oak tree where the Acadian girl met Gabriel.

Shadows-on-the-Teche, left, is named after the towering live oaks that shade the plantation grounds. The mansion acquired its name in the 1920's when it was restored to its former glory.

THE SANDHILLS

*Undulating sand dunes anchored
by tough grasses meet the sky
in America's heartland.*

The slightest hint of light touches the eastern sky. Soft mewing sounds fill the dark, cold air. A dozen people plod in silence across a Nebraska cornfield to a wooden observation blind, constructed on a gently sloping riverbank. Crowding inside, the dawn pilgrims peer expectantly through small portholes at countless gray islands resting on the surface of the silver waters 200 yards in front of them. The islands shift and change shape, revealing their true identity: they are birds, thousands of sandhill cranes packed body to body on sandbars in the shallow waters of the Platte River.

The birds become more distinct in the growing light. Slender, long necks. Knobby, stiltlike legs. Pale gray plumage. Red-feathered caps on their heads. Singly and in twos and fours, birds flap into the air. Their trumpeting cries merge, increasing in volume and urgency until together they reach a nearly unbearable cacophony. Then, without warning, an explosion of cries sends wave after wave of birds into the sky, the beating

WATER WORLD
The shallow, reedy potholes of the Valentine National Wildlife Refuge, above, make ideal rest spots for thousands of waterfowl on their journey south for the winter.

STRENGTH IN NUMBERS
Overleaf: Clusters of sandhill cranes line up along sandbars in the Platte River. These regal birds grow up to four feet tall and may live 30 years.

of their wings like the sound of slapping water as it splashes over a river gravel bar.

Each spring, as they travel from their southern wintering grounds to northern breeding sites, the sandhill cranes pause to rest on this 75-mile stretch of the Platte River between Overton and Grand Island in central Nebraska. The river marks the southern boundary of a vast region known as the Sandhills. From the Platte north to the Niobrara River, the Sandhills occupy nearly 19,000 square miles of Nebraska's western panhandle. Endless dunes of fine beige sand were formed eons ago from the weathered granite slopes of the Rocky Mountains. The sand was washed eastward down rivers and streams, picked up by the wind, and deposited as dunes. While most dunes are about 50 feet high, some reach as high as 400 feet.

	The rolling contours of the
GRASS-COVERED DUNES	Sandhills hint at the existence of the accumulation of sand beneath. But it takes a well-worn trail, a river's bare slope,

or a dune blowout to reveal this geological phenomenon. In most places, the sands are hidden and held together by tough grasses. Wind, fire, and native grazing, originally sculpted this countryside.

The dry surface of the land conceals an extensive natural reservoir called the Ogallala aquifer. The aquifer is a water-bearing stratum of porous rock that underlies not only Nebraska but the states of Kansas, Oklahoma, and part of Texas as well.

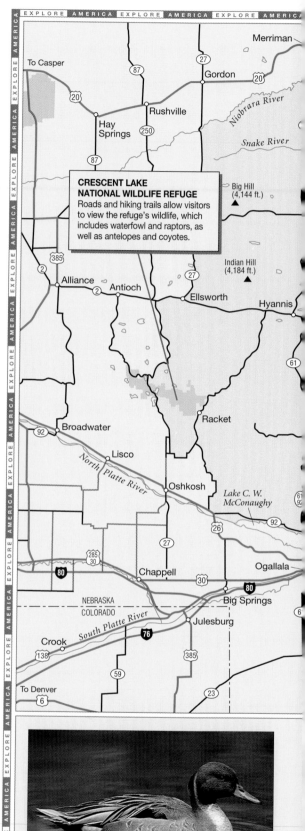

CRESCENT LAKE NATIONAL WILDLIFE REFUGE
Roads and hiking trails allow visitors to view the refuge's wildlife, which includes waterfowl and raptors, as well as antelopes and coyotes.

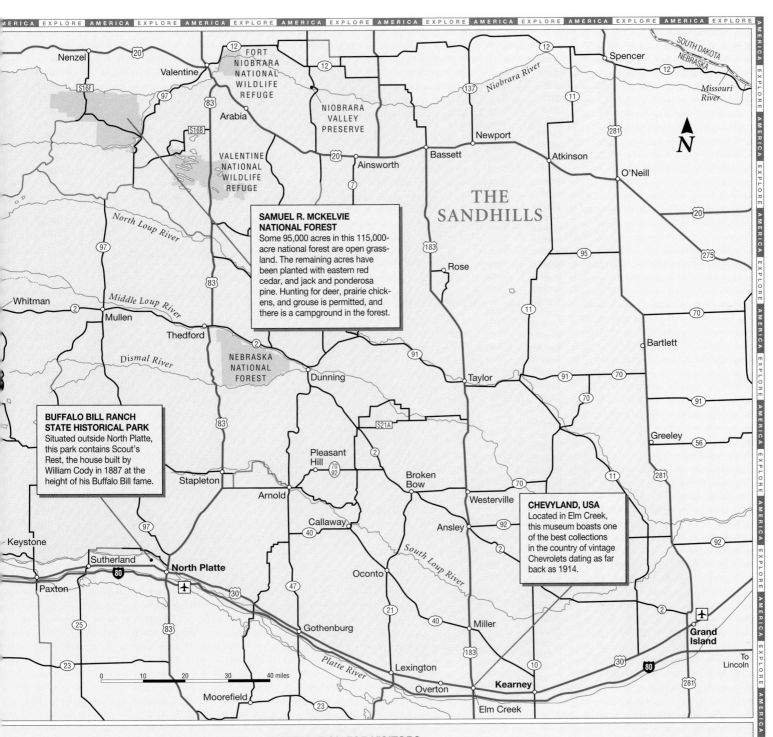

SAMUEL R. MCKELVIE NATIONAL FOREST
Some 95,000 acres in this 115,000-acre national forest are open grassland. The remaining acres have been planted with eastern red cedar, and jack and ponderosa pine. Hunting for deer, prairie chickens, and grouse is permitted, and there is a campground in the forest.

BUFFALO BILL RANCH STATE HISTORICAL PARK
Situated outside North Platte, this park contains Scout's Rest, the house built by William Cody in 1887 at the height of his Buffalo Bill fame.

CHEVYLAND, USA
Located in Elm Creek, this museum boasts one of the best collections in the country of vintage Chevrolets dating as far back as 1914.

THE SANDHILLS

DABBLING WATERFOWL

A northern pintail duck, left, paddles along a tranquil Nebraskan waterway. Pintails are dabbling ducks that, unlike divers, tip their tails skyward and dunk their heads underwater to pull small plants from the river bottom.

INFORMATION FOR VISITORS

The Valentine National Wildlife Refuge is located in the Sandhills, south of Valentine on Hwy. 83. Public roads are generally passable by two-wheel-drive vehicles, except in snowy or wet weather. Peak duck-watching months are May and October. Fort Niobrara National Wildlife Refuge is located on the edge of Valentine off Hwy. 12. Both refuges are open during daylight hours. The headquarters of the Niobrara Valley Preserve is located north of Ainsworth off Hwy. 20. The preserve's bison herd can be seen by arrangement with the preserve manager. Several outfitters, located in the town of Valentine, as well as at other outposts farther downstream, rent canoes and offer guided excursions along the Niobrara River. The nearest airport is in Grand Junction.

For more information: Nebraska Division of Travel and Tourism, Ferguson House, 700 South 16th St., P.O. Box 94666, Lincoln, NE 68509-4666; 402-471-3796 or 800-228-4307.

AMERICA EXPLORE AMERICA EXPLORE AMERICA EXPLORE AMERICA EXPLORE AMERICA EXPLORE AMERICA EXPLORE AMERICA EXPLORE AMERICA EXPLORE AMERICA EXPLORE

THE SANDHILLS 43

The porous rock acts like a sponge, soaking up snowmelt and rainwater and retaining the moisture close to the surface.

Here and there across the Sandhills, surface water nourishes an entire community of grassland and wetland creatures: prairie dogs, burrowing owls, bison, beavers, butterflies, elk, deer, fish, turtles, grouse, foxes, pronghorns, pocket gophers, and—once upon a time—wolves and grizzly bears. A multitude of small lakes and marshes provide a key habitat for the hundreds of thousands of waterfowl that converge here along the continent's great Central Flyway. Fantastic assemblages of snow geese, Canada geese, and teal, widgeon, gadwall, mallard, merganser, pintail, and shoveler ducks can be seen from the region's little-traveled coun-

ty roads. But what draws bird-watchers here from all over the world is the extraordinary sight each spring of nearly half a million gangly sandhill cranes as they congregate on the Platte River.

BIRDS OF WONDER

The cranes gather along the river during their northward migration, forming what is the densest concentration of lesser sandhill cranes in the world. The birds are joined by greater and Canadian sandhill cranes, as well as the occasional rare whooping crane. Temperatures and snow conditions govern the pace of the cranes' impressive 5,000-mile journey to their North Platte resting spot. They fly north from Mexico and Texas and usually start to arrive in Nebraska sometime during the month of February. Their numbers reach a peak by mid-March.

Hungry sandhill cranes spend their Nebraska days feeding on grain waste in the cornfields, situated mostly south of the river. The fat they store up during this stopover sustains them for the remainder of their migration to northern Canada, Alaska, or even Siberia, where they breed, nest, and raise their young with lifetime mates.

Signaled perhaps by light or by hunger, the cranes disperse into the fields each morning. At sunset they return to their river roosts to rest and sleep. The roosts protect the cranes from their primary land predator—the coyote. Unlike the frenzy of the sunrise gatherings, the evening get-togethers are quiet and leisurely. The flocks fly in disorganized skeins, blackening the sky like plumes of smoke, the whoosh of their wing beats as soft as a breeze. They circle over the river, searching for a place to alight, then lower their legs, flare their broad wings, and float to the ground.

The cranes are compressed into a smaller reach of the Platte River than in centuries past. Once a braided, shallow river a mile across, the Platte is now less than half that width. The river's flow has been drastically reduced by irrigation diversions upstream; and because big floods no longer scour the river, the banks are filling with cottonwoods and shrubs. The wide-open sandbars the birds require are few and far between. Who knows how long the cranes will continue their annual rite.

In the northern Sandhills sits the 71,516-acre Valentine National Wildlife Refuge, located near the town of the same name. Amid the hills, a multitude of prairie potholes gleam like shiny mirrors, beckoning blue-winged teals, gadwalls, canvasbacks, and beautiful ruddy ducks.

Tepee-shaped beaver lodges built of carefully laid cattails and bulrushes rise above the surface of small lakes. Their tireless architects ply the waters, poking their heads through floating mats of cattails to scan the surroundings. Muskie, bass, and muscular northern pike glide in the deep water below. On shore, red-winged blackbirds perch on the ubiquitous fencerows, giving voice to a cheerful Sunday chorus. A grasshopper sparrow alights atop the spiky stalk of a nearby yucca. In April and early May, male prairie chickens and sharp-tailed grouse strut and stomp in courtship rituals. The brightly colored sacs on both sides of their necks amplifying their calls to a boom.

ENDLESS GRASSLAND

Grass is the ecological foundation of the Sandhills. Before the arrival of the first homesteaders in the 19th century, the hills were covered by short-, mixed-, and tallgrass species—big and little bluestem, grama grasses, switchgrass, cordgrass, and the Sandhills specialties: sand lovegrass, prairie sandreed, and sand bluestem. In spite of the expansion of croplands and the growth of nonnative grasses and woody plants such as red cedar, much of the original grass remains. In June, the "green-up" month, the hills are transformed from umber and gold to emerald hues. Prairie roses, paintbrushes, coneflowers, and sunflowers brighten the ridges and the watery swales with their annual bursts of color.

MIRROR IMAGE
The still surface of the Platte River, below, reflects a cache of reeds painted by the golden brush of a brilliant sunrise.

The sky erupts over one of the thousands of waterways in the Sandhills area as a cloud of snow geese, right, takes wing at dawn.

TAKING A BREAK
In a state of alert repose, a pronghorn antelope, above, warily scans the horizon. North America's swiftest mammals, pronghorns can reach speeds of 60 miles an hour.

many as 60 million bison roamed the Great Plains in the year 1800. During the last three decades of the 19th century, hunters slaughtered the great herds until there were only a few hundred bison left. But at Fort Niobrara National Wildlife Refuge, located just east of Valentine, the nucleus of a bison herd was reintroduced, and it now numbers about 400 animals. Since the refuge's grassland can support only a limited number of bison, surplus animals are donated or sold each autumn in order to keep the herd in balance with its food supply.

MIGHTY BISON

Bison are built to withstand the harshest northwesterly winds Nebraska can deliver. When caught in a blizzard, they turn their massive wedge-shaped bodies, further protected by thick collars of brown fur, into the full force of the blast. They rub themselves against trees and wallow in the dust to shed winter fur and rid themselves of pesky insects. Mighty old bison bulls stand apart from the cows and calves, blinking their brown eyes in apparent indifference to anything going on around them. But observers are advised never to approach a bison, or any wild animal for that matter; a confrontation with a one-ton bull is not a fair contest.

Through the Fort Niobrara refuge flows the beautiful Niobrara River, now a federally designated Wild and Scenic River. This prairie river rises in Wyoming and threads eastward through the Sandhills. Niobrara is an Omaha-Ponca Indian word, variously translated as "plentiful water" or "running water." Near Merriman to the west of

Twenty thousand years ago, these prairie grasses fed herds of grazing mammals, including mammoths, mastodons, camels, antelopes, rhinoceroses, and horses. Fossilized evidence of these animals is buried in the banks of streams and in beds of volcanic ash throughout the region. With the extinction of the megafauna at the end of the Ice Age, elk, white-tailed deer, mule deer, and bison filled the ecological niches left by their predecessors.

Bison still live in Nebraska's Sandhills, though no longer in large numbers. Estimates claim that as

the refuge, the river flows through a canyon and begins to move downstream at a steady clip. Canoeists come from miles around to navigate a 25-mile section of the Niobrara below Valentine. Overwintering bald eagles proudly survey the surrounding land from their perches in the cottonwoods that line the river.

Farther east, the river wanders through the Niobrara Valley Preserve, which is administered by The Nature Conservancy. The preserve protects a fascinating intermingling of flora and fauna. Here along the famous hundredth meridian, east meets west and north meets south. For biologists and ecologists, this valley is a dream come true because plants and animals of various regions occur together or in close proximity. The West's great ponderosa pine grows directly across the river from stands of paper birch, the lovely white-barked tree of northern boreal forests. The birches grace spring-branch canyons and moss-lined streams, broken here and there by a rushing waterfall. These spring-branches arise on the southern side of the Niobrara due to a happy geological coincidence: ground-water hits an impermeable rock layer forcing the water to burst forth as a spring.

The birdlife reflects an intriguing mix of species not normally observed together: Western birds, such as black-billed magpies live side by side with ovenbirds of the eastern deciduous forests. Brown creepers and red-breasted nuthatches, birds common to the northern forests, reach their farthest southern limits here. Some animals, such as the eastern woodrat, make an unexpected appearance in this part of the Niobrara valley hundreds of miles from their usual habitat. This is also a rich zone for hybridization—quaking aspen cross with big-tooth aspen, for example, as nature continues to experiment in coming up with new species.

On a day in early April when the wind blows out of the south, the sandhill cranes leave their Platte River staging area. Their bodies fortified by feeding, the birds take flight and move in an efficient V-shape formation for their trip north. Below them bison graze, a prairie dog sniffs the air from atop a grassy mound, and a beaver slips into a cool prairie river. Next year the birds will retrace their monumental journey, flying back over the green sea of grass that hides the shifting sand. It is, in the words of biologist Paul Johnsgard, "a fragile land, a land of no straight lines, where wind becomes artist and sand has metamorphosed into art."

HAZARDOUS SHOALS
Ripples in the Niobrara River, left, indicate where the waters run shallow. Experienced canoeists must be on the lookout for these natural signposts to avoid running aground on the sandbars that lurk beneath the surface.

THE SANDHILLS 47

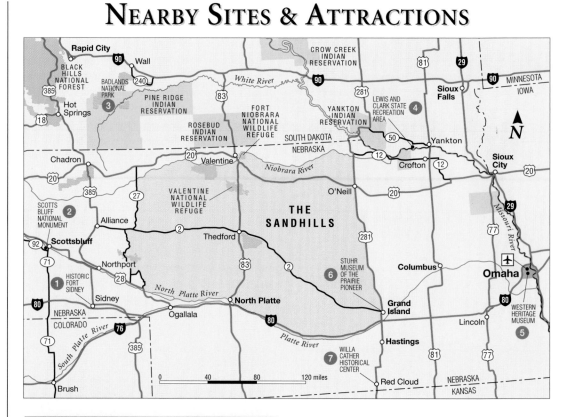

The Art Deco interior of Union Station, right, was designed by Los Angeles architect Gilbert Stanley Underwood. The building houses the Western Heritage Museum.

1 HISTORIC FORT SIDNEY, NEBRASKA

Standing guard over the broad Nebraska plain, Fort Sidney operated as a military barracks and freight depot for 25 years. Although only two of Fort Sidney's 40 original buildings remain, they are in mint condition. The Fort Sidney Post Commander's Home contains period furnishings, and the authentically restored officers' quarters, with its double front doors and two interior staircases, is maintained as a museum. The fort was established in 1867 to protect Union Pacific surveyors and work crews that were extending the rail lines westward from attacks by the Cheyenne, Sioux, and Arapaho Indians. After 1875, the fort functioned as a waystation for transporting supplies by horse-drawn freight wagons to mines and trading posts in North Dakota. The returning wagons were loaded with raw gold, which was sent East for processing. Cavalry units were dispatched from Fort Sidney during the 1876 Indian campaigns, but shortly thereafter the military outpost became obsolete. The fort closed in 1894, and some buildings were auctioned off five years later and removed from the site. Located in Sidney.

2 SCOTTS BLUFF NATIONAL MONUMENT, NEBRASKA

For pioneers traveling west along the Oregon Trail, 800-foot-high Scotts Bluff was a welcome change to the broad, flat expanse of the prairies. Millions of years ago the top of the promontory was even with the high Plains floor. While erosion lowered the level of the plain, the sandstone, volcanic ash, and silt-stone layers of the bluff were left virtually intact. Today it is the centerpiece of the 3,000-acre Scotts Bluff National Monument, which also preserves more than one-and-a-half miles of the Oregon Trail. A paved road and hiking trails take visitors to the top of the bluff, which opens up to spectacular views of the North Platte River. The visitor center presents a slide show on the history of the area and displays paintings and photographs by the renowned pioneer artist and photographer William Henry Jackson. Swifts and cliff swallows nest in the region during the summer months, and coyotes, foxes, rattlesnakes, white-tailed and mule deer, rabbits, and prairie dogs are some of the wildlife that may be spotted in the vicinity of the monument year-round. Located 2 miles south of Scottsbluff off Hwy. 92.

3 BADLANDS NATIONAL PARK, SOUTH DAKOTA

Wind, rain, and frost carved the canyons, spires, knobs, and sawtoothed ridges that gave Badlands National Park its name. Erosion also exposed layers of sediment, which range in color from ivory white to bright orange and deep pink. Animal fossils, dating back 25 to 40 million years, include sea turtles, and *brontothere*—the 10-foot-tall ancestor of the modern rhinoceros. Today the park is home to bison, coyotes, bighorn sheep, and yellow-bellied racers. Cliff swallows and rock wrens find refuge in the rock crevasses. The area receives little rainfall, but enough to support yuccas, skunk-bush sumacs, and stands of cottonwoods. The 33-mile Badlands Loop takes in this dramatic scenery. Located 7 miles south of Wall on Hwy. 240.

4 LEWIS AND CLARK STATE RECREATION AREA, NEBRASKA

The rocky bluffs that surround Lewis and Clark Lake are an abrupt change from the flat banks of the Missouri River. The Lewis and Clark Recreation Area stretches for 22 miles along the southern coast of the lake. Power boating and sailing are popular activities, and the park's sandy beaches are enjoyed by swimmers and sunbathers alike. A network of hiking trails allows visitors to explore the rolling woodlands around the lake. There are also four miles of equestrian trails and six miles of biking trails. Located 5 miles west of Yankton on Hwy. 52.

5 WESTERN HERITAGE MUSEUM, NEBRASKA

Housed in the 1931 Art Deco Omaha Union Station, the museum specializes in the history of Omaha and the railroad. The building's cream-colored terra-cotta exterior features many of the decorative elements of this architectural style. The interior of the building is virtually intact. In the station's waiting room, original chandeliers hang from the ceiling and stained-glass windows color the natural light. Visitors to the main level are greeted by interactive mannequins who describe what day-to-day life was like during the Great Depression, World War II, and the 1950's. Railroad exhibits include six turn-of-the-century train cars and a model railroad display measuring 85 feet long. Temporary exhibits include antique cars and motorcycles, and robotic dinosaurs. Located at 801 South 10th St. in Omaha.

6 STUHR MUSEUM OF THE PRAIRIE PIONEER, NEBRASKA

This 200-acre museum dedicated to 19th-century pioneer life consists of a museum, re-created rural towns, and a railroad town. The museum's main building illustrates the history of Nebraska through displays of period tools, household articles, and furnishings. Native American and Old West memorabilia are on exhibit at the Fonner Memorial Rotunda, and visitors can view a 1909 Model T and an 1880 threshing machine at the Antique Farm Machinery and Auto Exhibit. A 19th-century railroad town has been re-created from 60 structures, including a farmstead, bank, church, general store, and the house in which actor Henry Fonda was born. Three other rural settings are reconstructed here. The Pioneer Settlement is a complex of eight mid-19th-century buildings that served travelers moving West by rail; Runelsburg, a struggling community that was bypassed by the railroad, contains a country church, a school, and several other buildings; the Taylor Ranch and Ovina Station includes the original store from the 10,000-acre sheep ranch in Hall County. Located in Grand Island.

7 WILLA CATHER HISTORICAL CENTER, NEBRASKA

Willa Cather's novels evoke the hardships and challenges of late 19th- and early 20th-century prairie life. Although Black Hawk, Frankfort, and Sweet Water are fictional communities in Cather novels, visitors to Red Cloud will immediately recognize the inspiration for these places in the town where she was raised. The Willa Cather Historical Center preserves the sites in and around Red Cloud associated with Cather's books. The 1889 Farmers' and Merchants' Bank Building was owned by Silas Garber, a prominent Red Cloud resident and the model for Captain Forrester in the novel *Lady Lost*. Cather's first novel, titled *O Pioneers!*, describes Red Cloud in winter. The author's 1878 childhood home, a two-bedroom house built for her grandparents, contains original period furnishings, some of which are mentioned in her novels. Trains no longer stop at the Red Cloud depot, which was described in *My Ántonia*, considered to be Cather's best literary work. In 1923 Willa Cather was awarded the Pulitzer Prize for *One of Ours*. Red Cloud is also home of the largest circular barn in the nation. The Historical Center is located at 326 North Webster St. in Red Cloud.

The North Unit of Badlands National Park, above, is a jumble of eroded hills and gullies patched with low-growing vegetation.

Covered wagons lumber past Eagle Rock in Scotts Bluff National Monument, left, evoking the days when pioneers crossed the region by way of the Oregon Trail.

MOUNTAIN OASIS

---

*Once covered by an ancient sea,
the Guadalupe Mountains are
the remains of a giant reef.*

Wild tales about the rich veins of gold to be found in the Guadalupe Mountains of western Texas had circulated since the time of the Spanish conquistadors. Somewhere in one of hundreds of densely wooded canyons and gorges, or deep inside a cave, or buried in the rocky bed of a mountain stream lay an extensive mineral deposit of unimaginable worth.

But even at the height of the prospecting days, treasure hunters seldom ventured into this forbidding range, because it was the domain of the Mescalaro Apaches. Towering palisades and sheer, jagged escarpments discouraged all but the most intrepid adventurers from trying to breach these walls. Once, a cavalry patrol in pursuit of a band of Apaches became so hopelessly lost in the unforgiving mountains that they abandoned their horses and climbed out on foot.

This landscape is also the backdrop for the story of William C. Sublett—a fortune hunter who became a legend. In the 1880's, Sublett, whose nickname was Old Ben, took a job laying steel

for the Texas and Pacific Railroad. As the line pushed into West Texas, Old Ben started to skip work and venture into the Guadalupes. One day he returned with his pockets full of gold nuggets and the well-liquored boast that a friendly Apache had shown him a gold lode that was, according to local lore, the richest in America. As Sublett's excursions became more frequent, other gold seekers tried to pry the secret from him; but when Sublett refused even their bribes, they followed him deep into the mountains. The wily old prospector always eluded his dogged pursuers in the maze of chasms, ridges, and plateaus. Old Ben kept his secret for the rest of his years, the story goes, and was unwilling to reveal the precise location of the gold even as he lay dying. "You'll have to find it like I did," he said. His son tried, without success, well into the 20th century. Other fortune seekers, too, lusted after the gold and searched high and low, only to return empty handed.

ANCIENT FOSSIL REEF

This is an appealing legend, but modern geology reveals that wherever Old Ben managed to find his secret cache of gold, it most certainly was not extracted from this mountain range. The Guadalupe Mountains—which rise dramatically above the Carlsbad plains of southeastern New Mexico and climb to spectacular heights over the desert of remote West Texas—are not the sort of geological terrain in which gold is formed. Although the Guadalupes make up the

A STUDY IN CONTRASTS
Sunshine bathes Bone Canyon, right. The steep-sided walls of this deeply cut canyon, located on the western face of the Guadalupe Mountains, give a cross section showing the geological history of the range.

FROM OCEAN BED TO SKYSCRAPER
Overleaf: A light dusting of snow powders the craggy face of El Capitan in Guadalupe Mountains National Park. Part of a prehistoric sea wall, this striking landmark is one of the most famous peaks in the Southwest.

52

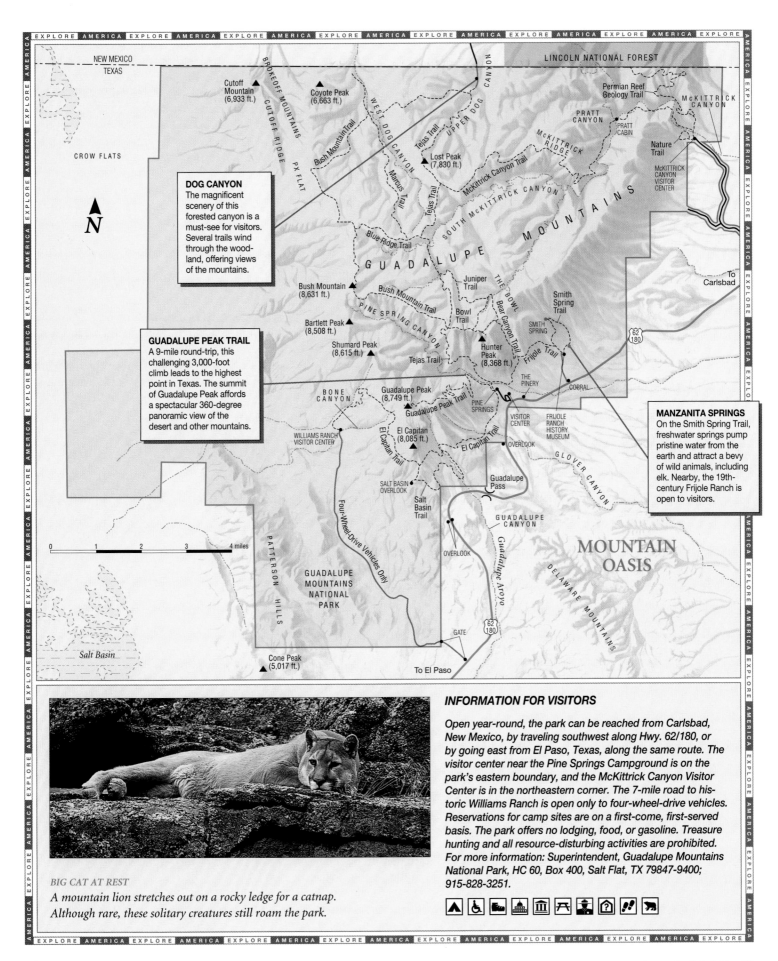

NEW MEXICO
TEXAS

LINCOLN NATIONAL FOREST

Cutoff Mountain (6,933 ft.)

Coyote Peak (6,663 ft.)

Permian Reef Geology Trail

McKITTRICK CANYON

CROW FLATS

BROKEOFF MOUNTAINS

CUTOFF RIDGE

PX FLAT

WEST DOG CANYON

UPPER DOG CANYON

Bush Mountain Trail

Tejas Trail

Marcus Trail

Tejas Trail

Lost Peak (7,830 ft.)

McKITTRICK RIDGE

PRATT CANYON

PRATT CABIN

Nature Trail

McKITTRICK CANYON VISITOR CENTER

McKittrick Canyon Trail

SOUTH McKITTRICK CANYON

N

DOG CANYON
The magnificent scenery of this forested canyon is a must-see for visitors. Several trails wind through the woodland, offering views of the mountains.

Blue Ridge Trail

G U A D A L U P E   M O U N T A I N S

THE BOWL

Bear Canyon Trail

To Carlsbad

Bush Mountain (8,631 ft.)

Bush Mountain Trail

Juniper Trail

Smith Spring Trail

SMITH SPRING

GUADALUPE PEAK TRAIL
A 9-mile round-trip, this challenging 3,000-foot climb leads to the highest point in Texas. The summit of Guadalupe Peak affords a spectacular 360-degree panoramic view of the desert and other mountains.

Bartlett Peak (8,508 ft.)

PINE SPRING CANYON

Bowl Trail

Shumard Peak (8,615 ft.)

Tejas Trail

Hunter Peak (8,368 ft.)

Frijole Trail

62 180

BONE CANYON

Guadalupe Peak (8,749 ft.)

Guadalupe Peak Trail

THE PINERY

PINE SPRINGS

VISITOR CENTER

CORRAL

FRIJOLE RANCH HISTORY MUSEUM

MANZANITA SPRINGS
On the Smith Spring Trail, freshwater springs pump pristine water from the earth and attract a bevy of wild animals, including elk. Nearby, the 19th-century Frijole Ranch is open to visitors.

WILLIAMS RANCH VISITOR CENTER

El Capitan Trail

El Capitan (8,085 ft.)

El Capitan Trail

OVERLOOK

SALT BASIN OVERLOOK

Salt Basin Trail

Guadalupe Pass

GUADALUPE CANYON

GLOVER CANYON

MOUNTAIN OASIS

Four-Wheel-Drive Vehicles Only

0 1 2 3 4 miles

PATTERSON HILLS

GUADALUPE MOUNTAINS NATIONAL PARK

OVERLOOK

Guadalupe Arroyo

DELAWARE MOUNTAINS

Salt Basin

Cone Peak (5,017 ft.)

GATE

62 180

To El Paso

BIG CAT AT REST

A mountain lion stretches out on a rocky ledge for a catnap.
Although rare, these solitary creatures still roam the park.

INFORMATION FOR VISITORS

Open year-round, the park can be reached from Carlsbad, New Mexico, by traveling southwest along Hwy. 62/180, or by going east from El Paso, Texas, along the same route. The visitor center near the Pine Springs Campground is on the park's eastern boundary, and the McKittrick Canyon Visitor Center is in the northeastern corner. The 7-mile road to historic Williams Ranch is open only to four-wheel-drive vehicles. Reservations for camp sites are on a first-come, first-served basis. The park offers no lodging, food, or gasoline. Treasure hunting and all resource-disturbing activities are prohibited. For more information: Superintendent, Guadalupe Mountains National Park, HC 60, Box 400, Salt Flat, TX 79847-9400; 915-828-3251.

Capitan glows in the morning sun like a gilded battlement, towering above the fingers of salt flats that extend toward the mighty Rio Grande.

In these mountains—a place of optical illusions, geological oddities, and climatic paradoxes—fact and fiction converge as if in a dream. Mythology and legend beg to be invented here, and phantom gold is not the only allure of this rocky vault.

WILDLIFE AND RARE TREES There is an old cowboy saying that goes, "Everything that grows west of the Pecos either sticks, stings, or stinks." A casual trip through the broad expanse of the Trans-Pecos and New Mexico badlands certainly deepens the impression of utter desolation. Yet in the middle of the bleak terrain lie these striking mountains that tens of thousands of years ago marked the southern extremity of an opulent forest running unbroken all the way to the Arctic tree line.

Rising about a mile or more above the surrounding wasteland, where summer temperatures

HIDDEN SPLENDORS
A lovely trail leads to Smith Spring, above, a tiny green oasis surrounded by trees and maidenhair ferns. Dragonflies and birds flit through the vegetation, and larger animals drink at the spring in the early morning and evening.

southernmost tip of the Rocky Mountains, they were created by far different forces than those that forged the rest of the range. The Rockies were born in a collision of continental plates; however, the Guadalupes are the remains of the world's largest fossil reef, dating back some 250 million years to the time when the Permian sea covered most of Texas and New Mexico. For eons lime-secreting algae, sponges, and other invertebrates were compacted and compressed into limestone formations that remained after the sea had evaporated. The soft floor of the reef eroded into the Rio Grande rift and the Gulf of Mexico.

This 350-mile-long fossil reef begins to reveal its magnificence in New Mexico, where extinct ocean currents incised swirls on the surface of a broad expanse of low, bald mounds. As the mountains move south into Texas, they grow taller and begin to converge in a V-shaped wedge, their steep outer slopes battered and scarred by the pounding of ancient tides. In the middle of this wedge is Guadalupe Peak, at 8,749 feet the highest point in Texas. Farther to the south, the reef ends abruptly, and the most familiar monument in the entire range comes into view. The craggy face of El

of 115°F bake the earth, the highest peaks conceal an enormous bowl of land supporting diverse wildlife. A Rocky Mountain conifer forest thrives here, nursed by cooling clouds carrying vital moisture from the Pacific Ocean. This is the heart of the park, a luxuriant highland oasis of green splendor. Douglas firs, junipers, and ponderosa pines blanket the knolls and plateaus. Canyons soar and lowlands stretch

out below, splashed with aspens, bigtooth maples, walnut trees, and a variety of ferns.

This unique habitat is home to the rare and striking Texas madrone tree, which keeps its thick coat of leaves year-round, blooms white flowers in the spring, and ripens with red berries in the fall. The agave also flourishes here, a desert lily that was arguably just as important to the mountain Apaches as bison once were to the Plains Indians. The Apaches made flour for bread out of the plant's starchy roots. They used its tough leaves and thorny tips for thread and needles, or ground them into soap. The seeds were converted to meal, and the petals were eaten raw.

More than 900 species of plants are found within the park's boundaries, along with 60 species of mammals, 289 of birds, and 55 of reptiles and amphibians. In the desert, lizards, snakes, kangaroo rats, coyotes, and mule deer can be seen foraging in the cool air at sunrise and sunset. When night falls, skunks and badgers cautiously make their rounds. Lush canyons teem with wildlife, including jackrabbits, porcupines, and gray foxes.

Noble-looking elk roam freely across the highland terrain as do black bears and the stealthy mountain lion. Great horned owls, red-tailed hawks, peregrine falcons, vultures, and golden eagles soar high above a land little changed since lumbering dinosaurs trod the earth.

A male wild turkey, below, displays his plumage to attract a female. Unlike their domesticated cousins, these birds are remarkably swift and agile. Benjamin Franklin thought so highly of the wild turkey that he wanted to make it the national bird.

VOLATILE ELEMENTS

Despite its being designated a national park in 1972, this 86,415-acre expanse of land is one of the least visited and least spoiled of America's wild regions. Its isolation and imposing mountain front have helped preserve its pristine character against the inexorable march of civilization. Driving along Highway 62/180 between El Paso and Carlsbad, travelers often pass within a few miles of El Capitan or Guadalupe Peak without realizing that just on the other side of the mountains lies a glorious land of scenic wonder. It is not surprising then, that the more accessible Carlsbad Caverns National Park toward the northern end of the range draws five times as many visitors as Guadalupe.

There are 80 miles of marked trails in Guadalupe Mountains National Park, but make no mistake, this is wild country. With no paved roads, the park must be explored on foot, and regardless of the path a hiker chooses, the way is not always easy. The longer rocky trails leading to the high country demand strong legs and sturdy boots. Temperatures vary widely from the lowlands to the mountaintops. Sudden afternoon thunderstorms make rain

SHEDDING ITS SKIN

The paper-thin red bark of a Texas madrone, right, peels away to expose its new growth. Found primarily in central Texas, the trees rarely reach heights over 20 feet.

gear a necessity. Reliable sources of water are scarce in the backcountry, and supplies must be carried in.

Wind, too, is unpredictable—and often violent. At the higher elevations, 70-mile-an-hour winds are common, and gales of more than twice that speed have been recorded. The winds come howling from the west, collide with the western escarpment, roil over the 8,000-foot rims of Bush Mountain and Bartlett and Shumard peaks, and pour through the canyons like angry seas. The U.S. Meteorological Service monitoring station on Guadalupe Peak once measured gusts of 170 miles an hour—just before the station was blown away.

Visitors to the region sometimes forget that this sublime landscape is also fragile. Precautions must be taken to protect the unspoiled beauty of the park. Open fires are prohibited, and refuse must not be left behind. For this reason, campsites are limited and the National Park Service discourages extended trips except by all but the most experienced and best-equipped backpackers.

Perhaps the most important equipment visitors can bring to this harsh land is an acceptance of the insignificant part they play in nature's scheme here. These are the people most likely to be rewarded.

OUTLAW'S HIDEOUT	Named after a bank robber, Kid McKittrick, who used to hide out here, McKittrick

Canyon is a labyrinthine passage that slowly unfolds its wonderful secrets to the patient explorer. Bubbling streams rise intermittently along the twisting canyon bottom and disappear again beneath the earth. In autumn, oak, walnut, and maple leaves light the landscape in hues of amber and red that turn iridescent in the sunlight. A 10.9-mile trail, beginning at the McKittrick Canyon Visitor Center, passes two picnic areas on its way to McKittrick Ridge, which

rises 2,300 feet in elevation. It's a tough climb, but worth the effort. The ridge offers a sweeping vista of the forested depression known as the Bowl and of the mountains to the south.

The caves and recesses that bore through McKittrick Canyon hold the remains of Arctic mammals—musk-oxen, saber-toothed tigers—pushed south by the last ice age. Artifacts fashioned by nomadic tribes of hunters and gatherers, nearly 10,000 years ago, have been found at the head of the canyon and in other neighboring canyons. These include wicker baskets, stone implements, fire pits, and at least 20 pictographs on the walls of McKittrick Canyon. Hermit Cave in Last Chance Canyon contains 12,000-year-old spearheads buried among wicker cases.

At Pine Springs, located just east of Guadalupe Peak, the signs of more recent human intrusion are evident. Mescal pits mark the former presence of the Apaches—driven into these mountains by the U.S. Army after clashing with settlers in the 1850's and 1860's. Stone-and-mud ruins are all that remain of a way station of the Butterfield Overland Mail stagecoach line in service during the mid-1800's. A 9.4-mile trail, which skirts the base of El Capitan, leads to the now-deserted Williams Ranch, built in 1908 at the base of a 3,000-foot rock cliff on the west side of the park. Once homesteaders tried to make a go of it here, ranching up to 3,000 head of longhorn cattle on the mountain slopes nearby.

But these man-made constructions are subjugated by the stark, timeless mountains and the deserts that surround them. This strange terrain—a prehistoric seabed that now reaches toward the sky—is a keeper of the earth's secrets. Here the fossils of creatures that lived 350 million years ago bear witness to the mystery of a world gone by. But, as anyone who crosses this range will attest, the splendors of yesterday live on today.

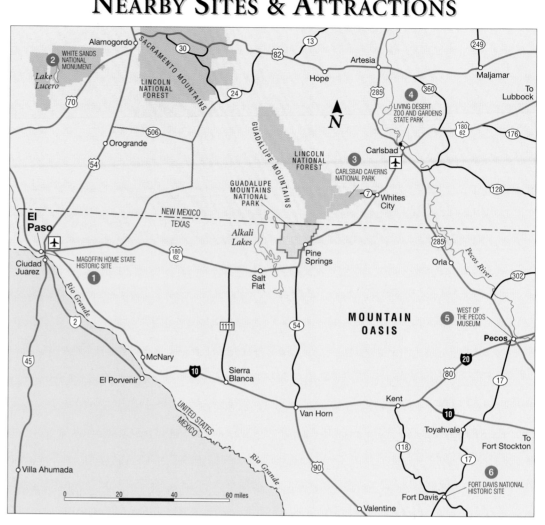

Formed over millions of years by the gentle trickle of water, the stalagmites and stalactites of the Carlsbad Caverns, below, create an unearthly subterranean world.

The porch of the post commander's house in Fort Davis, right, is painted orange by a Texas sunset.

① MAGOFFIN HOME STATE HISTORIC SITE, TEXAS

One of the best surviving examples of Southwest Territorial architecture is the 19th-century home of pioneer Joseph Magoffin. A county judge, customs officer, and four-term mayor of El Paso, Magoffin built his 19-room house between 1870 and 1890. The three-foot-thick walls are made of adobe—sunbaked bricks of earth and straw—covered in plaster, and scored to simulate Greek Revival stonework. Wood for floors and ceiling beams was hauled from New Mexico's Sacramento Mountains. The rooms of the house are filled with Victorian furniture. Located at 1120 Magoffin Ave. in El Paso.

② WHITE SANDS NATIONAL MONUMENT, NEW MEXICO

These 275 square miles of dunes make up the world's largest gypsum dune field. Over the centuries, rain and melted snow transported gypsum from the San Andres Mountains to dry Lake Lucero. Evaporation then transformed the dissolved gypsum into crystals, which the wind carried into the dune field. Rising as high as 60 feet, the sand dunes receive enough moisture for yucca, saltbush, and cottonwood to grow. Lizards, mice, and insects have adapted to the surroundings by camouflaging themselves to blend in with the sand. Geology and biology exhibits at the visitor center provide an excellent introduction to dune diversity. Located 52 miles northwest of Las Cruces on Hwy. 70.

3 CARLSBAD CAVERNS NATIONAL PARK, NEW MEXICO

Once described as the Grand Canyon with a roof on it, the park's largest cave contains more than 30 miles of passageways. Some 250 million years ago the area was a giant limestone reef on the edge of an inland sea. As the sea disappeared, the reef crumbled under its own weight. Hydrogen sulfide gas rose, dissolved the limestone, and created huge hollow expanses with spectacular nether formations. Although most of the caves are reserved for experienced spelunkers, three miles of paved trails in the main cave are open to the public. Visitors journeying underground will marvel at the unique formations of stalagmites, stalactites, columns, and helictites in each of the cavern's main chambers. The Big Room is the largest subterranean chamber in North America: measuring some 1,800 feet long, 1,100 feet wide, and over 200 feet tall, it is the size of 14 football fields and takes one hour to tour. Highlights of this chamber include the crystal-clear Mirror Lake and the Bottomless Pit—a 140-foot-deep hole. The caverns were discovered in the 19th century when settlers noticed a large number of bats flying out of the earth's core. Each day at dusk more than 1 million Mexican free-tailed bats pour from the cave in search of insects. Visitors can watch the bats' spectacular flight—over 5,000 bats come out per minute—from a nearby amphitheater. Park headquarters are located 6 miles west of Whites City off Hwy. 62/180.

4 LIVING DESERT ZOO AND GARDENS STATE PARK, NEW MEXICO

The animals living in this park have been brought here because they were injured or ill. Some 40 species of animals, birds, and reptiles can be found recuperating in this protected environment, including mountain lions, Mexican wolves, rattlesnakes, bison, badgers, eagles, and roadrunners. Once the animals are healthy again, they are returned to the wild. Those whose injuries make them unfit for the rigor of the Chihuahuan Desert become permanent residents of the park. Visitors stroll along a pleasant 1.3-mile self-guiding trail through a varied landscape of gypsum hills, sand dunes, pines, and arroyos. Sotol, cholla, prickly pear, agave cactus, yucca, and over 450 other plant species grow within the park's boundaries. A visitor center contains mineral and paleontological exhibits, and a greenhouse is stocked with succulents and desert cacti. Located 1 mile north of Carlsbad off Hwy. 285.

5 WEST OF THE PECOS MUSEUM, TEXAS

This impressive collection of frontier artifacts, housed in a restored 1896 saloon and 1904 hotel, brings to life the Western heritage of the Pecos area. The museum contains some 50 rooms that focus on aspects of 19th-century life in a railroad town. A doctor's office, church, and schoolroom are all re-created and contain various 100-year-old artifacts. Several rooms are devoted to ranching and to the West of the Pecos Rodeo, which has been in existence since 1883. Cowboy clothing, saddles, and Western art, as well as the new women rancher and cowgirl collections are also on display here. Other fascinating exhibits include a replica of the famed Judge Roy Bean's saloon and courthouse, built in 1936, and the grave of the Gentleman Gunfighter, Clay Allison. Located on First and Cedar streets in the town of Pecos.

6 FORT DAVIS NATIONAL HISTORIC SITE

Military authorities built Fort Davis in 1854 when the Apache and Comanche Indians launched raids on travelers heading to California. During the period 1854 to 1891, soldiers served as escorts for mail and freight trains through the area. The cavalry also used the fort as a base for its occasional offensives against Indian forces. Named for Jefferson Davis, before he became president of the Confederacy, the fort was one of many Western outposts to accept black soldiers. The fort originally housed 200 to 300 soldiers in 20 buildings. Today half of those buildings have been restored, including the officers' quarters, enlisted men's barracks, servants' quarters, commanding officer's quarters, officers' kitchen, and the post commissary. During the summer months, costumed interpreters help re-create the frontier spirit of this historic fort. Located in Fort Davis.

A solitary yucca, below, pokes through the rippled desert floor of White Sands National Monument in New Mexico.

BOB MARSHALL COUNTRY

*Straddling the Continental Divide,
this rugged Montana wilderness
is nature at its most sublime.*

Forester and writer Bob Marshall once declared that "a man must work hard for his wilderness enjoyment." Taking his own words to heart, the young Forest Service official was famous for his long walks; he would regularly cover 40 to 50 miles on a hike, and he was known to clock 70 miles in a single day. Marshall believed that nature areas should be big enough so that a hiker could travel for two weeks without recrossing his or her own tracks. Due in large part to his tireless efforts to preserve the wild, there is enough wilderness left in western Montana for a visitor to do just that. A 950,000-acre preserve called the Bob Marshall Wilderness was established the year after his death in 1939; the surrounding country bears the imprint of his powerful influence.

Approaching Bob Marshall country from the east, where prairie rolls up and breaks against the mountains, a traveler experiences the first impact of the dramatic sights in store. In one of the

LONE WOLF

Peering cautiously from behind a tree, a shy gray wolf, right, looks nothing like the man-eater of folk-lore. In reality most wolves will go miles out of their way to avoid contact with humans.

CALM BEFORE THE STORM

The quiet waters of the Freezeout Lake Wildlife Management Area, below, become a flurry of activity during the spring and fall, when up to a million waterfowl throng the area.

continent's grandest gestures, the Rocky Mountain Front rises nearly unbroken from the plains of central Montana and marches steadily northward. For several hundred miles, this rampart of rock presents a single facade of jagged peaks.

Breathtaking to behold, these snow-capped behemoths present an imposing natural barricade. On the flats, roads scurry every which way. However, through the expanse from Montana to the Yukon, only six highways cross the Continental Divide. This translates into some big stretches of roadless land—none more sizable than the wild country that sprawls on either side of the Continental Divide south of Glacier National Park. Bounded by a million or so acres of national forest on three sides, the region measures roughly 65 miles from east to west and 100 miles from north to south.

UNSPOILED OASIS

Overleaf: The crystalline waters of a small alpine pool in the Ahorn Basin of the Bob Marshall Wilderness sparkle like a rare gem within a mountain vault.

Three federally designated wilderness preserves lie in the heart of this area, comprising the wildest region of the Rocky Mountains in the nation: the Great Bear, the Scapegoat, and, foremost among them, the Bob Marshall (affectionately dubbed The Bob by locals and nature lovers). Together these areas form the Bob Marshall Complex, which amounts to some 1.5 million acres and is run by a management team from the Flathead, Lewis and Clark, Helena, and Lolo national forests.

Down the backbone of this American wilderness system run several entire mountain chains, all of them subranges of the Rockies. The high peaks rise dramatically from 8,000 to 9,400 feet in elevation; major interior valleys lie at elevations of 3,500 to 4,500 feet. Valleys tend to be broad and generously supplied with large trees, water, and open meadows. Distances are long and ideal for intrepid walkers or horseback riders.

MOUNTAIN WEATHER

The mountains receive plenty of precipitation, most of it in the form of snow, with an annual average of around 300 to 500 inches. There is no such thing as a typical year, though some patterns are reliable: dry years frequently follow wet years. Moisture levels vary, depending on elevation, aspect, and season. High elevations get more precipitation than low areas; many ranges are so high they make their own weather, producing coniferous forests of spruce, fir, cedar, pine, and larch. The eastern side of the mountains is drier than the western side, which is in the rain shadow of the Continental Divide. Westerly airflows from the Pacific determine the weather on the western side of the Rockies, and along the Rocky Mountain Front occasional warm winter winds called chinooks or snow eaters moderate the arctic air that sweeps down from the north across the plains east of the Front.

In spring and summer, the deep snow of the range melts, feeding a multitude of sparkling alpine streams that join to form powerful rivers flowing through Bob Marshall country. To the east the Teton, Sun, and Dearborn waterways carve their way through narrow limestone canyons and churn

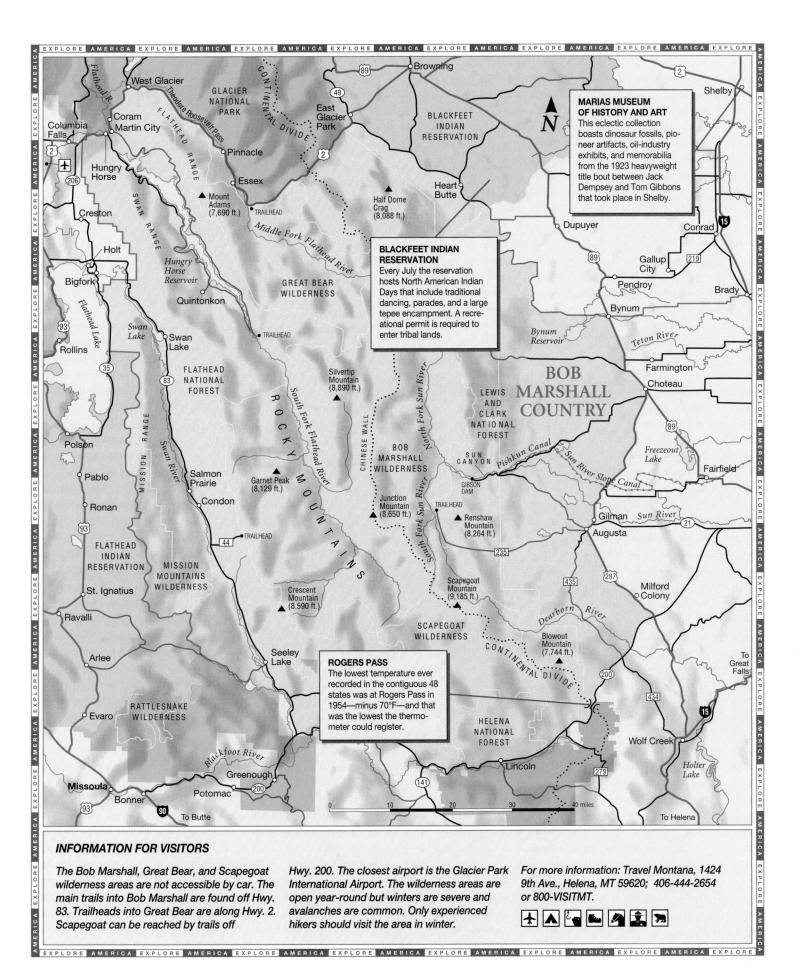

MARIAS MUSEUM OF HISTORY AND ART
This eclectic collection boasts dinosaur fossils, pioneer artifacts, oil-industry exhibits, and memorabilia from the 1923 heavyweight title bout between Jack Dempsey and Tom Gibbons that took place in Shelby.

BLACKFEET INDIAN RESERVATION
Every July the reservation hosts North American Indian Days that include traditional dancing, parades, and a large tepee encampment. A recreational permit is required to enter tribal lands.

ROGERS PASS
The lowest temperature ever recorded in the contiguous 48 states was at Rogers Pass in 1954—minus 70°F—and that was the lowest the thermometer could register.

BOB MARSHALL COUNTRY

INFORMATION FOR VISITORS

The Bob Marshall, Great Bear, and Scapegoat wilderness areas are not accessible by car. The main trails into Bob Marshall are found off Hwy. 83. Trailheads into Great Bear are along Hwy. 2. Scapegoat can be reached by trails off Hwy. 200. The closest airport is the Glacier Park International Airport. The wilderness areas are open year-round but winters are severe and avalanches are common. Only experienced hikers should visit the area in winter.

For more information: Travel Montana, 1424 9th Ave., Helena, MT 59620; 406-444-2654 or 800-VISITMT.

Quaking aspens stripe a mountainside in Sun Canyon with the golden yellows of fall, below. Keen-eyed visitors to the region may notice deep black scars on some of the tree trunks, left by the playful swipe of a passing bear.

across the plains toward the Missouri River. On the western slope, the south fork of the Flathead, fed by the Spotted Bear River, makes a slow journey through the Hungry Horse Dam Reservoir before joining the other two forks at Bad Rock Canyon. The middle fork of the Flathead originates in the heart of the Great Bear Wilderness, but it gains its fearsome reputation in the narrow canyon that separates the Flathead National Forest from Glacier National Park. Attracted by the frothing whitewater, rafters come from all over to ride the challenging rapids with names such as Bonecrusher and Jaws. Meandering through the Flathead Valley, the river empties into Flathead Lake, the largest freshwater lake west of the Mississippi River.

SPIRIT OF THE WILD

The spectacular terrain of Bob Marshall country is home to a variety of animals, and it is this wildlife that defines the stirring spirit of the land. A number of species now classified as threatened or endangered find refuge in this untamed world. Their names have become synonymous with the wild: grizzly bears, gray wolves, bald eagles, and peregrine falcons. Equally wild, though not in immediate danger of extinction, are wolverines, bighorn sheep, mountain goats, elk, and moose.

Here in this mountain wilderness, thick-coated grizzlies ramble across meadows, turning over rocks and pulverizing logs with their scythelike claws in search of rodents and other edibles. Black bears keep more to the deep forest, along with lynx, pine martens, and cheeky red squirrels. Wolves, once nearly eliminated from the area, are gradually reestablishing themselves. Lithe mountain lions rule a craggy domain, where they silently stalk mule deer, white-tailed deer, and the occasional elk. Herds of elk, some numbering around 10,000, wander the land in small bands like slow-moving shadows. Massive moose, though less common, are sometimes spotted picking their way through the moist forests of the western slope. Bighorn sheep,

An elk, right, conserves its energy by bedding down in a soft blanket of snow to masticate regurgitated food. Stags measure up to five feet at the shoulder and can weigh more than 1,000 pounds.

mountain goats, pikas, and hoary marmots lay claim to the high country. Peregrine falcons and golden eagles haunt the jutting cliffs. Powerful bald eagles and swift ospreys stay closer to water, where they can sometimes be seen tussling over a fish.

The verdant region is fed by the streams that tumble from the high tundra, frothing and sending up clouds of mist as they reach for the valley floor. Pouring off cliffs and giant boulders, the streams slide over gravel bars and filter through meadows of sedge before entering the forest where they curl around the roots of great firs and hemlocks and settle in deep pools. From the edge of a pool at twilight, visitors can watch great bull trout stirring the depths. The hypnotic silence of the forest is broken now and then by the soft splash of a fish as it rises to the surface in search of the insects that make up part of its diet.

| WILDERNESS AT DUSK | As the sun dips low in the sky, the terrain takes on a new personality, changing the very texture of the air. A figure in the |

dusk lifts off, drifts ghostlike across the water, and melts into the branches of a century-old fir tree; it's a great gray owl, the silence of its winged flight almost treacherous. The rustling sounds of animals creeping through the dry grass rouses the still forest. Perhaps it is a deer or an elk. But bear tracks on the trail remind visitors that this is grizzly country. The thought gives rise to an edgy sense of excitement and unease, a prevalent feeling in places still inhabited by the great bear.

Of all the inhabitants of Bob Marshall country, grizzlies are the most famous. Yet they are not the ferocious beasts of legend. Although tremendously strong, they are surprisingly shy when not threatened. The bears' diet varies by the season, and includes everything from winter-killed elk consumed in early spring to huckleberries, which ripen

in the late summer. Herbs, roots, grass, insects, rodents, elk calves, and pine nuts are other important food staples. Unfortunately grizzlies tend to develop a taste for food and garbage left around by humans, so residents and visitors are urged to properly store items that could attract bears. This is important to ensure the well-being of both visitors and bears.

Grizzlies travel up to 40 miles a day and they need plenty of space to roam: males require areas of 600 to 1,000 square miles, and females up to 100 square miles. The grizzlies' survival depends on how much territory humankind is willing to set aside for them. So far that has not been much. The bears of Bob Marshall country are living in one of the five remaining areas in the lower 48 states with remnant grizzly populations. Today this region is the last place in the nation where grizzlies can range from the mountains to the open plains, a habitat they once shared with the buffalo.

Gray wolves also roved the territory until they were eliminated by human settlement and predator control efforts. Occasionally a hiker has reported hearing a howl in some high remote area, giving rise to rumors of their return. In recent years wolves from Canada have returned to the ecosystem and have been spotted loping through the region. Currently, several packs of these wary beasts inhabit the country drained by the northern fork of the Flathead River and another pack roams the foothills of the Rockies just west of Augusta.

Along the Continental Divide near the center of The Bob stands what is perhaps its most famous geological feature—a sinuous 13-mile-long limestone cliff called the Chinese Wall. The western side of the wall is a gradual slope covered with small trees and littered with the fossilized remains of seashells. Its spectacular eastern face, riddled with caves, plunges 1,000 feet to rolling meadows of creamy white bear grass blossoms and to forests

PATIENT REWARD
A snowshoe hare, above, waits for nightfall to begin its search for food. Each winter the tip of the hare's brown fur turns white, camouflaging it when it crouches in the snow.

The nimble-footed mountain goat kids, above, are practiced climbers, having followed their mother over rugged terrain since they were just a few days old.

a summer spent just below the timberline in high country. The bulls arrive, their new antlers polished from hours of thrashing the trunks of small conifer trees. Their hormone levels are high and the air rings with their bugle calls. No sound is more characteristic of fall in the Rocky Mountains: the bulls let out a high-pitched squeal that rises to a clear whistle, then drops to a resonant deep-chested grunting. Females and juvenile elk add their distinctive mewing sounds to the chorus. When the moon is full, this comic opera might continue throughout the starlit night.

PROTECTING THE ELK | The elk that gather below the Chinese Wall belong to the Sun River herd, one of four major herds that inhabit Bob Marshall country and were once the object of a famous conservation effort. In 1912 long before the wilderness areas were designated, Montana established the Sun River Game Preserve. In the safety of this environment, the elk herd increased and soon became a nuisance for local ranchers. During the long winter, hungry elk would spill out of the high country looking for food on land that the ranchers had designated for their cattle.

Game wardens tried herding the wayward elk back into the mountains above the Sun River.

occupying the upper reaches of the Sun River drainage area. It is glorious to behold a sunset spreading across the horizon and bathing the sheer cliffs in a delicate pink light.

Every fall the meadows at the foot of the Chinese Wall become the mating ground for elk back from

GREEN, GREEN VALLEY
The dark mass of Scapegoat Mountain, right, stands guard over a swatch of green forest in the Scapegoat Wilderness.

BEAR GRASS IN BEAR COUNTRY
A lush field in the Bob Marshall Wilderness, opposite page, is spiked with pale yellow stalks of bear grass. Reaching heights of three feet, this wild grass got its name because bears enjoy eating its long, grasslike leaves.

snug in their homes among the boulders of the talus slopes, colonies of rabbitlike pikas devour the vegetation they so energetically collected and dried over the summer. Mice, voles, and pocket gophers live in a muffled world beneath the insulating snow blanket. Their tunnels are revealed in spring when the snow melts, uncovering banks riddled with passageways. The extensive labyrinths provide a getaway from the powerful talons of owls, but they are no deterrent against the long-tailed weasels who easily snake through the twisting burrows in search of tasty morsels.

Winter in high mountain country is so harsh and unforgiving it is a mystery that any animals survive at all. The long-legged moose stomp unperturbed through deep snow, managing to live on a strict diet of conifer needles and frozen willow sticks. Sheltered within the cavities of trees, the tiny nuthatch endures frigid nights of minus 40°F.

WINTER SURVIVAL

Some animals survive the winter by migrating to warmer climes rather than struggling to locate food buried beneath the six or seven feet of snow that regularly carpets the area during this season. Elk and deer travel to ranges outside the wilderness with their predators following close behind. Hungry grizzlies leave their hibernation dens and move to lowlands each spring to forage for food and to raise their young, following the snowline as it recedes upward. And many species of birds head south, some as far as Central and South America.

The millions of acres within the Bob Marshall Complex may not be enough to accommodate the seasonal migrations of its wildlife, but several smaller, and critically important wildlife reserves have been established nearby that do. Preserves such as Sun River and Ear Mountain offer refuge to animals that migrate seasonally in and out of these mountains, and migratory birds make safe pit stops here in spring and fall. Mule deer and elk find winter ranging grounds in the Blackleaf Wildlife Management Area. Grizzly bears return yearly to their last protected prairie habitat in Pine Butte Swamp Reserve. And at Freezeout Lake Wildlife Management Area, some 25 miles east of the mountains, some 1 million

A GAGGLE OF GEESE
Exploding into the sky, a flock of snow geese shows off their striking black-tipped plumage, above. Each spring and fall, hundreds of thousands of these birds pass through the region during their migration.

PROTECTIVE MOTHER
A female bobcat keeps a close eye on her curious kitten, right, in the Bob Marshall Wilderness. The most common wildcat in North America, the bobcat gets its name from its short—bobbed—tail.

Unfortunately this wintering ground had been taken over by bighorn sheep. A shared habitat was hard on both species, particularly the less assertive sheep, whose population suffered serious declines. The solution came in 1948, when the state of Montana bought two foothill ranches that the elk favored during the winter and turned them into a 20,000-acre elk range. With the elk no longer competing for space with the sheep, both species began to thrive. The sheep herd increased to between 700 and 900 animals, making it one of the biggest of its kind in North America.

Although the sheep prefer areas near rocky cliffs, they don't spend much time there. The precipices are populated by mountain goats, who are superbly adapted to life on the narrow ledges and even winter on the heights. The goats are tough, but the vertical range does exact a heavy toll. Mountain goats have among the highest natural mortality rates of North America's big mammals. They fall off cliffs, go hungry in winter, and suffer from disease. Still the herds manage to thrive.

Apart from the surefooted goats, there are few outward signs of animal life on the desolate slopes in winter. Yet under the thick cover of snow,

waterfowl belonging to more than 150 species pay regular visits. At the height of the spring migration, some 10,000 tundra swans and 300,000 snow geese, along with white-faced ibis, sandhill cranes, and long-billed curlews, are drawn to the lake.

Humans give names to preserve and wilderness areas and neatly partition them on maps but the land is all part of the same fabric. It is a place of absolute unity, where blue sky meets mountain, stream runs into river, and animals move freely across the grass and mountain. Here in Bob Marshall country, humans are transient guests invited to walk through the great expanse of wilderness and then bidden farewell.

ONE TOUGH CUSTOMER
A wolverine, below, bares its formidable teeth, warning the world not to get too close. Although mostly a scavenger, the wolverine, which weighs up to 60 pounds, is strong enough to fell a deer.

A RIVER RUNS THROUGH IT
Fed by rain and melting snow, the South Fork Sun River, left, winds lazily through the refuge. Miles of unspoiled rivers make the region popular with nature lovers and canoeing enthusiasts alike.

NEARBY SITES & ATTRACTIONS

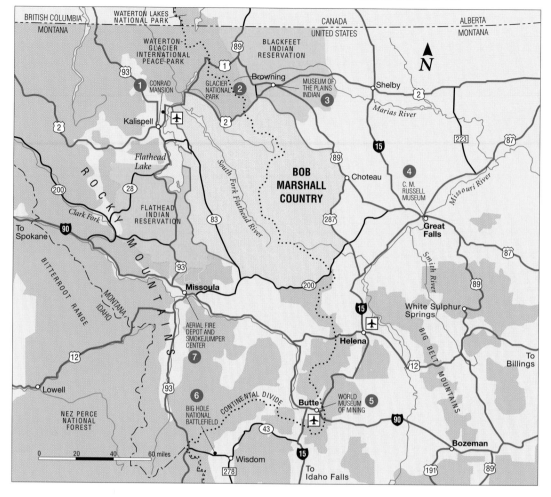

Antique ore wagons, above, are on display at the World Museum of Mining. In the background, the reconstructed headframe, or hoist, of the Orphan Girl Mine looms 100 feet above the old site.

① CONRAD MANSION

With its original facades, gardens, and furnishings, the Conrad Mansion is one of the finest surviving 19th-century buildings in Montana. The house was constructed in 1895 by a Missouri River entrepreneur named Charles Conrad, who moved west with his fortune and founded the town of Kalispell. The Norman-style building's furnishings include a Chippendale table and chairs, canopied four-poster beds, sleigh beds, and imported marble sinks in the bedrooms. The kitchen has a custom-made range, a Southern beaten biscuit machine, and a servants' call board. The exquisite golden oak woodwork of the Great Hall is dominated by a massive stone fireplace. The ceiling of the Great Hall is high enough to accommodate a two-story Christmas tree, which is decorated with hundreds of beeswax candles each year. Located on 4th St. East in Kalispell.

② GLACIER NATIONAL PARK

Spanning the Continental Divide, Glacier National Park covers more than 1 million acres of high mountain peaks, glaciers, alpine lakes, and thick forest, and is home to a wide array of wildlife. The landscape was shaped by glaciers more than 10,000 years ago. Today, 50 of these once-great rivers of

ice remain within the national park. Dense forests of Douglas fir, lodgepole pine, red cedar, and quaking aspen cloak the mountain slopes. More than 700 miles of trails bring hikers, horseback riders, and cross-country skiers to the nesting grounds of more than 200 species of birds, including the bald eagle. The park has a significant population of black bears and gray wolves. Other animals spotted here include moose, white-tailed deer, badgers, and coyotes. Going-to-the-Sun-Road, the main route through the park, is one of the nation's most spectacular scenic highways. Glacier was linked with Waterton Lakes National Park in Alberta in 1932 as the Waterton-Glacier International Peace Park. Visitor centers are located near the west entrance off Hwy. 2, at the St. Mary entrance off Hwy. 89, and at Logan Pass on the Going-to-the-Sun-Road.

③ MUSEUM OF THE PLAINS INDIAN

Located in the town of Browning on the Blackfeet Indian Reservation, the museum is devoted to exhibiting Native American artwork from the past, and promoting contemporary Native artists. Two galleries are set aside for temporary exhibits and special events. The permanent gallery focuses on the artwork of the tribes of the Northern Plains, among them the Blackfeet, Crow, Sioux, Arapaho, and

Northern Cheyenne. Native Americans are responsible for some of the museum's design, including the carved wooden panels of the front door. A five-screen movie and multimedia presentation titled "Winds of Change" introduces the viewer to the history of the Northern Plains. Its dual purpose is to educate the public and inspire contemporary artists. During the summer the museum grounds are used for an exhibit of painted tepees. In July Browning sponsors the North American Indian Days festival, which features games, parades, dancing, and sporting events. Located on Hwy. 89 west of Browning.

4 C. M. RUSSELL MUSEUM

Dedicated to Charles M. Russell, America's foremost Old West painter and sculptor, the museum includes a permanent collection of his works, the log cabin that served as his studio, and his home. Russell lived in his Great Falls home from 1900 to 1926. Apart from his paintings, the permanent collection includes bronze sculptures, personal objects, and the Browning Firearms Collection. The walls and floor of the studio are covered with objects depicted in his paintings: cowboy gear, buffalo skins, and Native artifacts. The cabin, built with old telephone poles and furnished with period pieces, evokes the 19th-century charm that Russell conveyed in his works. Located at 400 13th St. North in Great Falls.

5 WORLD MUSEUM OF MINING

This 12-acre national historic site, established in 1965, comprises both indoor and outdoor exhibits and includes a mine shaft, mining equipment, and Hell Roarin' Gulch, a re-created 19th-century mining town. The museum's goal is to preserve the history of mining and the heritage of mining communities. Prospectors flocked to Butte in the early 1870's after large deposits of silver were discovered there. Further mining unearthed even larger deposits of copper. The museum's indoor exhibits include hundreds of photos, a double-drum hoist, gold bullion scales, and subterranean firefighting equipment. The outdoor exhibit is highlighted by the 100-foot-tall headframe of the Orphan Girl shaft. Other displays

include a stagecoach, an armored pay car, and an electric ore truck. Hell Roarin' Gulch, with its cobbled streets and 37 re-created businesses, brings bygone days to life. Among the establishments are a saloon, funeral parlor, and sauerkraut factory. Located at the end of West Park and Granite St. in Butte.

6 BIG HOLE NATIONAL BATTLEFIELD

The Big Hole Valley lies just east of the Bitterroot Mountains of southwestern Montana. It was the site of a bloody engagement between Nez Perce Indians and the U.S. Army during the Nez Perce War of 1877. The Nez Perce were attempting to evade pursuing U.S. troops under orders to relocate the Natives on a reservation. The battle took place on August 9–10, 1877, with the loss of about 60 to 90 Nez Perce, and some 29 soldiers. A tour of the battlefield includes the Nez Perce campsite, siege area, and the Howitzer capture site, where the Nez Perce seized a cannon. Trenches dug by soldiers during the siege are still visible. A visitor center interprets the history of the war and the battle at Big Hole. Located 10 miles west of Wisdom on Hwy. 43.

7 AERIAL FIRE DEPOT AND SMOKEJUMPER CENTER

One of 10 smokejumper bases in the nation, the Missoula depot also houses a museum devoted to the highly specialized firefighters who parachute into remote areas to contain forest fires. Smokejumping was first employed in 1940 in Idaho's Nez Perce National Forest. Today there are 400 smokejumpers, and each makes an average of 10 jumps per season. Their history is brought to life for visitors through a display of dioramas and photographs, as well as video presentations. Guided tours include a look at the parachute loft and training facilities. The depot is also the site of the National Wildland Firefighters Memorial, which honors all smokejumpers who have lost their lives in the line of duty, among them 13 jumpers who died in a 1949 forest fire in Montana. Located in Missoula on Hwy. 93.

Jagged, glacier-carved peaks are mirrored by the still waters of Lake McDonald, above, in Glacier National Park.

The Conrad Mansion, above, was built for Charles Edward Conrad, a merchant who in 1891 founded a trading post that eventually grew into the town of Kalispell.

COCHISE COUNTY

---

*Mountain kingdoms, bordered
by grassy plains and arid desert,
conceal myriad forms of wildlife.*

More than a century ago a young man rode wearily across the San Simon Valley in southeastern Arizona on his way to Fort Bowie to enlist in the U.S. Cavalry. "A terrible place with no water and cactus all over," the soldier remarked dismissively years later. "It wasn't even a good place for snakes."

Struck by the outward barrenness of this "wild empty country," the recruit did not appreciate its spare beauty. He never suspected that the bleak desert and mountain landscape concealed a tremendous bounty of life; it is a variety matched by few other places in North America.

The profusion of life results from the geological rhythm of a land where dramatic shifts in elevation occur over short distances. Mountains pitch above the plains in a succession of isolated ranges, each claiming its own color, shape, and character. They rise from the surrounding sea of desert and grassland like so many islands. Some have a wrinkled aspect, others roll. Some are dark with evergreens. Others are spiked with yucca,

prickled with mesquite, or so devoid of vegetation that the whole mountainside takes on the somber hue of the underlying rock.

APACHE HOMELAND

Bordered on one side by New Mexico and on the other by Mexico, this southeastern corner of Arizona is called Cochise County after the leader of the Chiricahua Apache Indians native to the region. Across its southwestern flank runs the San Pedro River, the last undammed river in the state and the central artery of the county. Meandering through meadow and mountain ranges, the river drops about 2,500 feet on its journey from Mexico to the Gila River 100 miles to the north. Although the river sometimes dwindles to a fraction of its normal flow just before the summer rainy season, there has always been enough water to support the wildlife that is drawn to the river's shores.

Forty miles of this streamside habitat have been set aside as a national riparian, or waterside, preserve by the Bureau of Land Management. This avian migratory corridor lures bird-watchers from around the world. Some 400 species of birds have been sighted along the banks of the river, drawn by the ribbon of water below them. The rare green kingfisher and 36 species of raptors, such as the gray hawk and crested caracara, are the most exciting to birders. The bird list is lengthy and filled with evocative names, such as the red-faced warbler and the flammulated owl, the greater pewee and the yellow-bellied sapsucker, the bufflehead and the American coot.

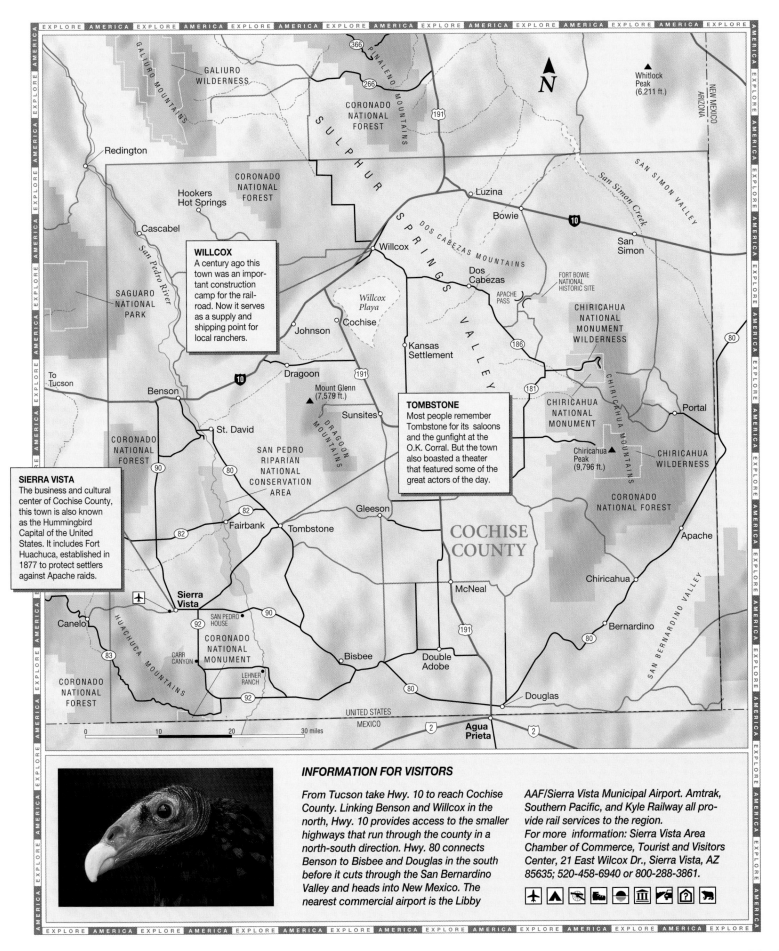

N

Whitlock
Peak
(6,211 ft.)

NEW MEXICO
ARIZONA

GALIURO
WILDERNESS

GALIURO MOUNTAINS

PINALENO MOUNTAINS

366

266

CORONADO
NATIONAL
FOREST

SULPHUR

San Simon Valley

San Simon Creek

Redington

CORONADO
NATIONAL
FOREST

Hookers
Hot Springs

191

Luzina

Bowie

10

San
Simon

Cascabel

DOS CABEZAS MOUNTAINS

SPRINGS VALLEY

San Pedro River

Willcox

Dos
Cabezas

FORT BOWIE
NATIONAL
HISTORIC SITE

APACHE
PASS

WILLCOX
A century ago this town was an important construction camp for the railroad. Now it serves as a supply and shipping point for local ranchers.

SAGUARO
NATIONAL
PARK

Willcox
Playa

Johnson

Cochise

Kansas
Settlement

186

CHIRICAHUA
NATIONAL
MONUMENT
WILDERNESS

80

To
Tucson

10

Dragoon

191

Mount Glenn
(7,579 ft.)

181

CHIRICAHUA
NATIONAL
MONUMENT

CHIRICAHUA MOUNTAINS

Portal

Benson

Sunsites

Chiricahua
Peak
(9,796 ft.)

CHIRICAHUA
WILDERNESS

TOMBSTONE
Most people remember Tombstone for its saloons and the gunfight at the O.K. Corral. But the town also boasted a theater that featured some of the great actors of the day.

St. David

CORONADO
NATIONAL
FOREST

90

SAN PEDRO
RIPARIAN
NATIONAL
CONSERVATION
AREA

DRAGOON MOUNTAINS

80

CORONADO
NATIONAL
FOREST

SIERRA VISTA
The business and cultural center of Cochise County, this town is also known as the Hummingbird Capital of the United States. It includes Fort Huachuca, established in 1877 to protect settlers against Apache raids.

82

Fairbank

82

Gleeson

Tombstone

**COCHISE
COUNTY**

Apache

Chiricahua

Sierra
Vista

SAN PEDRO
HOUSE

92

90

McNeal

191

Bernardino

SAN BERNARDINO VALLEY

Canelo

HUACHUCA MOUNTAINS

80

83

CARR
CANYON

CORONADO
NATIONAL
MONUMENT

LEHNER
RANCH

Bisbee

Double
Adobe

80

Douglas

CORONADO
NATIONAL
FOREST

92

UNITED STATES
MEXICO

Agua
Prieta

2

2

0   10   20   30 miles

INFORMATION FOR VISITORS

From Tucson take Hwy. 10 to reach Cochise County. Linking Benson and Willcox in the north, Hwy. 10 provides access to the smaller highways that run through the county in a north-south direction. Hwy. 80 connects Benson to Bisbee and Douglas in the south before it cuts through the San Bernardino Valley and heads into New Mexico. The nearest commercial airport is the Libby

AAF/Sierra Vista Municipal Airport. Amtrak, Southern Pacific, and Kyle Railway all provide rail services to the region.
For more information: Sierra Vista Area Chamber of Commerce, Tourist and Visitors Center, 21 East Wilcox Dr., Sierra Vista, AZ 85635; 520-458-6940 or 800-288-3861.

ONCE IN A LIFETIME
The parched deserts of southwestern Arizona are home to the agave, right, which takes so long to bloom that it is called the century plant. Some species die after a single flowering. This member of the amaryllis family is pollinated by bats drawn to the nectar of its tubular flowers. The spearlike leaves are the source of sisal, a strong fiber that is used to make rope.

The cattle that used to graze within the San Pedro conservation area were removed in 1988. Since that time, the riparian habitat has begun to recover. It is seen as one of the great modern conservation success stories—some bird populations have increased by as much as 6,000 percent.

Near the middle of the conservation area sits San Pedro House, a historic ranch house serving as the visitor center. Desert scrub of creosote bush, tarbush, and thorny mesquite covers the uplands above it. Tall sacaton grass, straw yellow in winter, grows in the bottomlands. Herds of snout-nosed javelina, a desert peccary, have flattened broad swaths of grass where they bedded down.

TRANQUIL BEAUTY

A narrow ribbon of Fremont cottonwood and Goodding willow runs along the river, screening the water from view. Early morning walkers, strolling the well-beaten path that winds through the trees, hear the rustling of birds in the verdant thickets. The path skirts some long pools and leads to a clear pond crowded with a flotilla of canvasback ducks and mallards. Startled, a great blue heron spreads its wings and lifts off, flying low to the water until out of sight.

While birds are the area's major draw, more than 80 species of mammals also live along the San Pedro River. Among these large and small four-legged inhabitants are coatimundis (also known as coatis) and ringtail cats, mountain lions and bobcats, Sonora white-tailed deer, and desert mule deer. Within the conservation area biologists have recorded more than 40 species of reptiles and

amphibians, such as spadefoot toads, Gila monsters, and Mojave green rattlesnakes.

Dozens of rare or endangered species also have found refuge in San Pedro. Among them are two native fish—the longfin dace and the desert sucker. On a tributary of the river farther north, five species of native fish swim in the spring-fed streams of Muleshoe Ranch, which is managed by The Nature Conservancy.

Near St. David, the Bureau of Land Management preserves a cienaga. A significant remnant of the San Pedro River valley's original marshes, cienagas are formed by the constant upwelling of small springs and seeps or in places where impervious clay or layers of rock retain water at the surface. The saturated ground supports a rare and fragile botanical community of sedges, grasses, and cattails. Until trappers eliminated beavers at the turn of the century, these dam builders helped to maintain the valley's system of cienagas. Their reintroduction, now in the planning stages, may help to restore something of what has been lost.

The lowlands were marsh 11,000 years ago when bands of Ice Age hunters tracked their quarry along the river. These Paleo-Indians belonged to what is now called the Clovis Culture, named after the handsomely crafted spearpoints they used to hunt big game. At Lehner Ranch and Murray Springs, archeologists have excavated the bones of extinct mammoths, bison, camels, North American horses, lions, and dire wolves. The hunters' distinctive fluted spearpoints, their butchering tools, and charcoal from their fires also have been uncovered nearby. These sites remain among the few where artifacts of the Clovis people have been found alongside the bones of the big game they hunted. Archeological evidence suggests that the people of

DECEPTIVE BEAUTY
The tricolored Sonora mountain king snake, below, preys on lizards and rodents, and the occasional rattler. Its red and black stripes give it an appearance similar to that of the deadly coral snake.

this culture ate meat almost exclusively, so much so that they may have overhunted these animals, contributing to their extinction.

| EUROPEAN ARRIVALS | Sobaipuri and Apache people were living here when the first major European expedition into the American Southwest |

took place in 1540. Led by Francisco Vásquez de Coronado, the intent of the expedition was to discover the mythical Seven Cities of Gold. Other Spanish explorers followed, establishing visitas and missions in the area. Near the ghost town of Fairbank, adobe ruins mark the site of Santa Cruz de Terrenate, a Spanish fort built in 1775. An assignment to this presidio was tantamount to getting a death sentence. During the Spanish garrison's five-year tenure, more than 80 soldiers stationed here were killed by Apache Indians.

West across the valley rise the steep Huachuca Mountains, which are scarred by a ragged band of cliffs that cuts across the face of the range. Floodwater flowing out of ravines at the foot of the mountains has deposited clay, silt, and sand in alluvial fans, which then join together in broad sloping deposits called bajadas. Canyons twist through the steep uplands, linking mountain with desert to form corridors used by wildlife to move from one elevation to another.

A long and winding mountain road leads up Carr Canyon. The road begins in open grassland and passes through oak woodland and a streamside riparian area before reaching towering pine forests at the peak of the canyon. Much of this densely forested range belongs to the Coronado National Forest, which is scattered in sizable patches across the higher elevations of southeastern Arizona. Travelers leave their vehicles at the trailhead and hike into the forest on foot.

TWIN PEAKS
Looming hazily in the distance, the Dos Cabezas Mountains (Spanish for two heads), above, provide a picturesque backdrop for the grassy plains.

LONG IN THE TOOTH
Sharp upper canine teeth earned the collared peccary, left, the name javelina. Unlike its more docile cousin, the pig, this mammal has a reputation for belligerence, particularly when cornered.

RIPARIAN HABITAT

One mile north of Carr Canyon lies Ramsey Canyon, a key wildlife sanctuary and botanical preserve. Protected by The Nature Conservancy, this lush riparian habitat attracts a brilliant throng of migrating birds in spring and summer, including 14 species of hummingbirds. Broad-tailed, black-chinned, and magnificent hummingbirds are the most likely to be sighted here. Birders can listen to the shrill trilling of a hummer or watch as one hovers over a bright flower, delicately sipping its sweet nectar.

Around every bend of Ramsey Canyon lies another biological niche. The trail wends its way through streamside sycamores and bigtooth maples, among lemon lilies and Tepic flame flowers. In some areas the division between desert and riparian zones is sharply drawn: hardy agave and cactus abruptly give way to clumps of moisture-loving horsetail weeds and canyon grape.

Apache bands once fiercely defended the entire region from occupying Spaniards, Mexicans, and Anglo-Americans. Chief Cochise based his operations in the core of the Dragoon Mountains, east of the San Pedro River at what is now called Cochise Stronghold. The legendary Apache lies buried somewhere within this cluster of rock sentinels and stands of oak and juniper. More than a century after Cochise agreed to a truce with the United States, a peacefulness still prevails in this natural fortress. What once served as Apache headquarters has now become the domain of hikers, birders, and rock climbers.

In the basin country to the east, the fields and pastures of Sulphur Springs Valley offer ideal territory for nesting raptors. Among the birds of prey encountered here are ferruginous and red-tailed hawks, kestrels, golden and bald eagles, and merlins. Pockets of marsh draw thousands of sandhill cranes in the winter.

EROSION'S HANDMAIDENS
Carved by wind and water, a volcanic rock grotto on the Echo Canyon Trail in Chiricahua National Monument, below, conjures up the magic of ancient fables.

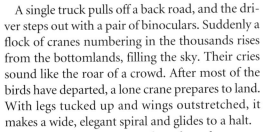

A WELCOME RETURN
The thick-billed parrot, left, the only parrot native to North America, is being reintroduced to its original habitat, the pine forests of southeastern Arizona. The bird uses its powerful bill to crack open Apache pinecones for food.

A single truck pulls off a back road, and the driver steps out with a pair of binoculars. Suddenly a flock of cranes numbering in the thousands rises from the bottomlands, filling the sky. Their cries sound like the roar of a crowd. After most of the birds have departed, a lone crane prepares to land. With legs tucked up and wings outstretched, it makes a wide, elegant spiral and glides to a halt.

More than 25,000 cranes have been known to winter in the valley. Some roost in the wetter margins of the Willcox Playa. Once covered by water, the parched lakebed stretches as flat as a tortilla across 50 square miles. The military claims most of the playa as a bombing range, but the northwestern corner has been set aside as a natural area.

On the eastern edge of the valley, farmland turns into grasslands, bristling with palmilla yucca. The scrubby grassland rolls upward to the base of the Chiricahuas, a mountain range presenting a wall across the horizon in a 40-mile front.

A creek from the high country spills into Chiricahua National Monument near the entrance. Pale-limbed sycamores twist massive roots into the bank to support their full girths. These riparian trees blend into a dense woodland of alligator juniper, Mexican piñon, Arizona cypress, seven species of oak, and the madrone with its papery red outer bark and pale underbark, smooth to the touch. Thickets of manzanita and buckthorn climb toward the ridgetops of the canyons. Higher elevations, reaching 9,796 feet in the Chiricahua Wilderness south of the parklands, support conifer forests of ponderosa pine and Douglas fir.

Deep within the monument lies the Wonderland of Rocks, formed 27 million years ago by a violent volcanic eruption. Dramatic rock spires and rocky cliffs break through the chaparral cover. Eroded deposits of rhyolite tuff have created an obstacle course of pinnacles, balanced rocks, hoodoos, and narrow slots. Black bears thrive in the thickets and broken terrain, a place the Chiricahua Apaches named the Land of Standing-Up Rocks.

MEXICAN INFLUENCE

In the cool moist forests of the the Chiricahua Mountains flourish plants and animals common not only to the Southwest but also to Mexico. Here the coatimundi, a southern relative of the raccoon, reaches the northern limits of its range. The male coati usually travels alone but bands of as many as 30 female and juveniles are sometimes seen, padding down a trail with their long snouts pointed down and their stiff tails straight up. The Apache fox squirrel, with its gray coat and red belly, lives only in these mountains. Rare birds, such as the brightly colored elegant trogon and the sulphur-bellied flycatcher, also have been sighted here.

Scientists have studied this living mosaic of biological communities for decades. Much of their research is conducted from a small field station run by the American Museum of Natural History, along Cave Creek on the eastern side of the Chiricahua Mountains.

At the northern end of the range, the highlands taper off to Apache Pass, which demarcates the Chiricahuas from the Dos Cabezas Mountains. A bald mass of rock, divided into twin knobs, tops this drier range. On a windy mesa overlooking the pass are the ruins of Fort Bowie. Soldiers once stationed here guarded a vital water source on the mail route across the desert. On a hot day nothing moves in the pass below these towering rocks but a roadrunner. It zips across the road with its head leaning forward, tail stretched out behind, and feet pedaling at cartoon speeds.

LOOK, BUT DON'T TOUCH
The alluring crimson blossoms of the nearly invincible hedgehog cactus, above, dazzle the eye.

Nearby Sites & Attractions

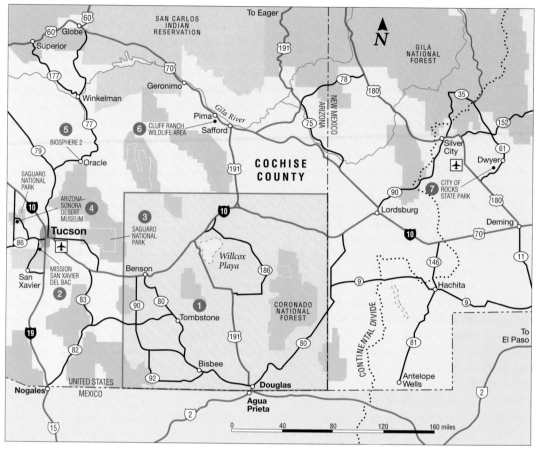

The tightly clustered blossoms of the saguaro cactus in Saguaro National Park, above, herald the appearance of its fruit. Local Indians make wine from the figlike fruit.

① TOMBSTONE, ARIZONA

A thriving mining town during the 19th century, Tombstone was the site of the famous 1881 gunfight at the O.K. Corral. The town was named by its founder Ed Schieffelin who, upon arriving in search of silver in 1877, was told the only thing he would find besides Apaches and rattlesnakes was his own grave. This colorful history has been kept alive by the preservation of a large number of old Tombstone buildings. Not far from the O.K. Corral stands *The Tombstone Epitaph* building, where the oldest continuously published newspaper in the state is still cranked out. An exhibit on the history of Western printing includes the original 1880 printing press. Outside the Rose Tree Inn Museum, the world's largest rose tree spreads its canopy over 8,000 square feet. The Bird Cage Theatre, built in 1881, contains its original furnishings and fixtures. The walls of the onetime saloon, dance hall, brothel, and gambling house are pockmarked by some 140 bullet holes. Located 26 miles north of Bisbee on Hwy. 80.

② MISSION SAN XAVIER DEL BAC, ARIZONA

In daylight or darkness the white stucco facade of this 18th-century church glows like a beacon in the middle of the desert. The original mission was established in 1700 by Jesuit priest Eusebio Francisco Kino to minister to the Tohono O'odham Indians. This structure was heavily damaged during the Pima

Indian revolt in 1734 and again in 1751. Construction of the existing structure was completed by Franciscan missionaries in 1797 and is one of the most outstanding examples of Spanish colonial architecture in the nation. Its thick walls and elegant bell towers are made of adobe bricks, which are painted a gleaming white. Above the altar is a statue of St. Francis Xavier. A museum displaying religious art, photographs, and architectural plans chronicles the history of the mission. Located 10 miles south of Tucson off Hwy. 19.

③ SAGUARO NATIONAL PARK, EAST UNIT, ARIZONA

Covering 67,293 acres, the eastern section of this national park is dedicated to protecting the giant desert cactus, the saguaro, found only in the Sonoran Desert in Arizona, California, and Mexico. The saguaro is able to retain large quantities of water, can live up to 200 years, and grows as tall as 50 feet. Its white blossom—Arizona's state flower—appears in early May. The Gila woodpecker and northern flicker live in nest holes that they excavate in the trunks and large branches of saguaros. Educational exhibits on the many plants and animals of the region are housed in the visitor center. The nine-mile Cactus Forest Drive and several hiking trails take visitors through the desert and grassland past the park's six campgrounds to the pine forests of the Rincon mountains. The area is home to coyotes, tarantulas, scorpions, and 50 species of reptiles, as well as roadrunners and hawks. Located 17 miles east of Tucson off the Old Spanish Trail.

4 ARIZONA–SONORA DESERT MUSEUM, ARIZONA

The museum displays flora and fauna of the Sonoran Desert primarily through a complex of realistic outdoor exhibits. A one-and-a-half mile path winds through the 30-acre museum where some 1,300 species of plants, including 200 species of Sonoran Desert cacti, are exhibited in their natural surroundings. These plants and 300 species of animals are displayed in various desert ecosystems. Ocelots, bobcats, and jaguarundis use their powerful legs to bound across the cliffs in Cat Canyon. In the Reptile Room, visitors see rattlesnakes, scorpions, and Gila monsters. The Desert Grassland, with 36 types of grass, is also inhabited by rattlesnakes, along with prairie dogs and burrowing owls. River dwellers, such as beavers and otters, that long ago left the Sonoran Desert, can be viewed behind underwater panels. Desert birds fly freely in the museum's walk-in aviaries. Although the birds are usually easy to spot when in motion, when still, their colors camouflage them in the desert environment. Located 14 miles west of Tucson on Kinney Rd.

5 BIOSPHERE 2, ARIZONA

This massive structure, designed to be a living laboratory, rises like a strange space station from the desert floor. Biosphere 2 was the home of crews of "bionauts" who lived inside the structure for up to two years and conducted research on the future of our planet. A three-quarter-mile walking tour circles the complex. Visitors can look through the greenhouse windows at its various ecosystems,

which include a tropical rain forest, savannah, desert, tidal estuary, a farm, and a 25-foot-deep ocean with a coral reef. A 15-minute multimedia show features a video of the bionauts. Located in Oracle.

6 CLUFF RANCH WILDLIFE AREA, ARIZONA

First used as a recreational site in the 1880's, then as a plant nursery and bird farm, Cluff Ranch has been a fish and wildlife habitat since 1949. The area, located at an elevation of 3,000 feet and covering 1,300 acres of upland and riparian woodland, provides an ideal setting for fishing, hiking, swimming, and bird-watching. With a total surface area of 18 acres, its three man-made lakes are rife with largemouth bass, trout, and bluegills. The lakes are surrounded by lush stands of cottonwood, ash, and willow. Also abundant are cactus, saltbush, and jimmy weed. Hiking trails cut through the forest, home to foxes, coyotes, mountain lions, and white-tailed deer. Some orphaned or injured birds and animals have been brought here from other parts of the state. Located 5 miles south of Pima on Hwy. 70.

7 CITY OF ROCKS STATE PARK, NEW MEXICO

City of Rocks was established in 1956, but the park's natural features were created millions of years ago. What look like giant boulders scattered over an area of 40 acres are actually the eroded remains of an ancient ash flow. Snow, wind, sand, and rain have molded the volcanic rock into distinctive outcrops. Some of the rocks rise as high as 50 feet, providing excellent shelter for camping and picnicking. Trails that wind between the monoliths resemble narrow city roadways, giving the park its name. Squirrels, chipmunks, bull- and rattlesnakes, cactus wrens, and house finches make their homes in the nooks and crannies of the rock face. Although the area receives little rain, volcanic rock holds water well, and the park has a bounty of oak, yucca, juniper, and a variety of shrubs and wildflowers. Located 23 miles north of Deming off Hwy. 180.

Looking like something out of science fiction, Biosphere 2, above, is the largest self-sustaining ecosystem ever built.

An arched entranceway leads to Mission San Xavier del Bac, left, which still serves as a spiritual center for the Tohono O'odham people. The church is called the White Dove of the Desert because of its immaculate exterior.

THE MOJAVE DESERT

*This desolate expanse supports a surprising
variety of animals and plants that have
adapted to the cruel heat of the high desert.*

California's Mojave Desert, located in the southeastern corner of the state, is just a two-hour drive from the bustle of Los Angeles. All the more striking that the desert is a sea of tranquillity, a study in natural contrasts. The Mojave is a place of eternity and evanescence, of giant and miniature wonders, of loners and community. Here the elements of heat and light have generated a fascinating array of complex adaptations to sustain life. The Mojave is a whisper of a place that reverberates long after the clamor emitted by other less subtle landscapes has died down.

Wedged between the cool, sage-clad Great Basin to the north and the scorching saguaro forests of the Sonoran Desert to the south, the Mojave is a unique ecological zone that defies easy classification. It is often referred to as high desert, because elevations here generally range between 2,000 and 7,000 feet. Yet it also encompasses Death Valley, which dips at Badwater to 282 feet below sea level—the lowest point on the North American continent. The Mojave is sometimes called a cold desert, but much of its expanse is a harsh, lunar landscape swept by infernal gusts and seared by a silver sun. The key to understanding the Mojave Desert lies in its contrasts, which have been shaped by its geological history.

Some 30 million years ago, the North American continental plate moved westward creating its characteristic accordion topography of basins and ranges. In the Mojave alone, there are 26 distinct mountain ranges, from the billion-year-old layered metamorphic rock, or gneiss, of the Old Woman Mountains to the bubbly rhyolite caps of the Providence Range. At the same time, the Pacific plate has slipped northward along the mighty San Andreas Fault, pulling the Mojave into the shape of a giant fan—tapered where it points toward the Tehachapi Mountains, opening out toward the northeast—and wedging it between cooler and hotter deserts.

Overleaf: The shadows of hardy desert grasses lengthen as a sunset colors the Kelso Dunes in Mojave National Preserve.

The Mojave is a relatively young desert. As recently as 10,000 years ago, the desert was a marshy woodland populated by tapirs, mammoths, and rhinoceroses. The glaciers that had carved out the landscape in the Pleistocene epoch were receding from the Sierra Nevada, leaving behind a milder, wetter climate for a time. Today's dry basins were the arms of a single immense body of glacial meltwater, Lake Manix, that emptied into the Gulf of Mexico. As the climate became hotter and drier, the Mojave, cut off from the moisture-laden air currents of the Pacific Ocean by the rain-shadow of the Sierra Nevada, gradually evolved into the desert of today, an inland reservoir of heat and dust.

Discovering the Mojave can mean an easy drive in the country or a demanding scramble up a sand dune. Interstates 15 and 40 bore into the heart of

WEATHERED SPHERE
The combined forces of wind and water have whittled and shaped a granite boulder into an eye-pleasing spherical sculpture, above, in Joshua Tree National Park.

the desert, passing close to lava beds, cactus forests, and dinosaur tracks. The freeways also provide access to Death Valley and Joshua Tree national parks. Secondary roads such as the Kelbaker or Cima scenic loops lead into the newly created Mojave National Preserve (formerly the East Mojave National Scenic Area)—a 1.4-million-acre jewel in the mountains east and south of Baker. Numerous dirt roads offer backcountry adventures to those equipped with high-clearance vehicles.

The best way to experience the ever-changing beauty of the Mojave is to explore it on foot. Only

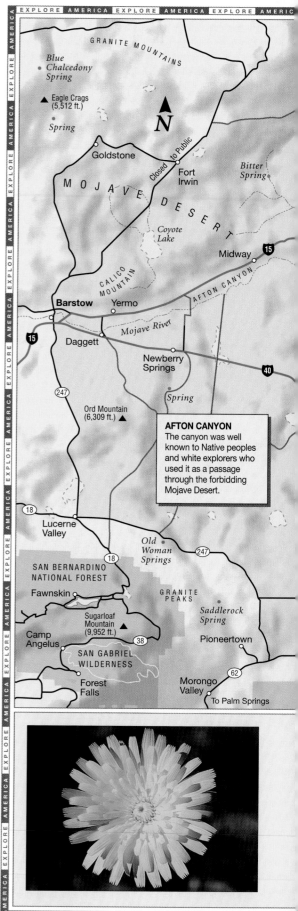

AFTON CANYON
The canyon was well known to Native peoples and white explorers who used it as a passage through the forbidding Mojave Desert.

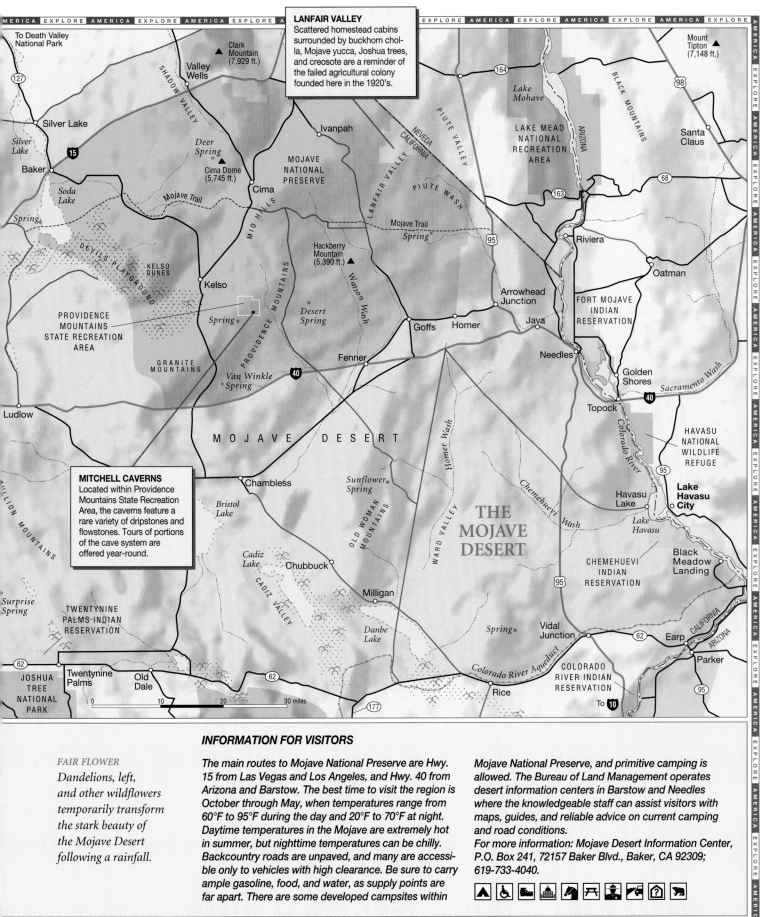

LANFAIR VALLEY
Scattered homestead cabins surrounded by buckhorn cholla, Mojave yucca, Joshua trees, and creosote are a reminder of the failed agricultural colony founded here in the 1920's.

MITCHELL CAVERNS
Located within Providence Mountains State Recreation Area, the caverns feature a rare variety of dripstones and flowstones. Tours of portions of the cave system are offered year-round.

INFORMATION FOR VISITORS

FAIR FLOWER
Dandelions, left, and other wildflowers temporarily transform the stark beauty of the Mojave Desert following a rainfall.

The main routes to Mojave National Preserve are Hwy. 15 from Las Vegas and Los Angeles, and Hwy. 40 from Arizona and Barstow. The best time to visit the region is October through May, when temperatures range from 60°F to 95°F during the day and 20°F to 70°F at night. Daytime temperatures in the Mojave are extremely hot in summer, but nighttime temperatures can be chilly. Backcountry roads are unpaved, and many are accessible only to vehicles with high clearance. Be sure to carry ample gasoline, food, and water, as supply points are far apart. There are some developed campsites within

Mojave National Preserve, and primitive camping is allowed. The Bureau of Land Management operates desert information centers in Barstow and Needles where the knowledgeable staff can assist visitors with maps, guides, and reliable advice on current camping and road conditions.
For more information: Mojave Desert Information Center, P.O. Box 241, 72157 Baker Blvd., Baker, CA 92309; 619-733-4040.

oases like Piute Creek. They climb steeply to the white pines atop Clark Mountain or mount the saddle of the Mid Hills, with its unobstructed panoramas of the surrounding terrain.

LAND OF BAJADAS

The Mojave receives less than five inches of precipitation per year. The weather station in Death Valley records an average of 1.63 inches, less than any other station in the United States. Long droughts are interrupted by sporadic cloudbursts that pound down the hillsides in flash floods, pool in salt flats on the valley floor, and evaporate. During cloudbursts, rivulets of water stream down every slope, joining together in cascading torrents that scour the gullies and canyons. After many such episodes, the boulders, stones, and particles torn from the slopes are deposited in fan-shaped formations, with boulders at the apex and finer particles at the base. Where several of these alluvial fans overlap, a long gently sloping sheet, or bajada, forms. It is these bajadas that give the desert its characteristic shape; a vast expanse of land that is simultaneously being eroded by water and buried by debris.

The Mojave features both the cold winters of the Great Basin and the hot summers of the Sonoran Desert, making its temperature range one of the widest on earth. The extremes in temperature and scarcity of moisture force every creature to meet two fundamental challenges: keeping body temperature within a favorable range and minimizing water loss. Dramatic temperature differences from mountain peak to valley floor are reflected in a corresponding change in vegetation that divides the bajadas into distinct zones. Piñon-juniper forests, which thrive on the summits, give way to Joshua tree forests, cactus and creosote scrub, and to saltbush, which surrounds the soda flats.

Animals employ survival strategies just as the desert plants do. Large animals, such as coyotes and bighorn sheep, travel great distances seeking cooler air. Most creatures are active only at night. As darkness falls, the air fills with the flap of bat wings, the howl of coyotes, the scratchings of rodents, and the buzzing of insects. As the sun rises, these night creatures take refuge underground, turning the soil into a honeycomb of burrows, from the sloping incisions of scorpions to the cupboard-size dens of badgers.

Some Mojave dwellers have developed unique adaptation strategies to meet the demands of an arid climate. Scorpions, spiders, and beetles derive moisture from their prey, and burrow to get away from the heat. Most have waterproof skins or hard, heat-resistant shells. Desert hummingbirds, bats, and ground squirrels are able to lower their body

GRANITE GLORY
Swordlike leaves surround the lush blossoms of the Mojave yucca, above, blooming amid the shattered splendor of the Granite Mountains. Yuccas flower only at night and are pollinated by a single species of moth.

by roving freely across open ground can visitors take in the immense space, the vast reaches of time, and the mutations of light that are the essence of this haunting landscape. To follow spinning dust devils across the salt flats, to smell the sour-sweet scent of creosote after a spring rain, to amble across a field of wildflowers in full bloom: these are the magical moments of desert life that reveal themselves to the visitor who leaves the beaten track for an hour or two. Abandoned roads and hiking trails lead to hidden pockets of biodiversity, such as Carruthers Canyon, and to petroglyph-decorated temperatures when at rest, thus conserving energy and water use.

Despite their many ingenious adaptations, desert life is extremely fragile. Food and water sources are scarce, and animal populations are very thinly distributed and easily disrupted. Yet the various life zones of the region sustain dynamic and surprisingly diverse communities of plants and animals.

JOSHUAS OF THE DOME

The sun burns like a red ember behind translucent streaks of ash-colored mist. Long shreds of cloud drift through the hollows, taking on the ruddy morning hues. To the northeast the heights of Clark Mountain are still shrouded in thunderclouds. As the sun begins its ascent, the clouds open to reveal an unusually deep blue, and the air fills with the spectral radiance of blowing ice crystals. Snow blankets the world of Cima Dome, bundling up the Joshua trees in whimsical winter clothing.

Only from a distance can Cima Dome's blister shape be appreciated. It rises so gently that it appears to incline to nowhere, an ascent without a

summit. The dome is a little-understood geological oddity, measuring some 10 miles in diameter and 75 square miles in area. It is made of granite that has been carved by wind and rain into the most symmetrical dome of its kind on the continent. The evenly eroded rocky gullies on the slopes support the world's largest, densest, and highest forest of Joshua trees.

The Joshua is a symbol of the Mojave, growing in groves at moderately high elevations that receive above average moisture, often in the form of snow. On Cima Dome, the Joshua forest is an endlessly fanciful display of tree personalities that charm, amuse, spook—or overwhelm. The Joshua is the largest of the yuccas, members of the lily family, a lineage demonstrated by the tree's clusters of creamy white flowers. Before it blossoms, a Joshua sends out the long, grizzly arms that led explorer John C. Frémont to call it "the most repulsive tree in the vegetable kingdom."

To Mormon settlers bound for California, the strange tree was seen as a benign apparition, promising water and relief from the heat. They named it after the Old Testament prophet Joshua who raised his arms to God in prayer. A host of other species depends on the Joshua, and Joshua tree woodlands support a sturdy web of life that includes prickly pear cacti, woolly bur sages, and spiny blue yuccas. Over 25 bird species nest in the Joshua's soft wood, including the northern flicker, a type of woodpecker found here and in only one other California location. Fallen limbs and downed trunks support colonies of termites that are eaten by desert lizards.

A chuckwalla lizard basks in the glow of a spring morning. From its perch on a huge egg-shaped granite boulder, this largest of all Mojave lizards soaks up enough warmth to raise its body temperature to the optimal 100°F, before it goes foraging in the creosote bushes for food. With its reddish black hide, the lizard looks part stone and part shadow. If threatened, it slithers into a crack in the rock, where it inflates itself until it fills the fissure like a plug and cannot be pried loose.

The Granite Mountains are located some 35 miles south of Cima Dome. A dreamscape of immense burnished bulb-forms, these mountains were created by ancient flows of magma and tens of millions of years of relentless erosion. Several hundred feet below the piñon-juniper woodland and Joshua groves, a cactus scrub community offers many protective nooks and crannies for plants and animals.

Barrel cacti, right, grow near Fort Piute in the eastern Mojave. The cactus's grooved surface and layer of sharp needles help reduce its exposure to the sun.

THE CIRCLE OF LIFE

When desert wildflowers bloom, Mojave insects such as the sphinx moth caterpillar, above, have only a short time to feed on the flowers' precious nectar. The riotous colors of wildflowers among the rocks after a spring rainfall contrast sharply with the forbidding expanse of Soda Lake, opposite page, bleached white by alkaline salts and soda.

Although it receives less moisture and more solar radiation than the upper bajada, this elevation is rich in succulents, from bunches of cushion cactus to extensive patches of beavertail and portly barrel cacti. The cacti bloom in winter, bathing the Mojave in the reds, pinks, and yellows of their tropical origins. Cacti are usually associated with the desert, but they are actually holdovers from wetter times. To survive the arid desert conditions, cacti have transformed their leaves into spines and turned their inner tissues into pithy reservoirs of water. The spines deter gnawing herbivores, but their primary function is to dissipate heat. They increase the surface area of the cactus, reducing the total amount of heat absorbed. At the same time, they shade the plant from direct rays.

When spring arrives, the cactus scrub and Joshua tree woodlands are suddenly awash in a blaze of color. Pink Mojave asters vie with bright yellow desert dandelions and sweet-scented white heliotropes. The dainty ghost flower, with its dusting of red inside a delicate golden bowl, rivals the beauty of the feathery Apache plumes and clusters of sand verbenas. Daturas, primroses, and poppies show off their splashy colors and opulent leaves. The air comes alive with the rumble of bees, the whizzing of hummingbirds, and the flutter of white skippers, desert orangetips, and other butterflies. Once they have germinated and before the driving heat of summer takes over, the wildflowers race to grow and reproduce, their leaves and petals moving with the sun across the sky in an effort to absorb every sparkle of solar energy. Only the most efficient will survive. One Mojave species, the brown-eyed evening primrose, photosynthesizes at the fastest rate ever measured.

At the foot of the Providence Mountains, the ground flattens out, lengthening the afternoon shadows. A black-tailed jackrabbit crouches in its form, a depression it has chewed out of the burrobush to hide from the sun and predators. The plant benefits from its tenant, who disperses burrobush seeds via its fur as it feeds on vegetation through the night. During the day the rabbit's long ears catch the sun, revealing a mesh of veins and vessels that help dissipate the intense heat.

KING OF THE BADLANDS There would be little life here were it not for creosote, the undisputed king of the badlands. The creosote bush is a relatively recent arrival, having moved into the Mojave from the south at the end of the Ice Age just as less adaptable plants were heading for more hospitable climes. The pitiless heat and sunlight of the lower Mojave suit the creosote just fine. It spreads out across hundreds of square miles of gravelly flatlands in monotonous uniformity, broken only by the occasional intrusion of burrobush, bur sage, and cholla. The creosote bush maintains its hegemony through sheer resourcefulness. It is a veritable chemical factory, producing more than 400 lignins, volatile oils, and other agents, mixed together in acrid resins for protection. Creosote root systems are extensive and astonishingly effective, sucking the soil around them dry so that the plant's own seeds rarely take root there. A creosote seed requires very wet conditions to germinate, but the Mojave Desert has not experienced an extended wet period in a long time. It should come as no surprise then that one creosote in the Mojave's Lucerne Valley has been dated at 11,000 years of age—the oldest living thing on earth by far.

The ground around the creosote's stem provides a habitat for burrowing rodents such as the kangaroo rat, a species that rivals the creosote in both determination and independence. This relative of the squirrel family, with its huge eyes, tufted tail, and powerful kangaroolike legs is a desert icon because of its ability to derive all of its water from food. Such a useful arid-land adaptation is partially due to highly developed kidneys and an absence of sweat glands, a characteristic that is unique to rodents. Furthermore, during the day the kangaroo rat holes up in its burrow recycling moisture created by its own breathing, which it then recaptures through glands in its nose.

The consummate desert predator, the Mojave rattlesnake, also known as the Mojave Green, is extremely vulnerable to both high and low temperatures. If exposed to the sun for more than 10 minutes, it dies, and if caught in the cold, it slips into paralysis. So the rattlesnake is active only during hours of moderate warmth, usually at night. After dark, the rattler moves slowly through the brush in search of prey. When a victim ventures too close, the rattler strikes, using a pair of fangs so long they hinge to fit inside the snake's mouth. The snake's venom—the most toxic of all the pit vipers'—enters its victim, paralyzing it. By day, the snake lies coiled beneath plants such as the cholla or creosote, or inside rocky crevices, where its greenish gray pallor provides camouflage.

BOOMING SANDS

On the Kelso Dunes, the twilight lingers long after the sun has set. The sand itself changes color in concert with the glowing sky, shifting from shimmering flax to misty blue as dusk washes across nearby Cima Dome. The Kelso Dunes rise more than 600 feet above Soda Lake, collecting sediments blown from the dry Mojave River into an area more than 45 miles square. People gather here to watch the sunset and to listen for the curious booming sound that emanates from the leeward slopes when conditions are just right. The rare phenomenon occurs when the moisture content of the dunes falls below one percent causing sand particles to slide downward. The vibration of the rolling sand is amplified by the giant sounding board of the stationary sand underneath, producing a counterpoint to the rich serenade of desert life.

The Kelso Dunes are home to more than 100 plant species, many of them native. Some, like the sand verbena and birdcage evening primrose, are low-growing wildflowers able to withstand strong winds and long dry spells. On the slippery slopes, dune panic grass grows to a height of three feet or more, its tendrils tracing arcs in the sand, a reliable natural compass of wind direction. The delicate golden fluff of Indian rice grass softens the gentle rise and fall of the dune's surface. Insects, including the native Kelso Dunes Jerusalem cricket, live among creosote and burrobush in sufficient numbers to support a thriving population of fringe-toed lizards. A streamlined shape and slippery skin enable this lizard to wriggle under the surface to cool off or keep out of sight. Overlapping eyelids, ear flaps, and special nasal valves shield its sense organs from the fine sand. When threatened by a sidewinder or kit fox, the kangaroo rat uses its serrated hind toes to increase its traction and scamper away upright at nearly 20 miles an hour.

RAVEN'S PROGRESS
*The tracks of a raven march
across the wind-rippled surface
of the Kelso Dunes, below.*

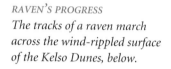

The mesquite tree creates its own oasis amid the dunes. Its immense root systems tap water 100 feet down, and its feathery boughs and prodigious flowerings offer shade and sustenance for numerous other plants and animals. It is estimated in fact that the mesquite attracts more kinds of animals than any other desert plant. Unlike the greedy creosote, the mesquite gives more to the soil than it takes. As a result the trees are often surrounded by a pleasant growth of wildflowers and grasses, alive with the hum of bees, mantids, and hummingbirds. Kangaroo rats and beetles feed on a steady supply of fallen mesquite pods, and larger mammals rest in the trees' welcoming shade.

A hot wind waltzes across Soda Lake as a distant mirage reduces the encircling cinder cones to a vague blur. The powdery earth radiates heat and light. Along the fringes of the flats, wisps of algae bring back the memory of water. Here the earth is cracked and peeling.

At the lowest point of the desert lie the playas and soda flats, which become temporary lakes when water from flood channels flows into them. The playas here are among the hottest and saltiest places on earth, where only a few plants and even fewer animals survive. Athol, also known as saltseeder, draws saline water through extensive root systems and excretes the salts through its leaves.

these specialized conditions, every pupfish population has evolved into virtually a different species, each indigenous to a small aquatic area. The pupfish burrows in the mud and hibernates when it gets too cold. By altering the thickness of its blood, the fish remains saltier than the water around it, avoiding thirst even in an environment three to four times as saline as seawater.

HUMAN TOUCH In the rainbow-hued Calico Hills near Yermo, where the Mojave looks its most ferocious, an archeological team under Dr. Louis Leakey has uncovered evidence of early human habitation. Leakey believed the digging implements, scrapers, and other tools his team found were made by people who lived along the shores of Mojave lakes and marshes more than 200,000 years ago—the earliest evidence of a human presence in North America.

In more recent times, the Mojave has been continuously, though sparsely, inhabited. Tribes such as the Paiutes and Chemehuevis crisscrossed the mountains and valleys, and explorers such as Kit Carson and John C. Frémont blazed trails, some of which, such as the Mojave Trail, are still passable. Later California-bound settlers couldn't get through the desert fast enough. Few people, aside from ranchers and miners, have withstood the rigors of desert life. Still, the Mojave is home to more people now than ever, especially on its western side, where the suburbs of Los Angeles spill over the San Gabriel Mountains into Antelope Valley.

A new awareness of the Mojave's fragility has inspired measures to protect the integrity of its complex ecosystems. Joshua Tree National Park, Death Valley National Park, and the Mojave National Preserve are vital refuges that reflect the evolution in our thinking about nature. Time has worked its magic on humanity, replacing initial indifference with a deep appreciation for the awesome beauty of this arid empire.

In the spring flash floods engorge the Amargosa River. Like all Mojave rivers, the Amargosa flows above ground for a time, then sinks into the sand, moving through the soil almost as a vapor, to reemerge in increasingly weaker increments until evaporating completely. River residents cope with many extremes: temperatures that swing from freezing to over 100°F in a single day, changing levels of salinity, and erratic water flow. No animal is more dauntless than the Amargosa River pupfish. This fish dates back to the Pleistocene era, when its habitat consisted of vast lakes with ocean outlets. Now it lives in a handful of holes and springs that may contain less than 100 gallons of water. Due to

STONE SCULPTURES
A pair of rock spires in the Granite Mountains, left, seem to survey the splendor of the Mojave Desert.

SLOW AND STEADY
The persistent desert tortoise, left, serves as a symbol of the Mojave. The animal carries its water supply in a bladder beneath its shell and spends the hottest part of the day in extensive burrows, which its powerful clawed forelimbs excavate in the sides of washes.

Nearby Sites & Attractions

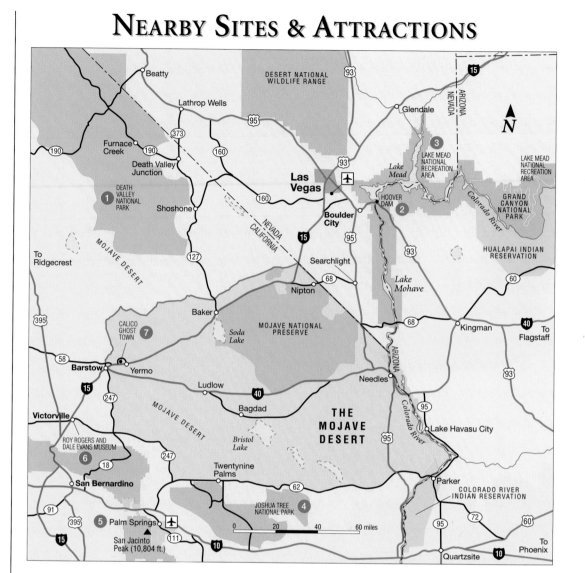

The beautiful flowers of the silver cholla, above, bloom among its fearsome spines in Joshua Tree National Park. Cactus wrens and thrashers manage to nest on the chollas, protected from predators by the long spines.

① DEATH VALLEY NATIONAL PARK, CALIFORNIA

This desert valley is one of the hottest places in the world. Called Tomesha, or "ground afire" by Native Americans, the hostile stretch of land was given its current name by early prospectors who barely survived crossing it in 1849. Surprisingly, the scorched valley supports a wide variety of wildlife and vegetation. More than 900 species of plants grow in the park, including 21 that are unique to the area. The region is home to bobcats and coyotes, 17 species of snakes, 17 species of lizards, and gives temporary haven to 230 species of migratory birds. Underground springs form lush oases. The Furnace Creek Visitor Center provides information about the region's history and natural history. Park headquarters is located at Furnace Creek on Hwy. 190.

② HOOVER DAM, NEVADA

One of the engineering feats of the Great Depression, Hoover Dam is 1,244 feet wide, 726 feet high, 45 feet thick at its crest, and 660 feet wide at its base. The dam was completed in 1935 at a cost of $165 million, using 6.6 million tons of concrete. Guided tours include an elevator ride from top to bottom and viewings of the 30-foot-diameter water pipes and the enormous turbines. Located 30 miles east of Las Vegas on Hwy. 93.

③ LAKE MEAD NATIONAL RECREATION AREA, NEVADA

This 1.5 million-acre recreation area began to take shape in 1935 when the completed Hoover Dam held back the waters of the Colorado River within Black Canyon. Within three years the dam created the largest man-made lake in the West—110 miles long and more than 500 feet deep. Davis Dam, built downriver from Lake Mead in 1953, created Lake Mohave, also part of the recreation area. Both lakes offer marine recreation for powerboats, houseboats, canoes, and sailboarders. Striped bass, largemouth bass, catfish, rainbow trout, and black crappie lure fishermen to the area. The clear waters of the lakes are ideal for swimming and snorkeling. Park headquarters is located on Hwy. 93 in Boulder City.

4 JOSHUA TREE NATIONAL PARK, CALIFORNIA

This 794,000-acre park straddles two deserts, making it a representative habitat for a variety of desert animals and vegetation. The western half of the park is home to the Joshua tree, a type of yucca plant. The eastern half, located in the Colorado Desert, is much drier and hotter. Creosote bushes grow in abundance here, along with cholla cactus and ocotillo. The park is an area of rugged beauty, highlighted by rocky outcrops, towering granite boulders, and 6,000-foot peaks and five oases. Wildlife includes bobcats, coyotes, roadrunners, and golden eagles. Park headquarters is located 2 miles south of Twentynine Palms off Hwy. 62.

5 PALM SPRINGS, CALIFORNIA

The natural springs of this resort attracted Native Americans long before the Hollywood crowd discovered the area. The Palm Springs Desert Museum's art collection ranges from 19th-century landscapes to modern sculpture. Its natural science section focuses on desert life shown in dioramas of Gila monsters, lizards, and scorpions. Just outside this bustling town, the nature trails of Indian Canyons wind past hundreds of species of plants, striking rock formations, and ancient Cahuilla rock art. A two-and-a-half mile tramway ride takes visitors almost to the top of 10,804-foot San Jacinto Peak where they can enjoy cool mountain air, nature trails, and picnic sites. Located on Hwy. 111.

6 ROY ROGERS AND DALE EVANS MUSEUM, CALIFORNIA

This lively museum is filled with photographs, costumes, fan mail, and artifacts documenting the personal and professional lives of legendary country singers Roy Rogers and Dale Evans. In the 1930's Roy Rogers, Hollywood's singing cowboy, made more than 100 films. He and his wife, Dale Evans, hosted the popular family television series, *The Roy Rogers Show,* in the 1950's. Rogers' faithful steed *Trigger* has been preserved and is on display. Located at 15650 Seneca Rd. in Victorville.

7 CALICO GHOST TOWN, CALIFORNIA

A booming mining center in the late 19th century, Calico became a ghost town virtually overnight when the price of silver plummeted. The town was named after the multicolored slopes that surround it. Tours take in the mine, saloon, theater, and a shooting gallery. Some 200,000 years ago the area was used as a stone quarry. Since 1964 more than 11,000 artifacts have been excavated at the nearby Calico Early Man Archaeological Site, including scrapers and hand axes. A mining shack has been converted into a museum. Located near Yermo off Hwy. 15.

The establishments along fashionable Palm Canyon Drive in the city of Palm Springs, above, cater to a clientele that includes many Hollywood celebrities.

Clumps of blond grasses bend in the warm desert breeze, left, at Death Valley National Park. The temperature on the valley floor reaches as high as 134°F.

THE FAR NORTH

It is the winter solstice in Alaska's Arctic National Wildlife Refuge, and no birds sing. No rivers flow. The land is plunged in darkness, and ice and snow lock everything in a frozen embrace. The sun has not broken the horizon since the last days of November, and will not rise again until late January. Inupiat Eskimos say experiencing winter on the northern edge of North America is like going through a tunnel—it is a long, cold, dark journey. The temperature drops to minus 40° on the Fahrenheit thermometer. Windchills knock it down another 40 degrees.

This is a netherworld, a sunless realm, more Jovian than earthly. But, even in the dead of winter, the refuge lives on. It is merely sleeping. When summer finally arrives everything will change. Sunlight will flood the land, signs of life will return, and the 19-million-acre Arctic National Wildlife Refuge—large enough to contain eight Yellowstone National Parks, nearly the size of South Carolina—will transform itself into an American Serengeti.

Overleaf: A midnight sun in June casts the shadow of the towering Romanzof Mountains across the Jago River valley. Continuous light prevails here from late April through mid-August. From mid-November to mid-January the sun hovers below the horizon.

COATS OF MANY SHADES

A gray wolf, cousin to the domestic dog, reclines on a blanket of snow, right. The wolves of the refuge sport gray, brown, black, or white coats.

BORN IN ALASKA

The speckled brown eggs of a willow ptarmigan, opposite page, lie safely ensconced in their shallow nest. The birds are seasonally monogamous, and the males take an active role in protecting the nest and rearing the hatchlings.

It is a slow and magical process. In January the rising sun casts a rose-colored hue on the icy summits of the Brooks Range, ancient peaks that slice in an east-west direction through the middle of the refuge. Sandwiched between the Beaufort Sea to the north and the Canadian border to the east, the refuge encompasses the Porcupine, Yukon, and Chandalar river basins. South of the mountains the land descends into a boreal forest of century-old spruce trees that stand less than 20 feet tall on either side of the Coleen, Sheenjek, and East Fork Chandalar rivers. Treeless Arctic tundra spills onto the vast northern slope of the Brooks Range, which descends to the Coastal Plain, ending on the frozen shores of the Arctic Ocean.

land carnivore, bringing both vitality and danger to the Arctic. Approximately 2,000 of these mighty animals roam a territory that extends more than 800 miles along the northern coasts of Alaska and Canada. Polar bears spend most of their time on the pack ice; pregnant females move onshore in late fall to dig dens in the snow for their cubs, which are born in December and January. The young are nursed until March or early April and then they leave the dens and make their way to the ice to hunt for ringed seals and other prey. During the summer months the bears travel hundreds of miles inland to feast on crowberries and blueberries.

A willow ptarmigan, its plumage turned from summer brown to winter white, moves among leaf-

Ravens soar overhead, their obsidian wings casting surreal shadows on the alabaster snowscape. They wheel in the air, squawking indignantly, and land by the remains of a dead caribou left exposed to fierce, ground-raking winds. The carcass has been picked clean by wolves, wolverines, arctic foxes, and a polar bear, whose tracks are still discernible in the heavy snow.

REALM OF THE ICE BEAR

"The polar bear is a creature of arctic edges," wrote Barry Lopez in *Arctic Dreams.* "He hunts the ice margins, the surface of the water, and the continental shore. The ice bear, he is called." The polar bear never seems to rest. In winter he hunts while other animals, such as the grizzly, sleep. Legend says the ice bear covers his black nose with snow as camouflage for hunting; that he can crush the head of a dog with one swipe of his paw. The bear is the world's largest

less willow trees in a frozen drainage. Its scientific name is *Lagopus lagopus,* Latin for hare's foot, a reference to the feathers that cover its legs and feet, affording insulation against the bitter cold. The state bird of Alaska and a member of the pheasant family, the willow ptarmigan proceeds with watchful caution. An arctic fox, sporting a white winter coat trots by and the ptarmigan freezes. But the bird fails to see the threat from above—a gyrfalcon, a year-round resident in the Arctic. More than a century ago John James Audubon, the dean of North American wildlife painters, described gyrfalcons as "warriors," saying they "descend like a streak of lightning." Indeed, this warrior of the air dives at breakneck speed and hits the ptarmigan with tremendous impact, sending feathers into the air and killing it instantly.

The silence here is so profound it seems to be another presence. The Arctic rivers, most of them less than waist deep, are partially frozen. Here and

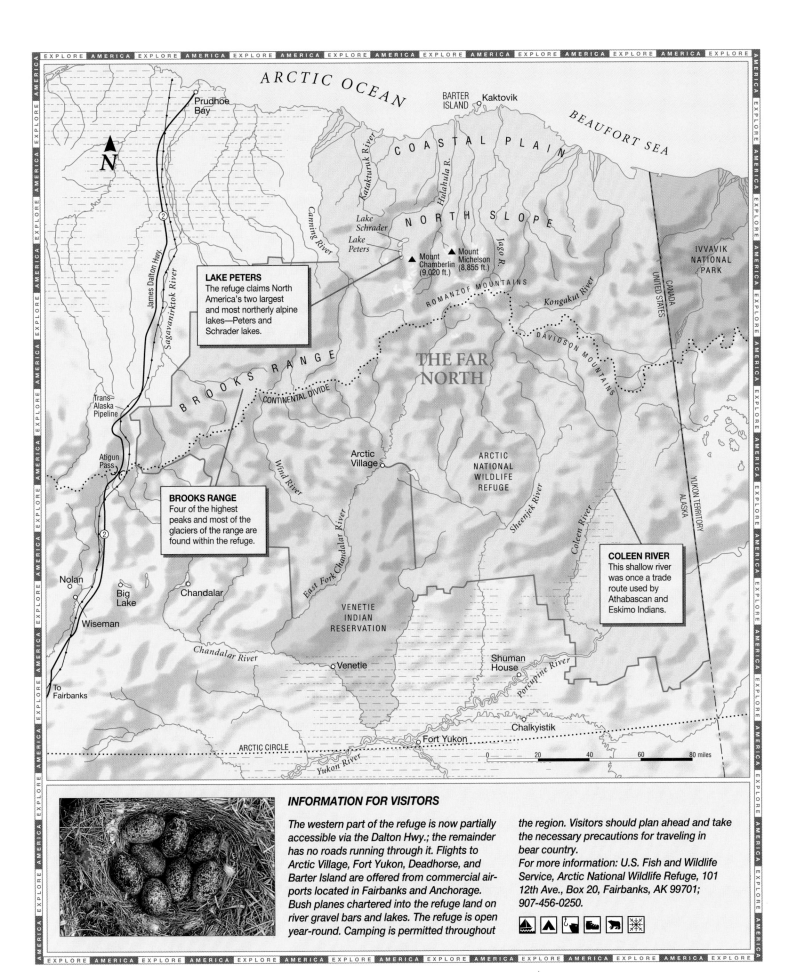

ARCTIC OCEAN

BARTER ISLAND   Kaktovik

BEAUFORT SEA

Prudhoe Bay

N

COASTAL PLAIN

NORTH SLOPE

Katakturuk River

Canning River

Hulahula R.

Jago R.

IVVAVIK NATIONAL PARK

Lake Schrader

Lake Peters

Mount Chamberlin (9,020 ft.)

Mount Michelson (8,855 ft.)

ROMANZOF MOUNTAINS

Kongakut River

DAVIDSON MOUNTAINS

LAKE PETERS
The refuge claims North America's two largest and most northerly alpine lakes—Peters and Schrader lakes.

James Dalton Hwy.

Sagavanirktok River

B R O O K S   R A N G E

CONTINENTAL DIVIDE

THE FAR NORTH

UNITED STATES

CANADA

Trans-Alaska Pipeline

Wind River

Arctic Village

ARCTIC NATIONAL WILDLIFE REFUGE

Sheenjek River

Coleen River

YUKON TERRITORY

ALASKA

Atigun Pass

BROOKS RANGE
Four of the highest peaks and most of the glaciers of the range are found within the refuge.

East Fork Chandalar River

COLEEN RIVER
This shallow river was once a trade route used by Athabascan and Eskimo Indians.

Nolan

Big Lake

Chandalar

Wiseman

VENETIE INDIAN RESERVATION

Chandalar River

Venetie

Shuman House

Porcupine River

To Fairbanks

Chalkyistik

ARCTIC CIRCLE

Fort Yukon

0   20   40   60   80 miles

Yukon River

INFORMATION FOR VISITORS

The western part of the refuge is now partially accessible via the Dalton Hwy.; the remainder has no roads running through it. Flights to Arctic Village, Fort Yukon, Deadhorse, and Barter Island are offered from commercial airports located in Fairbanks and Anchorage. Bush planes chartered into the refuge land on river gravel bars and lakes. The refuge is open year-round. Camping is permitted throughout the region. Visitors should plan ahead and take the necessary precautions for traveling in bear country.
For more information: U.S. Fish and Wildlife Service, Arctic National Wildlife Refuge, 101 12th Ave., Box 20, Fairbanks, AK 99701; 907-456-0250.

there deep pools remain unfrozen at the bottom. Below six feet of solid ice lives perhaps the most remarkable of 36 fish species in the refuge—the Arctic grayling, a freshwater cousin of the trout. It has an elegant sail-like dorsal fin and a supreme tolerance for low levels of dissolved oxygen. Having feasted on aquatic insects during the summer, the fish stores enough fat to survive eight long foodless months under the ice.

The colorful Dolly Varden, also known as the Arctic char, is distinguished by its bright green skin, which is speckled with red, and a red belly. The fish lives in the lagoons and northward-flowing rivers of the refuge where it spawns and spends the winters in the rivers' year-round springs. Dolly Vardens spend the summers in coastal marine waters.

The days lengthen as February stretches into March, still the refuge is bitterly cold. Bands of Dall sheep climb across the windswept, precipitous slopes of the Brooks Range to graze on grasses, lichens, forbs, and dwarf willows. Unlike caribou and moose—also members of the deer family—which shed their antlers every winter and grow new ones the following year, Dall sheep retain horns that lengthen each year. While Dall ewes have short,

pointed horns, rams develop beautifully curving ones that, in seven to nine years, form the full curl signifying dominance in the ram hierarchy. Wolves prey on the sheep, and occasionally a grizzly bear gives chase. The sheep, among nature's best mountaineers, scramble up cliffs only they can negotiate. Yet they are not so sure-footed as to avoid every rockslide, or so skilled that they never misjudge a climb. The greatest danger for the sheep is not the fierce cold or wind but a heavy snow followed by a temporary thaw or freezing rain that covers their food source with a thick mantle of ice. Unable to break through the ice, the animals starve.

By spring equinox the rising sun sends a faint yet unmistakable warmth to the land. The wind, still raw and biting, exposes patches of the tundra where wildlife forage. Feeding on one of these patches is a large herd of musk-oxen. "Omingmak, the bearded one," the Eskimos call them. If alarmed by a wolf or other predator, the musk-oxen will quickly form a defensive circle, standing shoulder to shoulder, horn to horn, to protect their calves, their long shaggy coats blowing in the wind. The animals seem to exist in a time warp 10,000 years back to the Pleistocene, or Ice Age, when mammoths and

WETLAND INHABITANT

Distinguished by its flat head, long bill, and rust-colored sides, a northern shoveler paddles across the shallow waters of the wetlands within the refuge, right.

CUBIST SCULPTURE

Gigantic blocks of overflow ice in the Hulahula River, below, seem chiseled as if by hand. These ice fields, known as "aufeis," are created by underground springs. The river water warms the ice fields in spring, causing layers to break off and slide into the water.

HISTORICAL SITES

A food cache, set up by Inupiat Eskimos in the early part of the century, lies abandoned in a cotton-wood grove, left. The refuge contains more than 300 important archeological sites, and fossils have been found in the streambeds. Long ago the area was covered by the Beaufort Sea.

BEAR FACTS

The grizzly, above, is one of three species of North American bears that inhabit the refuge. Grizzlies roam the entire region, black bears forage in the forests, and polar bears spend part of the year on land and part on ice packs.

mastodons roamed Alaska. The musk-oxen almost disappeared in the past century when hunters slaughtered them. But a few survived and in 1969 they were introduced back into the refuge from Nunivak Island; roughly 350 live here now. These are the only large mammals to inhabit the Arctic Coastal Plain year-round. Not only do the musk-oxen survive in this winterscape, which is so inhospitable to humankind, they thrive, protected by hairs and soft underfur eight times warmer than sheep's wool.

A TIME OF AWAKENING

In April the refuge awakens. To the east in the upper Porcupine River drainage of Canada's Northern Yukon National Park, 150,000 caribou begin an annual journey undertaken by generations of their antecedents. Among the caribou herd are thousands of pregnant females. They move north by northwest, slowly yet inexorably, their route varying from year to year depending on snow and weather conditions.

By the end of the month of April, birds from Asia and the Americas also begin their epic journey northward. From New Hampshire comes the dunlin; from Montana, the golden eagle; from Illinois, the dark-eyed junco; from Alabama, the ruby-crowned kinglet; from New Mexico, the sandhill crane; from Nevada, the green-winged teal. The list includes species from every state in the continental United States.

The ice melts in May, and the tundra, not yet green, emerges from behind winter's white veil. Nearly 140 species of birds arrive to feed, nest, and breed. The distinctive cry of the loon pierces the

The muted spectrum of a rainbow arcs the confluence of the Marsh Fork Canning and Canning rivers, right. The Canning River is one of 18 major rivers in the refuge.

SUMMER COLORS

A male ptarmigan, above, assumes reddish plumage in summer. When winter comes, its feathers turn white, except for the tail, which remains black.

silence. Snowy owls and jaegers glide like stealth fighters over the tundra on the hunt for lemmings, voles, and shrews. Gyrfalcons are joined by peregrine falcons, merlins, rough-legged hawks, and America's northernmost breeding population of golden eagles, all sailing on summer thermals in the Brooks Range. Some nesting pairs reunite and occupy the same aerie year after year.

After wintering on tidal flats and storm-battered beaches, countless shorebirds head for the middle of the tundra to find a mate and nest. At times the birds can be heard singing madly for a mate, at other times they quietly and inconspicuously guard their eggs. When a hiker comes upon a nesting plover, the bird will create a distraction by running away and peeping incessantly to divert the intruder from the location of the nest.

By early June caribou congregate on the refuge's Coastal Plain, located between the Katakturuk and Kongakut rivers. In this ideal nursery the pregnant females give birth to a single calf. The predatory grizzly bears, wolves, and golden eagles of the foothills to the south are relatively scarce here, and a wide array of plant life offers mothers and calves the necessary nutrition. For tens of thousands of years, the caribou have perfected their survival skills by outrunning wolves and bears and finding safe places to raise their young, just as the bison of the Great Plains once did.

WILDERNESS
BATTLEFIELD
The U.S. Fish and Wildlife Service describes the Arctic National Wildlife Refuge as America's "only national conservation area that provides a complete range of arctic ecosystems," and praises it for protecting "the greatest variety of plant and animal life of any conservation area in the circumpolar north." But the endless search for new sources of oil has culminated in one of the last wilderness battles of the 20th century in this remote corner of Alaska.

The caribou give birth in a part of the refuge's Coastal Plain that is as pristine as any place on earth. The oil industry is seeking permission to drill here. Conservationists oppose the development. In the words of U.S. Secretary of the Interior Bruce Babbitt, drilling "will inevitably shatter the delicate balance of land and life into a thousand fragments, like pan ice in the spring breakup . . ." Some Alaskan legislators, however, believe oil drilling would create jobs and spur economic growth. They also see an opportunity to link the declining oil fields of Prudhoe Bay, some 60 miles to the west, to the new oil fields in the refuge, thus increasing the total production in the region. They believe that no more than 23 square miles of tundra would be affected by oil drilling. Environmentalists, on the other hand, fear oil development would require a harmful network of roads, pipelines, airfields, pump stations, port facilities, drill pads, and seawater treatment plants.

Would caribou and other wildlife tolerate an oil complex on the Coastal Plain? No one is certain. If the caribou refused to calve near the complex, they might be forced to go south into the foothills or to migrate east toward Canada.

ABOVE THE TREE LINE
The brilliant red blossoms of the alpine bearberry, below, add a splash of color to the autumn landscape. These small plants grow above the tree line.

YEAR-ROUND RESIDENTS
The shaggy coats of the musk-oxen, left, provide the insulation they need to live on the refuge's Coastal Plains year-round. Their diet consists of forbs, sedges, and shrubs.

While most of the Inupiat Eskimos who live north of the Brooks Range favor oil development, the Gwich'in, Athabascan Indians living immediately south of the refuge and in Canada's Yukon Territory, oppose it. "The caribou is not just what we eat," says Sarah James, a Gwich'in leader, "it's who we are. It's in our stories, dances, songs, and the whole way we see the world. Caribou is our boots and mittens. Caribou is how we get from one year to another."

For now, the Arctic National Wildlife Refuge provides a safe nursery for the caribou. Newborn caribou calves, though wobbly, can stand minutes after being born, and in two weeks sprint alongside their parents. By that time in the young calf's life, the herd has usually migrated to the foothills to feed on blooming willows. One recent summer day biologists watched as four bears and a wolf attacked the herd. The caribou outran them every time. When a calf strayed too far from its mother, a magnificent blond grizzly closed in for the kill. Realizing its peril at the last moment, the calf bolted for the safety of the herd and barely escaped.

LAND OF THE MIDNIGHT SUN

The weather in the refuge fluctuates from year to year, but a wondrous, ancient consistency prevails overall. The soul of the earth rises and falls in a roadless, townless terrain that stretches beyond view. In June and July the tundra glitters with constellations of wildflowers: avens, arnicas, saxifrages, phloxes, lupines, and arctic poppies. The sun stays up all night, as the winter land of the afternoon moon becomes the summer land of the midnight sun. Unable to catch the increasingly fleet-footed

caribou calves, grizzlies feed instead on summer greens, berries, and arctic ground squirrels. A short feeding season and long hibernation period—up to eight months without food or drink—have caused bears this far north to stay small in size and suffer from low reproduction rates. Yet their populations remain stable.

SURVIVORS
IN THE WILD

Gray wolves can be legally trapped and shot in the refuge as well as elsewhere in Alaska. Still nowhere is the gray wolf more at home than in the Arctic National Wildlife Refuge, where five packs of about 30 animals patrol the North Slope and Coastal Plain. The wolves prefer to hunt in the foothills and along rivers in the mountains, rarely passing up an opportunity to catch small rodents and birds, an injured caribou, a distracted Dall sheep, or the biggest prize of all— a moose, the largest member of the deer family.

STAYING WARM
The arctic fox, left, is guarded from the cold by a thick coat that reaches all the way up to its ears, further reducing any loss of body heat.

SUMMER'S SURPRISES
Purple lupines dot the summer meadows leading up to the dramatic Brooks Range, left.

Wolf packs stick together throughout the winter, but in summer many wolves travel alone or in pairs. They always seem in a hurry, headed for a place only they know of and understand.

August brings a chill, and with it an early autumn that paints the tundra in successive shades of gold, sienna, and scarlet. Most of the nesting birds have left, but at the end of the month and in early September another spectacle of the air will unfold: the staging of the snow geese. Having raised their young in Canada, the geese arrive here in staggering numbers—up to 300,000—to fatten up on cottongrass in preparation for the flight south. They gorge themselves, feeding for up to 16 hours a day.

BOUNTIFUL LAND
A North American lynx sprawls on a lichen-encrusted rock, right. The Sheenjek River, below, meanders past the stunted trees and shrubs of a broad valley set among the peaks of the Brooks Range south of the Continental Divide.

ANNUAL MIGRATION
Herds of caribou, left, trek across the Coastal Plain, where, between May and July, they will bear their young. Their proximity to both the coast and the foothills enables the caribou to avoid insects and predators.

Their body fat increases by 400-fold as they fly from one cottongrass site to another, feasting on highly digestible underground stem bases. Then, as if choreographed, the geese call out in a cacophony and rise into the sky as one winged creature. They turn south, heading back to the Mackenzie Delta before beginning their 1,200-mile nonstop flight to the next resting and feeding area.

LONG DAYS OF WINTER

When old man winter returns to the area, bitter winds blow off the Beaufort Sea, some of which never thaws in summer. Ice forms anew. Once the ground freezes, grizzly bears seek out winter homes in rock caves or depressions of sandy soil capped by thick ice. The mantle of ice acts like a roof, preventing the dens from collapsing under the weight of the snow. The hibernating bears are able to survive the winter despite limited food resources.

Quiet reigns. The sun winks away toward the end of November, not to be seen for two months, and a billion stars appear, sparkling like diamonds on black velvet. A final stroke of magic, and great bands of green, yellow, and red flash and shimmer in the sky. It is the aurora borealis, the northern lights. Nature's light show takes many forms, creating elegant fans, curtains, and arches that sometimes brighten the entire sky.

The ancient drama of life and landscape is played out year after year; ever changing, ever the same. The Arctic National Wildlife Refuge is truly a last, great place—a reminder of North America as it once was and a vision of how it can forever remain if it is valued as a precious wildlife community rather than a commodity for development. For visitors to this northern domain, a sense of freedom, discovery, and wonder prevails.

FEATHERS AND FLOWERS
Snowy owlets peer over a garden of gay alpine flowers, above. The owls are among the few species of birds that stay in the Arctic year-round.

Nearby Sites & Attractions

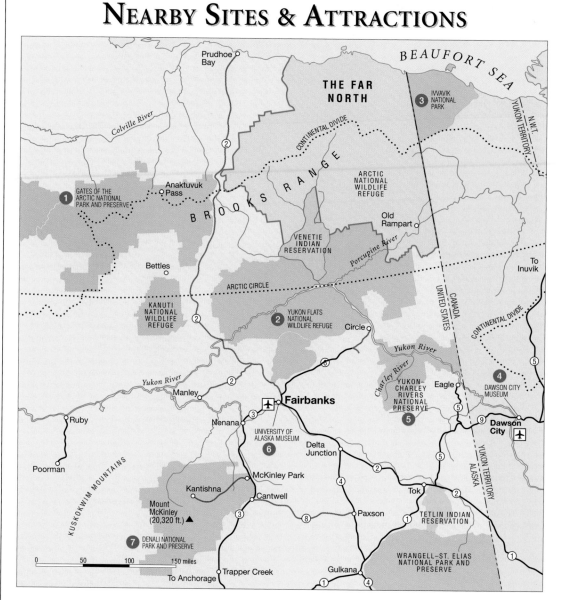

A mask, below, made of caribou skin and trimmed with fur, is displayed at the Eskimo Village at Anaktuvuk Pass, the northern entrance to Gates of the Arctic National Park and Preserve.

1 GATES OF THE ARCTIC NATIONAL PARK AND PRESERVE, ALASKA

Located in one of the most remote regions in the nation, this national park was created to preserve the heart of the Brooks Range. Gates of the Arctic is truly an untamed wilderness with no roads, facilities, hiking trails, or campgrounds. For veteran outdoor enthusiasts, hiking through this rough terrain is the experience of a lifetime. The rugged Arctic landscape was formed by the gouging of ancient glaciers and continues to be shaped by relentless wind and ice. Churning rivers and gentle streams dissect the treeless tundra, which is carpeted with wildflowers in the summer. Dramatic granite peaks jut more than 7,000 feet into the crisp Arctic sky. The southern slopes are cloaked with taiga—a sparse forest of dwarfed black spruce trees. Grizzly bears, wolves, moose, caribou, and wolverines are just some of the creatures that roam freely within the park's boundaries. Visitors must charter a small plane in Bettles to get to the park.

2 YUKON FLATS NATIONAL WILDLIFE REFUGE, ALASKA

The Yukon River reaches its most northern point within this 8.48-million-acre refuge and spreads into a vast flood plain for 200 miles. The refuge is dotted with some 40,000 ponds and lakes, and 25,000 miles of rivers and streams meander through the region. The wetland valley has one of the highest nesting densities of waterfowl in the nation. Each spring more than 1.5 million nesting waterfowl return to the area, including sandhill cranes, trumpeter swans, Canada geese, Pacific loons, and approximately 100,000 horned and red-necked grebes. Peregrine falcons, golden eagles, and red-tailed hawks nest on craggy rock ledges. Among the four-legged creatures of this refuge are black bears, Dall sheep, and the striking long-haired lynx. The best way to visit the region is by taking a float trip down one of the 10 major rivers that crisscross the refuge. Visitors must fly into the refuge; planes can be chartered in Fairbanks.

③ IVVAVIK NATIONAL PARK, YUKON TERRITORY

The spring thaw attracts huge numbers of caribou back to their traditional calving grounds, now protected within the boundaries of this Canadian national park. Massive grizzlies and polar bears are full-time residents here. Barely marked by man, the region has no visitor facilities. As the snow melts, rivers spill their banks and marshy ponds form on the tundra, beckoning a wide array of nesting waterfowl. One of the few regions of Canada that was never glaciated, the park lies in the northwestern corner of the Yukon and is accessible only by chartered plane from Inuvik in the Northwest Territories and Old Crow in the Yukon.

④ DAWSON CITY MUSEUM, YUKON TERRITORY

Housed in an elegant building that was first used as the Yukon's Legislative Assembly, the Dawson City Museum interprets the natural and cultural history of this colorful region. Ancient fossils and Han Indian artifacts tell the story of the Yukon's early days. Also on display are exhibits on the North West Mounted Police and a fully furnished 1896 miner's cabin. Located on 5th Ave. in Dawson City.

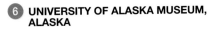

⑤ YUKON–CHARLEY RIVERS NATIONAL PRESERVE, ALASKA

Some 130 miles of the mighty Yukon River and the entire 118-mile length of its scenic tributary, the Charley River, churn through this expansive landscape. Canoeists and kayakers can test their mettle on various challenging waterways. Boaters find camping at its best on the open beaches and sandbars along the river, and can enjoy daytime hiking excursions through the bordering highlands. In springtime the region is alive with calving caribou,

grazing black bears, and nesting peregrine falcons, whose spectacular diving attacks on migrating birds thrill bird-watchers. Air taxis to the park leave from Tok and Fairbanks year-round.

⑥ UNIVERSITY OF ALASKA MUSEUM, ALASKA

A depository for the state's natural and cultural history for more than 60 years, the museum holds some of Alaska's deepest secrets. Visitors learn how solar winds and the magnetic field combine to create the haunting beauty of the northern lights; how the landscape was carved by glaciers and altered by volcanoes and earthquakes; and how Alaska's Native peoples have learned to adapt to the harsh climate. Organized by region, the museum's galleries display dinosaur bones, a mummified Pleistocene bison, and examples of the pink coral and sea anemones found beneath the polar ice pack. Alaska's Native heritage is explored through collections of Athabaskan beadwork, Eskimo carvings, and Tlingit and Haida potlatch goods. Located at 907 Yukon Dr. in Fairbanks.

⑦ DENALI NATIONAL PARK AND PRESERVE, ALASKA

The most outstanding feature in this remarkable terrain is Mount McKinley. Covered by ice fields more than 100 feet thick in places, this 20,320-foot granitic peak is the highest in North America. In spring massive glaciers on the northern face of the Alaska Range feed braided rivers and streams. Arctic poppies and saxifrage sprout in the tundra in late June; by early August cranberries and bog berries have burst on the scene. The park is equipped with campsites, a visitor center, hotels, tours, and shuttle buses that take passengers from the visitor center to Wonder Lake. Hikers can view local wildlife, including some 37 species of mammals. The park allows backcountry hiking and offers some of the most challenging mountaineering in the world. Located 120 miles south of Fairbanks on Hwy. 3.

Hundreds of small tundra ponds, such as the one shown above, are formed when melted snow pools in the lowlands and valleys of Denali National Park.

Wolf tracks on the shores of the Yukon River, left, in Yukon–Charley Rivers National Preserve, are a telltale sign that this is still wild country.

MOLOKAI ISLAND

---

*Golden beaches, sculpted sand
dunes, and lush rain forests make
this island a tropical paradise.*

Entering the misty Kamakou Preserve on the Hawaiian island of Molokai is like walking into a primeval jungle. The Pepeopae Trail, a narrow boardwalk, creaks through an ancient rain forest and then ascends to an equally old montane bog atop Molokai's tallest mountain, Kamakou. The unwitting visitor who steps off the wooden walkway could trample a rare species of plant whose leaves, buds, or bark hold the cure for a disease. Or the plant may serve as the host for an insect species eaten by a particular bird that pollinates a certain tree, and so on up and down the ecological chain.

This walk on Kamakou may stir up something of the exhilaration felt by the European explorers who first encountered the uncharted terrain populated by an unknown people. The explorers were enchanted by the numerous wondrous and alien sights they beheld and declared the land a paradise. The artists and scientists in their parties carried home proof of this claim in the exotic flora they replanted in foreign lands.

COLORFUL NATIVE

Sporting bright red plumage, an iiwi perches on an akala plant, above. A member of the honeycreeper family, the bird has a curved beak perfectly shaped to sip nectar from blossoming flowers.

ROYAL VALLEY

Overleaf: Waves lap the black-sand beach fringing the waters of Halawa Bay. Halawa means "curve," and this crescent-shaped beach, once popular with Molokai's chiefs for surfing, attracts surfers to this day.

The Hawaiian Islands are a unique natural showcase, a living museum of adaptation and evolution. They are the tops of a range of mountains formed by volcanic activity. Farther from a land mass than anywhere else on earth, they have never been connected to any continent. When the islands emerged from the ocean, the land was sterile and barren. Life came borne on the trade winds and jet streams, in the ocean currents, and in the feathers and digestive systems of migratory birds. The wildlife proliferated slowly, taking thousands of years to establish each new species.

EARLY COLONISTS

From a state of utter isolation, these colonizing seeds, spores, birds, and insects diversified into an astonishing variety of life, certainly the most unusual array of nature in the United States. All of Hawaii's native forest birds exist nowhere else in the world. The islands' more than 70 species and subspecies of birds arose from as few as 15 colonizing species. Unique birds include a type of hawk, owl, goose, crow, two thrushes, a warbler, a flycatcher, and an entire subfamily of 47 kinds of Hawaiian honeycreepers. Of the islands' insects and land snails, nearly 100 percent are endemic, as are almost 95 percent of flowering plants and 65 percent of ferns, some of which grow as tall as a tree.

Specialization is so complete that some species live on one island and not another, or in one valley but not its neighbor. With no predators to fend off, the plants developed neither thorns nor noxious odors, and some flying insects lost their wings.

The impact of Western man and the introduction of nonnative flora and fauna, however, have had disastrous effects on Hawaii's native species. Of the 70 kinds of birds known to exist at the time of Capt. James Cook's arrival in 1778, 23 have become extinct and 30 are classified as endangered. Hawaii, with 72 percent of the extinct species recorded in the United States, is the endangered species capital of the nation.

A bright spot in this sad story is Molokai and its many nature preserves. One of the smaller Hawaiian Islands—a mere 37 miles long and 10 miles across—it contains a superabundance of flowers, birds, and other wildlife. Two volcanic mountain ranges stretch along the eastern and western parts of the island, separated by the plain of Hoolehua. The island's diverse topography is virtually untamed. The most pristine natural areas on the island are Lehuula, the Waikolu Plateau, Olokui, and the deep green valleys of Pelekunu and Wailau. Molokai's steep mountain ridges and palisades are cloaked in rare native flora and offer shelter for much of the island's bird population.

N

Kaiwi Channel

MOOMOMI
DUNES
PRESERVE

ILIO
POINT

MOKIO

Kepuhi

Kakaako Stream

PAPOHAKU
BEACH

MOLOKAI
RANCH
WILDLIFE
PARK

Kaluakoi
Road

Maunaloa

Puu Nana
(1,381 ft.)

LAAU
POINT

HALEOLONO
POINT

Halena

INFORMATION FOR VISITORS

Hwy. 450, also known as the Kamehameha V Hwy., is the main thoroughfare on the island. This coastal road runs east from Kaunakakai to Halawa Valley and the Kapuaiwa Coconut Grove. The Molokai Ranch Wildlife Park is located off Kaluakoi Rd. Kamakou Preserve, accessible only to four-wheel-drive vehicles, is located about one-half mile south of the junctions of Hwys. 460 and 470 on Jeep Rd. The road is often impassable, and visitors should check road conditions with the preserve. To get to the Moomomi Preserve, take Maunaloa Hwy. to Kalae Hwy., then continue along Farrington Ave. until the pavement ends. Four-wheel-drive-vehicles can take the dirt road that leads to the preserve; other visitors must continue on foot. Hawaiian Air offers regularly

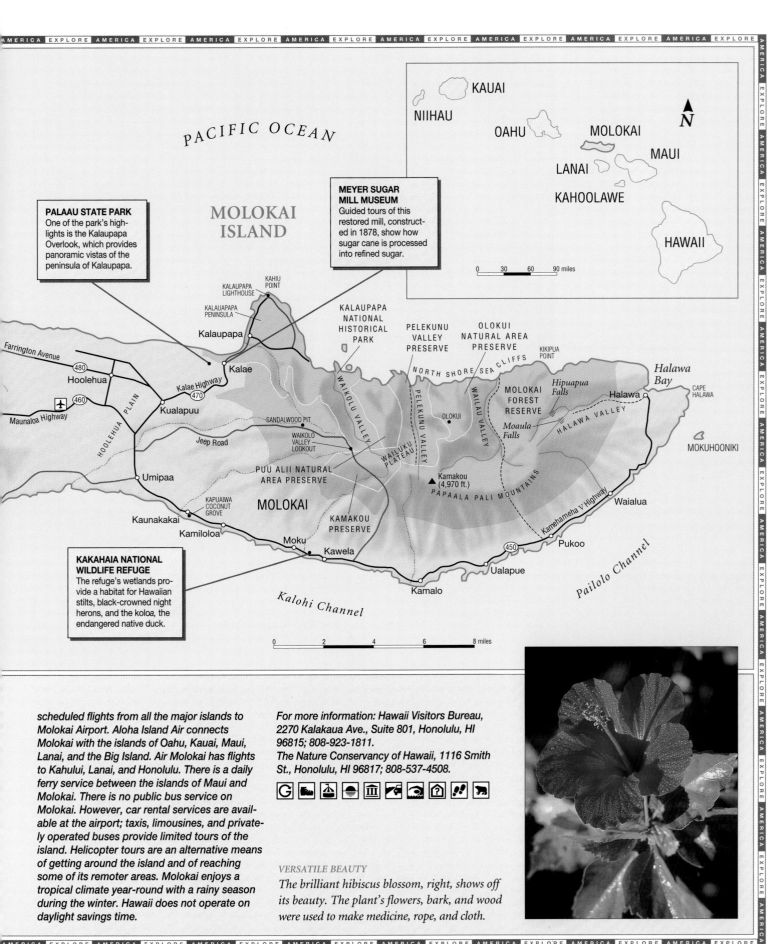

PACIFIC OCEAN

MOLOKAI ISLAND

KAUAI
NIIHAU
OAHU
MOLOKAI
MAUI
LANAI
KAHOOLAWE
HAWAII

N

0 30 60 90 miles

PALAAU STATE PARK
One of the park's high-lights is the Kalaupapa Overlook, which provides panoramic vistas of the peninsula of Kalaupapa.

MEYER SUGAR MILL MUSEUM
Guided tours of this restored mill, construct-ed in 1878, show how sugar cane is processed into refined sugar.

KAHIU POINT
KALAUPAPA LIGHTHOUSE
KALAUAPAPA PENINSULA
Kalaupapa
Kalae
Farrington Avenue
Hoolehua
480
Kalae Highway
470
460
Kualapuu
Maunaloa Highway
HOOLEHUA PLAIN
SANDALWOOD PIT
Jeep Road
WAIKOLO VALLEY LOOKOUT
Umipaa
KAPUAIWA COCONUT GROVE
PUU ALII NATURAL AREA PRESERVE
MOLOKAI
Kaunakakai
Kamiloloa
Moku
Kawela
KAMAKOU PRESERVE

KALAUPAPA NATIONAL HISTORICAL PARK
PELEKUNU VALLEY PRESERVE
OLOKUI NATURAL AREA PRESERVE
KIKIPUA POINT
NORTH SHORE SEA CLIFFS
WAIKOLU VALLEY
PELEKUNU VALLEY
WAILAU VALLEY
MOLOKAI FOREST RESERVE
Hipuapua Falls
Halawa
Halawa Bay
CAPE HALAWA
OLOKUI
WAILUKU PLATEAU
Moaula Falls
HALAWA VALLEY
MOKUHOONIKI
Kamakou (4,970 ft.)
PAPAALA PALI MOUNTAINS
Waialua
Kamehameha V Highway
450
Pukoo
Ualapue
Kamalo
Pailolo Channel

KAKAHAIA NATIONAL WILDLIFE REFUGE
The refuge's wetlands pro-vide a habitat for Hawaiian stilts, black-crowned night herons, and the koloa, the endangered native duck.

Kalohi Channel

0 2 4 6 8 miles

scheduled flights from all the major islands to Molokai Airport. Aloha Island Air connects Molokai with the islands of Oahu, Kauai, Maui, Lanai, and the Big Island. Air Molokai has flights to Kahului, Lanai, and Honolulu. There is a daily ferry service between the islands of Maui and Molokai. There is no public bus service on Molokai. However, car rental services are avail-able at the airport; taxis, limousines, and private-ly operated buses provide limited tours of the island. Helicopter tours are an alternative means of getting around the island and of reaching some of its remoter areas. Molokai enjoys a tropical climate year-round with a rainy season during the winter. Hawaii does not operate on daylight savings time.

For more information: Hawaii Visitors Bureau, 2270 Kalakaua Ave., Suite 801, Honolulu, HI 96815; 808-923-1811.
The Nature Conservancy of Hawaii, 1116 Smith St., Honolulu, HI 96817; 808-537-4508.

VERSATILE BEAUTY
The brilliant hibiscus blossom, right, shows off its beauty. The plant's flowers, bark, and wood were used to make medicine, rope, and cloth.

VERDANT PRESERVE
Moss-covered trees and giant ferns are among the splendors of the rain forest, which grows at elevations above 4,000 feet in the Kamakou Preserve, right. A boardwalk plunges deep into this lush landscape, which receives about 150 inches of rainfall a year.

WORLD IN MINIATURE
A carpet of fragile plant life, below, spreads over Pepeopae Bog, located within the Kamakou Preserve. Unique soil conditions stunt plant growth, creating miniature versions of island vegetation.

The 2,774 acres of the Kamakou Preserve, on the western flank of the 4,970-foot volcanic peak, range from gulch bottoms to summit rain forests and bogs. Of the 250 kinds of plants that grow here, 219 live nowhere else on earth. The plants support hordes of native insects, and together they provide a haven for Molokai's unique forest birds. The last known sightings of rare and endangered birds such as the Molokai thrush and the Molokai creeper occurred within this forest sanctuary.

Located just outside the preserve is an old sandalwood pit made in the days of China trade when the Hawaiians harvested iliahi—a fragrant variety of sandalwood—and tossed the logs into pits dug to the size of a ship's hull. When a pit was full, the logs were hauled down the mountain to vessels bound for the Orient, leaving behind a multitude of stumps. During the Depression, the Civilian Conservation Corps replanted vast numbers of trees in an attempt to control soil erosion in the area. Unfortunately for the native forest, the corps introduced nonnative species, including Norfolk pine, eucalyptus, Japanese cedar, Oregon ash, and even plum trees.

A closeup view of the trunk of the eucalyptus tree, left, reveals its multihued bark. The slopes of the Halawa Valley are covered with forests of this aromatic tree.

ferns, woven into the canopy of tall ohia trees. Near the top of Kamakou, the forest ends abruptly as if on command. This is the domain of Pepeopae Bog—a Lilliputian world of plant life. The ohia trees that towered in full glory in the forest, mature in the bog at a mere four inches tall but still send out full-sized scarlet blossoms. Plant growth is stunted here due to its particular soil conditions: underneath the surface lies a layer of lava that traps highly acidic, oxygen-deprived water. The grasses and mosses that carpet the bog range in colors from silver to viridian. Nurtured only by rain, swift ghostly mists, and golden sunshine, the landscape of Pepeopae Bog resembles a lovingly tended Japanese bonsai garden.

SHORELINE SAND DUNES

The Moomomi Dunes showcase another of Molokai's magnificent natural kingdoms. The coast of the island is wind scoured, salt-sprayed, bone dry, and uncompromising, asking neither for water nor nourishment. This wild shore fringes the northwestern corner of Molokai, in view of the tall Kalaupapa lighthouse. At one end, the ocean assaults jagged sandstone ledges, sending up plumes of foaming spray. A long scimitar-shaped beach is enclosed by rolling sand dunes. Powerful northeastern trade winds carry white coral sands far inland, where they settle and are attenuated into dunes a mile long and hundreds of feet wide.

The dunes are a last refuge for the Hawaiian flora of an ancient era. Clinging tenaciously to this untamed landscape are lovely low-level plants. The silvery green hinahina with its tight clusters of fragrant white blossoms covers the sand like a mat. The thick leaves of these sweet-smelling heliotropes are protected from the heat of the sun by delicate hairs. The leaves of another plant, the pale silver enaena, are as soft as the coat of a baby seal, yet the plant is able to take root in the dry sand and blooms in spite of the howling winds. Also dressing up the dunes are the lilac blooms of the beach morning glory and the coral blossoms of the ohai, an endangered beach legume.

KAMAKOU PRESERVE

The entrance to the Kamakou Preserve is at Waikolu Valley Lookout, which overhangs a green notch in the mountains where waterfalls plunge into unseen emerald depths and the ocean laps at the edge of the valley. The air is filled with the sweet fragrance of flowers and the melodic songs of birds. The Hawaiian owl still hunts in this place where vivid green amakihis flit through the trees, stopping to feed on fragrant blossoms, and scarlet apapanes sip sweet nectar from the brilliant red blossoms of the ohia.

Lush spongy mosses and lichens adorn the trees and forest floor. Peeking out are delicate orchids the size of a thumbnail and silver lilies that resemble fallen stars. Beyond its great beauty, the vegetation within the preserve is essential to the very survival of Molokai. A kind of sedge marsh plant also grows here whose white heart was once used by the early Hawaiians in weaving baskets. More importantly the rain forest of Kamakou supplies the island with more than half of its water.

The trail winds upward through this dense and leafy rain forest. There are entire thickets of tree

The native fiddlehead fern or amaumau, above, thrives within the mountainous forests of the Kamakou Preserve.

Hardiest of the beach plants is the naupaka shrub with its distinctive white berries and curly waxed leaves. Legend says that the blossoms of two types of naupaka, each of which looks like a half-bloom, represent a fisherman and the princess he loved, forever separated because of the difference in their stations. Undulating carpets of akiaki grasslands stabilize the shifting dunes, allowing rare native nightshades to take root. One vine that grows here, known as the pau-o-Hiiaka, spreads out its lacework of roots, helping to hold the dunes together. According to folklore, the vine first appeared at Moomomi when it adorned the goddess Hiiaka-i-ka-poli-o-Pele as she rested on the shore.

Within the sands of the Moomomi Dunes Preserve lie the secrets of the life forms that once inhabited the region. Some of the dunes have been petrified through the ages. Erosion reveals the fossils of extinct Hawaiian birds and the shells of land or tree snails, embedded in the hardened dunes. Deposits of bird bones found by paleontologists are evidence that these time-worn dunes were once hospitable to at least 30 bird species, of which approximately one-third are now extinct, among them a sea eagle, a falconing owl, a flightless ibis, and a giant flightless goose. One set of bird bones is estimated to be at least 25,000 years old.

HISTORY OF THE DUNES

As early as the 11th century, the ancient Hawaiians who inhabited the Pelekunu Valley came to Moomomi to fish, gather salt, and collect dense basalt for making adzes. They took up shelter in a cave at one end of the beach, and the charcoal-stained soil of the area marks the site of a coastal house. Important archeological excavations at the dunes have uncovered the hammerstones used to shape the adzes that were the Hawaiians' major hewing implement. Nearby are haunting reminders of World War II—the tangled barbed wire and cement platforms where heavy guns were mounted.

Today the tracks of native sanderlings, plovers, and seabirds, including the great frigatebird, are imprinted in the sand along the shoreline. Endangered Hawaiian green sea turtles and the Laysan albatross build their nests in peace at Moomomi, and the occasional rare Hawaiian monk seal hauls itself ashore. At one time, the dunes were succumbing to the depredations of

all-terrain vehicles. No longer—now that The Nature Conservancy of Hawaii has stepped in.

The third Molokai preserve managed by the conservancy is Pelekunu Valley, notched into the rugged north shore of Molokai and guarded by the tallest sea cliffs in the world. Accessible only by an arduous two-day hike across the East Molokai Mountains or by boat in low tide, Pelekunu shelters a lowland rain forest and one of Hawaii's last remaining free-flowing streams, which runs from the mountaintops to the sea. The preserve is home to at least seven native animals, including the rare oopu alamoo, a freshwater fish. The upper valley encloses a native forest in which endemic hibiscus and gardenias thrive.

Growing high on the coastal cliffs is a rare member of the bluebell family, the alula. This fragrant plant, which looks like a cabbage on the end of a baseball bat, illustrates the delicate balance of nature and human intervention. The plant clings to the sea cliffs, its thick stems strong and flexible in the wind. Its pollinator—thought to be a moth that has either become extinct or is extremely rare—has never been seen. The alula survives in the wild only because concerned botanists rappel down the face of the Molokai cliffs in order to pollinate it mechanically. Individual plants are also being cultivated in the controlled environment at the National Tropical Botanical Garden on the island of Kauai. The natural habitat of alulas continues to shrink on Molokai due to the grazing of wild goats and pigs.

Dividing the Pelekunu and Wailau valleys is the tallest of the sea cliffs, and at the top is Olokui, an area so inaccessible that even the feral pigs and goats that have caused so much havoc in Molokai's other wilderness areas have not invaded the area. The Olokui forest resembles Hawaii as it looked before the arrival of the first Polynesian voyagers. Set aside as a natural area reserve by the state, the forest is a restricted region, closed to the public, and the most pristine in the Hawaiian islands.

STATELY TREE

Some interisland airlines fly over Molokai's northern coast, with its cascading waterfalls and mysterious valleys. From the air the untrammeled forest unfolds in an awesome and unforgettable panorama of a hundred hues of green. Scattered splotches of silver among the green indicate stands of kukui trees, an 80-foot member of the Euphorbiaceae or spurge family. The tree was used by the ancient Hawaiians as a source of fuel, food, light, medicine, dye, and ornament, and is designated the state tree of Hawaii.

On the road to Halawa Valley, visitors will come upon a sacred kukui grove, in which the remains of Lanikaula lie. A famous 16th-century sorcerer, Lanikaula, or "one who knows the secrets," decreed Molokai a spiritual refuge where warfare was prohibited. Lanikaula was also hailed as the Prophet of Molokai. In fact, the ancient name of the island is Molokai Pule Oo, which means Molokai of the Powerful Prayer. Betrayed by a rival sorcerer from nearby Lanai, Lanikaula was killed, and his sons

WINDSWEPT BEAUTY
The island's western lowlands are protected within Moomomi Dunes Preserve, left. Steady trade winds sculpt the dunes into beautiful, undulating shapes.

FLOWER PLUMAGE
The feathery blossom of a bird-of-paradise, left, gracefully fans out in a spray of tropical colors.

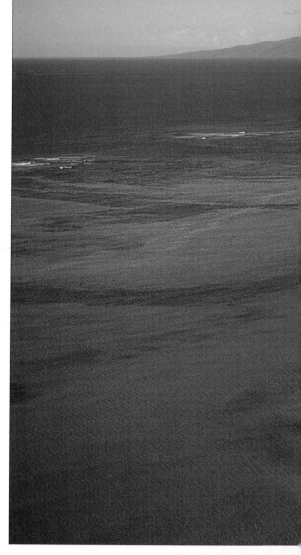

buried him. They hid the grave by planting groves of kukui trees around it so that Lanikaula's enemies would be unable to find his bones and use their power to control his spirit.

A system of aquaculture ponds once ringed all the Hawaiian Islands and some still scallop the shore of Molokai along the road to Halawa. In recent years this traditional method of stocking fish has been rediscovered, and an old fish pond is still in use at the Kakahaia Beach Park and National Wildlife Sanctuary. The sanctuary was once a puuhonua, a sacred and inviolable place of refuge for women and children in time of war. Now the tranquil grounds protect endangered waterbirds. Among them are the Hawaiian coot, gallinule, and the stilt—a long-legged wading bird that lures predators away from its nest by faking wing injury.

The beach park has fine examples of the tall niu, or coconut palm. The best place to find these majestic trees is within the Kapuaiwa Coconut Grove, located just outside Molokai's main town of Kaunakakai. A thousand trees were planted there in the 1860's for King Kamehameha V. Today the extensive grove contains approximately 2,000 trees, making it the largest preserve of these stately palms in Hawaii. Curlews, which breed in the Arctic and winter on Molokai and the neighboring island of Niihau, are often sighted on the mudflats along the waterfront during their sojourn.

OUT OF AFRICA
Imported zebras, such as the one below, can be spotted at the Molokai Ranch Wildlife Park. These animals graze in dry scrub plains that closely resemble their native landscape.

WRAPPED IN GREEN
A 750-foot-high promontory overlooks the seemingly endless mantle of green that cloaks Halawa Valley, right. The valley is one of three places in Hawaii settled by the earliest Polynesians to arrive in these tropical isles.

The first Hawaiian settlement on Molokai is believed to have been in Halawa Valley. Visitors can still see the lava rock walls that once enclosed patches of taro. Taro was used to make poi, an essential staple for these early inhabitants of Molokai. Now largely overgrown by the jungle, the remnants of ancient shrines and house sites are still visible. Groves of broad-leafed kamani trees mark the burial plots of the nobility. A trail leads through the jungle to Moaula Falls at the head of the valley. Unexpected clumps of impatiens interrupt the verdure of the path with their brilliant colors, and the scent of ginger fills the air. Mangoes, Indian mulberries, Java plums, Surinam cherries, and guavas also thrive in the valley. According to local legend, people discern whether it is safe to swim in the pool below the waterfall by placing a ti leaf on the surface of the water: If the leaf floats, swimmers may dive into the pool without fear of drowning; however, if the leaf sinks, a mountain spirit known as Moo is present and must be reckoned with.

The most curious preserve on the island is the Molokai Ranch Wildlife Park located on the parched western end. The Kaluakoi Road leading to the park wends its way through an arid landscape that closely resembles the African veldt. The road passes through sleepy Maunaloa, an old plantation town that sprang up during the days when the Dole pineapple company was the primary industry on the island.

In the 1960's, the ranch imported antelopes from Africa in the hope that the grazers would curb the encroachment of weeds and scrub, particularly kiawe, on pastureland. The ravines and dry plains of Molokai were similar to the antelopes' native habitat and they thrived, inspiring the importation of more exotic animals. Today, elands, ostriches, kudus, giraffes, zebras, Barbary sheep, and ibex roam the extensive grounds. These animals have become so at home on the range that many of them approach visitors' cars, providing some incredible photo opportunities.

From its lush rain forests and verdant valleys to its windswept dunes, dry grassy plains, and long stretches of white-sand beach, Molokai's diverse habitats are home to a splendid array of unique species of flora and fauna. Under the brilliant canopy of a night sky, a barely perceptible flutter of wings serves as a reminder that this lush oasis holds vast treasures well worth protecting.

OCEAN FISH POND
Coral and basalt walls encircle the blue waters of the Kapeke Fishpond, above, one of the many shoreline ponds built to raise fish for Hawaii's royalty. The island of Lanai is visible in the background.

NEARBY SITES & ATTRACTIONS

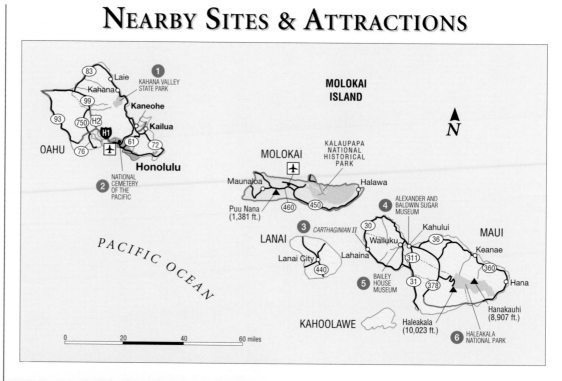

The hand-crafted masts of the Carthaginian II, a square-rigged brigantine, tower over Lahaina Harbor, above. The exhibits in this floating museum focus on whales and the whaling industry.

lookouts, each of which offers a spectacular vista of Kahana Bay. Hikers passing the Kahana Stream can swim in its cold mountain waters and pick mountain apples and guavas from the fruit trees that overhang the trails. Located south of Kahana on Hwy. 83.

2 NATIONAL CEMETERY OF THE PACIFIC, OAHU

One of the most tranquil spots on the island of Oahu is Puowaina, or the Hill of Sacrifice. More commonly known as the Punchbowl, this extinct volcanic crater is the place of interment for almost 40,000 Americans who died in armed conflicts dating from the Spanish-American War to Vietnam. A long roadway lined with Chinese banyan trees runs through the cemetery, where plumeria and rainbow shower trees are interspersed with flat granite headstones. The trees are commonly planted in Hawaiian cemeteries because their perennial flowers represent symbolic offerings from the living to the dead. The road leads to a monument dedicated to soldiers listed as missing in action (MIA). The monument includes a small chapel whose walls are covered with maps of the battles that took place in the Pacific theater during World War II. In the middle of the chapel stands a statue called *Columbia, Goddess of the Dead* that represents all the mothers of lost and fallen sons and daughters. Outside the chapel the names of 20,000 MIAs from World War II and Vietnam have been engraved on two marble slabs. Located in Honolulu off Hwy. 61.

1 KAHANA VALLEY STATE PARK, OAHU

Stretching from the mountainous Koolau Range to Oahu's east coast, Kahana Valley State Park is a place of natural beauty and archeological treasures. It is Hawaii's only publicly owned *ahupuaa*—one of the ancient land divisions that extended from the mountains to the ocean and marked off all the natural resources necessary for sustenance. The remains of a number of ponds formerly used to raise fish for food can be found within the park. Although many of the fish ponds are under renovation, they are still open to the public. Huilua Fishpond is located on the east side of Kahana Bay. The Kahana Valley receives approximately 75 inches of rainfall annually, and its dense tropical rain forest is home to a great number of bird species. Hiking trails lead visitors to two

3 CARTHAGINIAN II, MAUI

Humpback whales are annual winter visitors to Maui's offshore waters, and this museum, devoted to the study of whales and whaling, is appropriately housed aboard a 1920 schooner built in Kiel, Germany. On display are photographs, videos, whaling artifacts, and a 19th-century whaling boat discovered in an Inuit village in Point Barrow, Alaska, in 1973. The laborious task of refurbishing *Carthaginian II* was completed in 1980. Its lower deck was refitted with eucalyptus wood from Maui and its masts made of Douglas fir from Washington state. The ship's masts, yards, iron fittings, and spars were manufactured by hand, making it the world's only authentically refitted brigantine. Located in Lahaina Harbor.

④ ALEXANDER AND BALDWIN SUGAR MUSEUM, MAUI

Sugar was once Hawaii's primary export, and a visit to this award-winning museum transports visitors back to the plantation days of the early 20th century. Located across from an operational sugar mill, the museum is housed in the residence of its former superintendent, built in 1902. The collection includes artifacts, photographs, and scale-model exhibits on sugar production and on Maui's geography, climate, and water supply system. The museum's oldest artifact, an 1878 iron collar used to join two lengths of pipe, is on display in the Water Room. In the Mill Room, a working scale model of sugar factory machinery shows how cane is cut and crushed for its juice. A scale-model camp house, household artifacts, and a Japanese Buddhist altar are on display in the plantation life gallery. The museum is located at 3957 Hansen Rd. in Puunene.

⑤ BAILEY HOUSE MUSEUM, MAUI

Formerly an all-girls' school, this historic site now displays oil paintings by 19th-century Maui landscape painter Edward Bailey, as well as traditional Hawaiian art, including fine tapa cloth and calabashes, natural history and archeological artifacts, and an extensive photograph collection. Artifacts include quilts and china transported from Boston by missionaries early in the 19th century. Construction of the Bailey House began in 1833, 13 years after the first missionaries arrived in the Hawaiian Islands. Edward Bailey was the principal of the seminary until it closed in 1849. He continued to live in the house until 1890, using the dining room as his studio. Influenced by the Hudson River school of painting, Bailey spent the latter half of the century capturing the beauty of the Maui landscape in a collection of more than 100 paintings. The museum displays 26 of his works. Located at 2375-A Main St. in Wailuku.

⑥ HALEAKALA NATIONAL PARK, MAUI

The enormous depression in the middle of Mount Haleakala—actually a volcano—is the most impressive sight in Haleakala National Park. The craterlike bowl, called a summit valley, is 3,000 feet deep, 7.5 miles long, and 2.5 miles wide, and covers an area of 19 square miles. The entire park includes 28,665 acres and stretches from the volcano to Maui's east coast. Twenty-one cinder cones, some rising as high as 1,000 feet, form a mountain range on the floor of this yawning chasm. Hiking trails wind through a varied landscape of desert, rain forest, and dry forestland. Native trees blend with forests of introduced trees and plants, including pine, cactus, and eucalyptus. The silversword, a plant found only in Hawaii, grows in the park at elevations above 7,000 feet. The endangered nene, a wild Hawaiian goose that is the state's official bird, is also found here. Once abundant on all the islands, the nene is now found only on the Big Island, Kauai, and at Haleakala. Located off Hwy. 378.

A serviceman pays his respects at the National Cemetery of the Pacific, above. The cemetery is nicknamed the Punchbowl because it is located within the almost perfectly circular crater of a volcano.

An aerial view displays the moonlike landscape within Haleakala's summit valley, left. Designated an International Biosphere Reserve by the United Nations, the park protects the summit, the rain forest valley of Kipahulu, and Ohe'o Gulch.

Cloud Peak Wilderness in Wyoming's Bighorn Basin.

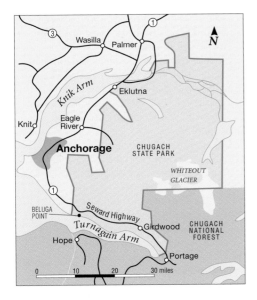

Lily pads mottle the tranquil surface of a beaver pond in Chugach National Forest, above. The region supports many species of animals in a variety of habitats.

Located north of Chugach National Forest, Chugach State Park is the perfect spot for those looking to get away from it all without traveling too far from civilization.

The landscape, chiseled thousands of years ago by massive glaciers, is dominated by snow-encrusted peaks that overlook ice fields, arctic tundra, and dense forests. A topographical mix of jagged peaks and deep valleys, the park's elevations range from sea level to 8,000 feet. Here where winter lasts up to 10 months, frigid temperatures cause entire waterfalls to freeze in dramatic ice sculptures. This sublime landscape is illuminated at night by the spectacular light show of the aurora borealis.

A wide variety of wildlife thrives in this bone-chilling cold. Dall sheep, mountain goats, wolves, wolverines, lynx, red foxes, porcupines, bald eagles, and sharp-shinned hawks are just some of the creatures that can be found here. Among the park's least popular inhabitants are mosquitoes, which proliferate during the summer months.

CLOSE ENCOUNTERS

Grizzlies, black bears, and moose also roam the park. While attacks are rare, it is important for visitors to exercise extreme caution and common sense if they encounter one of these large animals. The Potter Section House Historic Site and the Eagle River Visitor Center both mount interpretive displays and programs and offer travelers a wealth of useful tips on bear awareness and wilderness survival.

Its three campgrounds make the park a popular destination with outdoor enthusiasts. The Eklutna Lake and Eagle River campgrounds are located a short drive north of Anchorage, and the Bird Creek campground is about 20 miles southeast of the city, just off the Seward Highway. All three sites offer easy access to the park's major points of interest.

One of the park's most spectacular sights is the tidal bore in Turnagain Arm—a long fjord, which slashes into the park from the sea. Twice a day as the tide comes in, a roaring wall of water up to six feet high races up

the channel at speeds of 10 to 15 miles an hour. One of the best vantage points for this event is Beluga Point, located about halfway down the 9.4-mile-long Turnagain Arm Trail.

Popular winter activities include cross-country skiing, snowshoeing, dogsledding, snowmobiling, ice climbing, and tracking. Visitors should dress for extreme cold and educate themselves on emergency avalanche procedures before venturing into the backcountry during the winter.

Camping, rock climbing, mountain biking, horseback riding, boating, fishing, white-water rafting—even windsurfing—can all be enjoyed in the summer. As the days grow warmer, wild berries and mushrooms become plentiful, and a variety of wildflowers overtake the lower slopes of the Chugach Mountains.

The park has 28 hiking trails, ranging from easy walks on paved paths to steep trails with challenging river crossings and long climbs to solitary areas. Park rangers and naturalists conduct a variety of programs for visitors that cover topics like safe river crossing, wildflower identification, and bird-watching.

A unique place for people looking for a challenging vacation, Chugach State Park offers a chance to explore the wild and fragile beauty of the Alaskan landscape.

FOR MORE INFORMATION:
Chugach State Park, HC 52, Box 8999, Indian, AK 99540; 907-345-5014.

Moose graze peacefully in Chugach State Park, left. The largest species of the deer family, their antlers can grow to 78 inches in length.

If paradise can be defined as a place of unspoiled beauty and abundant wildlife, then the Yukon Delta National Wildlife Refuge qualifies as a Garden of Eden in the far north.

Spanning some 26 million acres, the refuge is one of the largest in the world—and one of the wettest. Encompassing the final stretch of the mighty Kuskokwim and Yukon rivers and their deltas, almost one-third of the region lies under water. This liquid landscape makes the area one of the most significant waterfowl breeding areas in North America. About 150 species of birds hatch their young within the refuge's expansive boundaries, including more than 500,000 swans and geese, 1.6 million ducks and millions of shorebirds and waterfowl. Large numbers of bristle-thighed curlews, white-fronted geese, tundra swans, and emperor geese nest here, as well as the world's entire population of cackling Canada geese.

Even a partial list of the refuge's feathered residents makes bird-watchers reach for their binoculars. Golden plovers, bar-tailed godwits, western sandpipers, red-throated loons, oldsquaws, surfbirds, and yellow wagtails are just some of the 220 species of birds that live in the refuge or that pass through the region each year on their annual migrations. With a diverse and seemingly endless supply of prey at hand, golden eagles, hawks, falcons, and other raptors can be seen soaring in the skies above certain bird of prey areas.

The countless lakes and ponds within the Yukon-Kuskokwim Delta, right, create the ideal conditions for waterfowl to raise their young.

Wildlife of every description thrives here on the vast, treeless wetland plain, nesting and feeding among the diverse vegetation of heath tundra, mosses, lichens, shrubs, and small willow and alder thickets.

The fast-flowing rivers teem with fish. Arctic char, whitefish, and northern pike lurk in the depths of the icy water. Each year millions of king, coho, sockeye, chum, and pink salmon churn their way up the Yukon and Kuskokwim rivers in order to spawn. Heeding a powerful, primeval instinct, the salmon battle the raging rapids in an heroic return to the waters where they were born. Completing this incredible cycle of life, the exhausted salmon die soon after they have spawned.

Springtime along the rivers also produces occasional sightings of ghostlike beluga whales and massive walruses. Along the coast harbor, ribbon, ringed, and bearded seals can be seen slicing through the waves in search of a watery meal.

MUSK-OX RESURGENCE

Almost all of the refuge's land mammals roam the mountains on its eastern and northern side. Black bears and huge hump-backed grizzlies pad through this continuously evolving habitat. Moose, caribou, wolves, red and arctic foxes, wolverines, tundra hares, minks, and muskrats also thrive in this isolated land.

Animal lovers get a rare treat on Nunivak Island, situated 20 miles west of the Alaska coast in the Bering Sea, where a herd of musk-ox lives in protected seclusion on the island's 1.1-million acres of volcanic cones and sea cliffs. Wiped out in Alaska by hunters in the late 1800's, 31 of these small, shaggy creatures were reintroduced to Alaska from Greenland in 1935. The herd has now grown to 500 and has been used as a breeding stock to establish herds elsewhere in Alaska and in the former Soviet Union.

Although the Yukon-Kuskokwim Delta provides a perfect habitat for wildlife, the demanding climate has proved to be too harsh for most humans—with the exception of the Yup'ik Eskimo culture. These aboriginal people enjoy a thriving existence in 42 small villages scattered throughout the delta, living in much the same way their ancestors did before them.

As with many of the protected lands of this unique region, the Yukon Delta is primarily wild country. Reached most easily by chartered plane, the refuge is known for its unpredictable weather and its lack of amenities. In order to get the most out of their trip, visitors should be self-sufficient and experienced backcountry adventurers. Those seeking the true wilderness will not soon forget the Yukon Delta National Wildlife Refuge.

FOR MORE INFORMATION:
Refuge Manager, Yukon Delta National Wildlife Refuge, P.O. Box 346, Bethel, AK 99559; 907-543-3151.

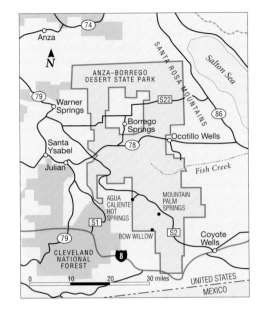

A Gambel's quail, below, surveys the surrounding terrain of the Anza–Borrego Desert State Park from its perch.

in the arid soil, which supports diverse vegetation ranging from creosote scrubs to conifer forests.

At the eastern end of the park, Fish Creek's raised fossil reefs are the petrified casualties of geological shifts. Despite its name, the region has been devoid of fish since 1914, when rock and debris from a huge tropical storm buried the creek. The fossilized remains of more than 100 species spanning 20 million years trace the area's metamorphoses from desert to marine estuary to savanna, and back to desert. Amateur geologists may be particularly interested in Split Mountain, a canyon formed by an ancestral stream, and the rock formations at Olla Wash.

LAVA FLOWS AND PALM OASES

In Bow Willow, the terrain varies from gloomy badlands to a landscape strewn with granite boulders as big as three-story houses. The volcanic hills between the dry stream beds of Mortero and Jojoba offer visitors a chance to explore the park's most accessible lava flow. When rain nourishes the flowering brittle bush, the purple-black lava fields are offset by yellow blossoms.

In Mountain Palm Springs, located just north of Bow Willow, visitors can camp near a complex of oases shaded by California fan palms. The spring-fed pools support lush vegetation, aquatic insects, and species of frogs and toads uncommon to the desert. Hikers can see elephant trees and six distinct palm groves.

Each spring the park's mountains are dappled with the reds, purples, oranges, and golds of blossoming cacti and wildflowers. The roselike flowers of hedgehog cacti are an exquisite rarity, and 20-foot agaves wait several decades to bloom. Common plants, such as ocotillo and beavertail cactus, set the desert ablaze with their fiery blossoms. The peak blooming period lasts approximately two weeks and takes place sometime between early March and late May depending on temperatures and rainfall.

The annual explosion of color is dazzling, and so are the subtly changing shadows created by the sun's advance over the buff-colored desert. The undulating slopes and zigzagging mountains play out rhythms that describe the beauty of the park in a way no words can express.

Located on the western edge of the park, Culp Valley, above, offers stunning vistas of the desert floor.

Encompassing sun-baked badlands, cactus-studded canyons, and sheer mountain peaks that rise to great heights, the breadth and variety of Anza–Borrego Desert State Park seem to defy the standard definition of a desert. Located just east of San Diego, the 600,000-acre region is a true geological oddity.

From Font's Point, visitors are afforded a 360-degree view of desertscapes that resemble surreal tableaus. Centered in the Borrego Badlands, the point overlooks the remains of a Pliocene epoch aquatic delta. Where nourishing wetlands and savannas once covered the region, waves of soft rock now ripple in rich mauves and reds.

In the distance, a rocky matrix of mountains stretches far and wide before meeting sharp ridges formed by massive fault lines.

Borrego Mountain splits into twin peaks along the southern horizon, and to the west, the granitic San Ysidro Mountains border the arid terrain. Facing north, the magnificent Santa Rosa Mountains soar 8,700 feet from the dusty desert floor.

Thrust upward in one mass as the result of geological upheaval, the Santa Rosas are among the most forbidding sights of the Anza–Borrego region. Visitors who trek through the surrounding area can spot bighorn sheep grazing in the desolate mountains, which harbor half of the park's population of these surefooted creatures. (*Borrego* is Spanish for sheep.) At night granite night lizards scurry among the rocks, while western mastiff and pocketed free-tailed bats fly by. Unique plants such as Parish's larkspur and Santa Rosa sage grow

FOR MORE INFORMATION:

Anza–Borrego Desert State Park, 200 Palm Canyon Dr., Borrego Springs, CA 92004; 619-767-5311.

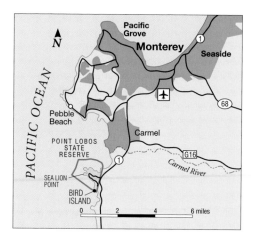

The dark forms of Brandt's cormorants speckle Bird Island, above. Located at the southern tip of the reserve, the island is crowded each spring and summer with thousands of nesting sea birds.

Legend has it that *Treasure Island*, Robert Louis Stevenson's classic, was inspired by the rocky shoreline of California's Point Lobos State Reserve. This dramatic landscape of rugged coves, sea cliffs, and lush kelp forests is indeed a marvel of coastal beauty and the perfect setting for a maritime adventure.

The region was dubbed Punta de Lobos Marinos, or Point of the Sea Wolves, for the hordes of sea lions that basked on the offshore rocks. Today visitors can still watch these agile creatures glide through the foaming surf at Sea Lion Point. Glossy-coated southern sea otters and harbor seals swim together among kelp forests, nibbling on mussels, crabs, snails, and sea urchins.

Established in 1933, the reserve was expanded in 1960 to include 750 submerged acres, making it the nation's first underwater reserve. In this watery realm the California gray whale is king. Between December and May, sightseers scan the ocean from Bird Island to Sea Lion Point, looking for the spouting mists or tail flukes that signal the presence of these giant creatures as they make their way up the coast. Fortunate visitors may also catch a glimpse of 40-foot-long humpback whales leaping headfirst from the water, as well as orcas and the rare northern elephant seal.

Divers and snorkelers can explore two rich offshore areas: Bluefish Cove and Whalers Cove. As they swim past 70-foot-high kelp beds, underwater enthusiasts will marvel at the lingcod, cabezone, and rockfish darting past unperturbed by the strangers in their midst. Visitors less keen to take the plunge might go see the cabin at Whalers Cove, which was constructed in the mid-19th century by Chinese fishermen. The floor joists of this structure are supported by whale vertebrae.

RUGGED COASTLINE

The reserve boasts rocky headlands and stark sea cliffs of granite and the soft sedimentary rock that was formed deep below the earth's crust millions of years ago. The steep cliff sides serve as nesting spots for pelagic cormorants, while their cousins, the Brandt's cormorants, prefer to construct their nests on Bird Island. While strolling along the shoreline, bird-watchers are also likely to see western gulls, white-crowned sparrows, brown pelicans, and black oystercatchers with bright-red bills.

Hiking is the best way to experience the wild at Point Lobos. A network of 13 trails takes visitors through pine woods, coastal scrub, sedges, and meadows adorned by California poppies and Indian paintbrushes. Highlights include the Carmelo Meadow Trail, where birds and small mammals attracts owls, bobcats, and coyotes. The Lace Lichen Trail is named for the gray-green lichen that hangs from the tree branches. Along the South Plateau Nature Trail visitors are likely to encounter gray squirrels, pygmy nuthatches, and black-tailed deer.

No trip to Point Lobos would be complete without venturing into its famed woods. One of the most popular routes is the Cypress Grove Trail, a half-mile loop that winds through stands of Monterey pine and leads past rare trees, including the Monterey cypress. Point Lobos and another grove across Carmel Bay at Cypress Point are the only spots on earth where Monterey cypress trees can be seen in their natural habitat. Like Robert Louis Stevenson before them, visitors to this unique land will find the experience truly inspirational.

FOR MORE INFORMATION:
California Dept. of Parks and Recreation, Point Lobos State Reserve, Route 1, Box 62, Carmel, CA 93923; 408-624-4909.

The cumbersome bulk and sleepy gaze of a northern elephant seal, left, belie the speed and power with which it slices through the water. Full-grown males reach lengths of 15 feet.

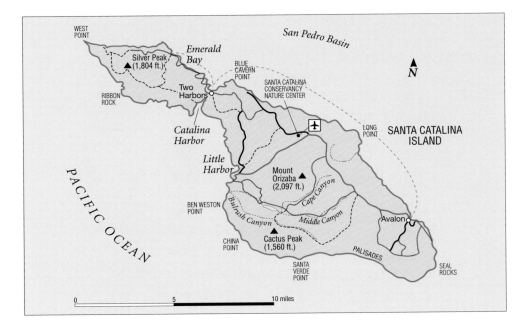

Just off the coast of southern California lie the scalloped shores of Santa Catalina Island, legendary playground of the affluent and influential. The island's crystal waters and pristine coves once drew the likes of Clark Gable, Teddy Roosevelt, Amelia Earhart, and Zane Grey, who built a house in Avalon in 1926. Today Catalina's image as a luxury resort is being overshadowed by its reputation as a place of carefully preserved natural beauty and bounty.

Discovered in 1542 by a Portuguese navigator named Juan Rodriguez Cabrillo, the 76-square-mile island has been a haven for smugglers, a range for cattle farmers, and a camp for Union soldiers. In the mid-1800's much of the island was ravaged by prospectors mining for gold, silver, and zinc. Chewing gum magnate William Wrigley, Jr., bought Santa Catalina in 1919 and developed a world-famous island retreat at the same time as he tried to preserve the land's natural beauty. His son Philip fulfilled that vision in 1972 by creating the Santa Catalina Island Conservancy.

The lengthy efforts to restore Santa Catalina to its natural state of splendor culminated in 1975 when 86 percent of the interior of the island was deeded to the conservancy. Today the hillsides are blanketed with prickly cacti, the lush valleys filled with chaparral, and the forested ravines speak of a land reborn.

The conservancy has reintroduced the bald eagle, rejuvenated coastal grasslands, and nurtured 15 species found nowhere else in the world. Among the plants and animals unique to the island are Catalina ironwood, St. Catherine's lace, Catalina mahogany, Catalina quail, and Catalina island fox.

During the summer, the conservancy introduces visitors to the natural treasures of this small island with organized walks led by experienced guides. Year-round Jeep tours take travelers into areas of Catalina's interior not normally open to the public.

An hour-long boat ride whisks visitors from Los Angeles to the tiny seaport of Avalon on the island where they are greeted by squadrons of gulls. Dotted with white houses sporting red-tiled roofs, Avalon is a place where leisure prevails and the sun shines an average of 267 days a year. The picturesque harbor is sprinkled with sailboats, and cobblestone streets lead from the palm-lined waterfront into town.

POSEIDON'S PARADISE
Catalina's sparkling waters are as clear as its blue skies. Bright orange garibaldi fish shine like beacons from lush underwater forests, where octopus, barracuda, calico bass, bat ray, and opaleye forage for food among the kelp forests and underwater caves. Among shipwrecks and massive rock pinnacles, scuba divers may come face-to-face with a playful harbor seal. An evening trip aboard a glass-bottomed boat reveals the island's nocturnal creatures, which include bioluminescent squids, bat rays, spiny lobsters, California morays, flying fish, cusk eels, and horn sharks.

Above water, intrepid kayakers paddle to Seal Rocks and watch the sleek animals lounge in the sun's orange glow or follow pebbled shores populated by curious brown pelicans. On Catalina's windward side, ocean rafters skim past towering cliffs to Ribbon Rock, where the island's geological history is visible in the bands of glorious silver quartz that stream diagonally between layers of dark metamorphic rock.

Nineteen miles from Avalon, the rugged verdant hillsides border wide canyons folded like creased fabric. Winding dirt roads take cyclists past buffalos, wild boars, deer, and wild turkeys that roam freely through the peaceful countryside.

Hiking trails lead to north-facing coastal bluffs where the air is scented with the aroma of sage scrub baked by the sun. Inaccessible to grazing animals, the area boasts the highest proportion of endemic plant species on the island. Amateur botanists may identify the delicate white flowers of St. Catherine's lace.

Other trails lead to the island's four campgrounds: one nestled in the hills between 2,000-foot peaks, and three others at seaside, where campers will be lulled to sleep by splashing surf.

Hikers should beware of rattlesnakes: Santa Catalina is the only Channel Island with a resident population of them. Herds of bison were introduced on the island in 1924 for the filming of a movie called *The Vanishing American* and today more than 400 of their descendants remain.

FOR MORE INFORMATION:
Catalina Island Chamber of Commerce and Visitors Bureau, P.O. Box 217, Avalon, CA 90704; 310-510-1520.

Set between the blues of sea and sky, the ragged coastline of Little Harbor on Santa Catalina Island, above, is a vision of paradise.

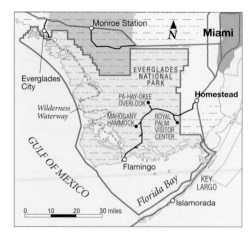

Wood storks, above, which still number less than a quarter of their 1930's population of 75,000, are making a valiant comeback in the Everglades.

Everglades National Park is a vast open wetland patched with small islands of stunted trees. Spread over 1.4 million acres in southern Florida, the glades are flooded by rivers, creeks, estuaries, sloughs, marshes, lakes, and ponds. Flowing across the Everglades' immense limestone bedrock, the water spreads through the sawgrass prairies, pine forests, oak hammocks, and mangrove swamps that border the ocean. The dense root system of the mangroves protects the coastline from erosion.

Pa-hay-okee, or "grassy water," is the Indian name for the Everglades. Today visitors can glide through this river of grass on rented canoes or skiffs. Water routes range from 3-mile loops to the park's 99-mile-long Wilderness Waterway. A seven-day canoe trip winds around bays, creeks, and estuaries fringed with mangrove thickets, which grow in the western portion of the park from Flamingo to Everglades City. One-hour sightseeing boat tours leave from the Gulf Coast Ranger Station.

On the eastern side of the park, Main Park Road runs through 38 miles of freshwater marshes, pinelands, hardwood hammocks, and coastal prairies. Inland areas are webbed by trails, while stretches of road near the town of Flamingo offer sparkling views of Florida Bay.

WADING BIRDS

Long-legged wading birds are a common sight in the park. Bright pink roseate spoonbills scoop up shrimp and small fish; graceful wood storks use their long bills to probe for food, their gray, featherless heads bobbing above the water; statuesque great egrets and great blue herons hunt for frogs; and little blue herons, snowy egrets, and tricolored herons stand nearly motionless as they scrutinize the water for prey. In spring wading birds perform courtship dances, announcing the spectacle with their shrill

cries. Bald eagles and the endangered snail kites are among the 326 bird species found in the park. The snail kite, also known as the Everglades kite, feeds on the tiny apple snails that cling to the blades of marsh grass. The kite's bill is designed to extract the snail from its shell.

The park also provides a habitat for about 60 species of amphibians and reptiles and 25 species of mammals. The endangered American crocodile skulks in saltwater estuaries, while bobcats, white-tailed deer, raccoons, opossums, and the extremely rare Florida panther hide in slash pine forests. Anglers can hook largemouth bass in fresh-

The brown-spotted yellow wing dragonfly, above, plays an important role in the wetland food web by feeding on mosquitoes. The dragonfly shapes its spindly legs in the form of a basket and scoops up its prey as it darts past.

water ponds or fish for saltwater snapper, redfish, and sea trout. Ranger-led tours from the Flamingo Visitor Center enable visitors to get close to the wildlife, including alligators and 27 species of snakes.

Seven marked trails showcase the park's distinct vegetation and wildlife. The Anhinga Trail—part boardwalk, part asphalt—allows visitors to see anhingas (also called water turkeys), which skewer fish with their sharp beaks, then swallow them head first. The Gumbo-Limbo Trail winds through royal palms and hardwoods strung with arboreal orchids and ferns. Local residents jokingly refer to gumbo-limbos as tourist trees because the red and peeling bark resembles sun-burned skin. Along the Mahogany Hammock Trail, hikers amble amid junglelike vegetation beneath a green canopy, walking past the largest mahogany tree growing in the United States.

Most visitors come to the park during the cool dry season, which lasts from mid-December to mid-April. This is also the time when the park records its lowest mosquito population.

FOR MORE INFORMATION:
Everglades National Park, 40001 State Rd. 9336, Homestead, FL 33034; 305-242-7700.

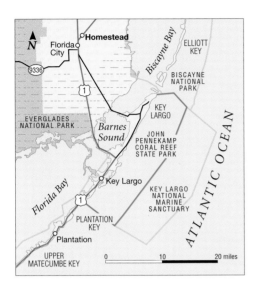

O ff the shore of Key Largo, iridescent fish dart through coral gardens teeming with multicolored marine animals. Sea anemones, sponges, jellyfish, snails, and crabs are just a few of the intriguing residents of this fragile underwater community. Blessed with a greater variety of life than any other marine environment in the nation, John Pennekamp Coral Reef State Park also protects a portion of the only living coral reef in the continental United States. Together with the adjacent Key Largo National Marine Sanctuary, the park covers approximately 178 nautical square miles.

Visitors come to these turquoise waters for the opportunity to go swimming, boating, lobstering, and saltwater fishing. But it is the coral reefs and their inhabitants that hold the greatest allure. The reef supports an incredible range of marine life, from microscopic organisms to giant manatees. From above the reef, snorkelers can view jewel-colored fish swimming amid vibrant coral formations shaped like antlers, fans, and brainlike domes. The tiny polyps that make up the coral reef feed by unfurling their tentacles to snag passing zooplankton that drifts in the water.

OCEAN THEATER

The drama of the ocean continues in the nearby seagrass beds, which help cleanse the waters that are critical to the survival of the coral reef. As the tide flows through the underwater meadows, the grass blades slow the currents, allowing sediments in the water to sink to the ocean floor. Crabs, pink shrimp, and lobsters scuttle through the nutrient-rich grass forests and starfish, queen conch, and urchins nibble on organisms living in the grass blades. Snappers, grunts, rays, and bonefish forage among the seagrass blades, while tarpons and barracudas circle the beds, poised to seize unwary fish. Lucky snorkelers may catch a glimpse of a manatee. This stout sea cow is a distant relative of the elephant and an endangered aquatic mammal. Some of these gentle giants weigh as much as 3,000 pounds.

Before heading to shore, divers should take a peek at the Marine Sanctuary's spectacular underwater monument: a nine-foot bronze statue called *Christ of the Deep*, created in Italy by sculptor Guido Galletti and submerged in 20 feet of water. The figure symbolizes peace for humankind.

No exploration of the ocean depths is complete without investigating a sunken ship. Resting in shallow waters 130 feet offshore, the park's reconstructed shipwreck is a tribute to the days when treasure-laden Spanish galleons once plied the Atlantic Coast. Among the authentic relics on display are 14 cannons from a Spanish fleet lost in a 1715 hurricane, an anchor from a 1733 shipwreck, and numerous ballast stones arranged in the shape of a ship's hull.

Back on land, visitors can follow a boardwalk nature trail through the mangrove forest and watch wading birds, such as roseate spoonbills, brown pelicans, snowy egrets, reddish egrets, and little blue herons fishing for their dinner. Red mangroves, the largest of the species, grow close to the water's edge, while the smaller black and white mangroves are found farther inland. Small crustaceans and fish search for food among the spiderlike roots of the red mangrove, and a rare American crocodile lurks in a nearby water channel.

The Wild Tamarind Trail, located in the park's 2,000-acre upland limestone area, winds through a tropical hammock. Native vegetation includes buttonwood, which was once used to make charcoal for smoking fish, and black ironwood, a heavy wood that will not float even in sea water. Nearby are clusters of green sea grape shrubs, which turn deep red in winter. The fruits of the native fig trees are a delicacy for wildlife, and the dense foliage of wild tamarinds provides a shady home for endangered tree snails. Schaus' swallowtails and Miami blue butterflies flit among rare wildflowers, such as butterfly orchids, wild cottons, and a night-blooming cactus called prickly apple.

The state park fosters natural habitats, from tropical hammocks to coral reefs, and offers a glimpse of how Florida may have looked when Europeans first laid eyes on it. Today visitors can view this underwater world from glass-bottom boats or by participating in scuba-diving and snorkeling excursions sponsored by the park. Visitors can rent motorboats, sailboats, and canoes at the marina. Diving and snorkeling equipment is also available for rental.

FOR MORE INFORMATION:
John Pennekamp Coral Reef State Park, P.O. Box 487, Key Largo, FL 33037; 305-451-1202.

A yellow stingray, above, lies half-buried in the sand in shallow water. A flat-bodied relative of the shark, the stingray is armed with venomous spikes along its whiplike tail.

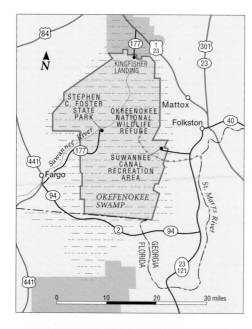

The murky water of an Okefenokee waterway, above, faithfully mirrors the robin's egg blue sky, fluffy white clouds, and surrounding green foliage, tricking the eye and delighting the heart.

In this predator's paradise, even plants are carnivorous. The hooded pitcher plant, above, consumes insects trapped in its sticky funnels.

At the headwaters of the Suwannee and St. Marys rivers in southern Georgia, slatted pine forests yield to brooding cypress stands, steamy marshes, and creeks as dark as strong tea. This is swamp country, where the alligators are known so well they have been given names and the night air is thick with mosquitoes.

The 396,000 acres of the refuge abound with bobcats, armadillos, black bears, white-tailed deer, and marsh rabbits. Countless other animals inhabit the swamp, including about 10,000 alligators, 37 species of snakes, and 11 lizard species.

Visitors can take a boat tour, stroll along boardwalks, or view the swamp from observation towers. But the best way to explore the exotic landscape is by canoe. Skimming along water trails cleared of floating lilies and aquatic sedge, canoes weave through the Okefenokee. Wooden platforms along the banks of the swamp indicate places to camp overnight, for which visitors must obtain permits.

Paddlers enter Okefenokee at Suwannee Canal, Stephen C. Foster State Park, or at Kingfisher Landing, between Folkston and Waycross. Once past the canal, the watery fields are choked with bladderworts, pipeworts, neverwets, and other species of swamp weeds. Egrets, ibis, storks, and crimson-crowned sandhill cranes build their nests here. Quiet canoeists observe the food chain in action: fishing spiders prey on insect larvae, herons feast on frogs, cormorants dive for fish, and alligators cruise the waters for turtles.

PEAT BOGS

Masses of decomposing swamp vegetation produce tannic acid, methane gas, and peat, which piles up in layers beneath the surface of the water. On occasion, gas rises from the depths of the bog with enough force to shoot chunks of peat up to the surface. Over time, many of the floating mats of peat are held in place by tree roots. Although some of the peat is firm enough to support a person's weight, it quakes at a footfall, which gave the area its Seminole name —"Land of Trembling Earth."

In damp hardwood hammocks of oak, swamp maple, and cypress trees, bird-watching enthusiasts can spot prothonotary warblers, brown-headed nuthatches, wood pewees, yellow-billed cuckoos, Carolina wrens, and chuck-will's-widows. Cypress stands draped with Spanish moss fill in approximately 80 percent of Okefenokee Swamp. Shading the bog with their thick canopy of foliage and curtains of hanging moss, the cypresses enhance the swamp's moody atmosphere.

With nightfall, the swamp becomes a noisy place. Chorusing frogs, bellowing alligators, chirping insects, hooting owls, croaking toads, and the steady drone of mosquitoes all add their voices to the darkness. When nighttime canoeists beam their flashlights on the water and the land, the gleam of many eyes—the red alligator, green-and-gold frogs, and the ebony eyes of raccoons—beam back.

Dyed black by the peat's tannic acid, the still waters of the swamp cast the silvery reflections of magnolia-fringed islands and fern-lined waterways. At day's end, the setting sun bathes sky and water in shades of magenta as flocks of snowy egrets take wing. It is a fitting conclusion to a day in this primeval place.

FOR MORE INFORMATION:
Okefenokee National Wildlife Refuge, Rte. 2, Box 3330, Folkston, GA 31537; 912-496-7836.

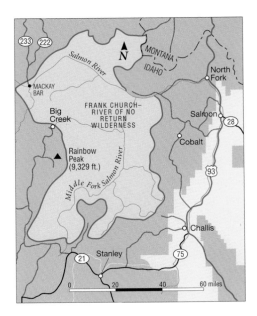

Covering 2.3 million acres of central Idaho, the Frank Church–River of No Return Wilderness is a lonely place where serious outdoor enthusiasts pit themselves against roaring whitewaters, steep volcanic slopes, sharp ridges, and glaciated subalpine lands.

Visitors must leave their vehicles at the wilderness boundary, then venture into the refuge by foot, horse, raft, or jetboat. Backpackers are advised to come equipped since few of the wilderness' 296 trails, most of which were created before 1930, offer facilities. Despite the 2,616-mile network of maintained trails, much of this wilderness kingdom remains virtually untouched.

MOUNTAINS AND BASINS

This is a landscape of sublime beauty. Mountain ranges soar from 2,000 to more than 10,000 feet. Rolling basin lands are covered with trees, brush, and grasses. At least 240 bird species are regular visitors to the area, including bald eagles, peregrine falcons, boreal owls, and belted kingfishers. Mule deer, white-tailed deer, elk, bighorn sheep, moose, and mountain goats range through deep canyons, and black bears, mountain lions, lynx, and wolverines prowl the forests. Wolves from Alberta have been recently reintroduced into the wilderness, and plans are under way to reintroduce the grizzly bear.

On fishing expeditions to the Bitterroot and Salmon forests, anglers can hook steelhead, cutthroat, rainbow, and brook trout.

The prospect of whitewater rafting lures the adventurous to the unbridled currents of Middle Fork Salmon River, right.

Elsewhere the water is burgeoning with game fish such as white sturgeon, arctic grayling, and mountain whitefish.

Outfitters lead expeditions into the region for hunting, fishing, camping, backpacking, cross-country skiing, horseback riding, photographing, and whitewater boating. Seasoned guides teach visitors how to camp in the wild and cook outdoors, and instill in them a healthy respect for the wilderness and the local ecology.

WILDFIRES

Naturally occurring fires in the wilderness are often beneficial because they help maintain the ecological balance and reduce the buildup of natural ground fuels. The area experiences about 100 fires each year. Although most of them—nearly 55 percent—are triggered by lightning—fires set by humans continue to be a problem in the wilderness. Experienced campers carry self-contained stoves to reduce the chance of escaped flames.

In 1805 William Clark and some fellow explorers on the Lewis and Clark expedition arrived in the region, becoming the first white men to see the Salmon River area. Their journals note the outstanding quality of the skins of beaver, buffalo, and bear worn by local Indians. Fur-trapping enterprises soon followed, but wildlife continued to flourish in central Idaho until 1860, when gold was discovered there. The mining communities that sprang up created an instant demand for readily available sources of food, resulting in a rapid decline of big game. Although mountain goat and bighorn sheep populations are still smaller than in the days before the mining camps arrived, most other big game has been restored through careful management.

Archeologists are just beginning to interpret their finds from area sites. Villages, rock shelters, rock art, and burial grounds, some of which may be linked to the Northern Shoshoni Indian culture, are scattered throughout the Frank Church–River of No Return Wilderness. Other historic sites are linked to the ranchers, trappers, and homesteaders associated with the region. Both the Jim Moore Ranch and Shoup Rockshelters are in the National Register of Historic Places.

This sprawling refuge in the heart of Idaho is bigger than Yellowstone National Park. The area is accessible at Mackay Bar off Route 222 and at access points near McCall, Salmon, Challis, and Stanley. The wilderness was named for Sen. Frank Church who believed that "the true meaning of wilderness will open our eyes like an Idaho sunrise on a summer day."

FOR MORE INFORMATION:

Salmon and Challis National Forests, R.R. 2, Box 600, Salmon, ID 83467; 208-756-5100.

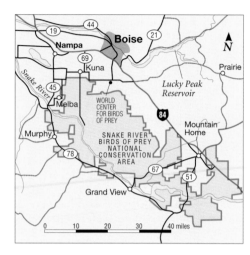

The prairie falcon, above, nests in the crevices of the high sheer basalt cliffs above the Snake River. There are some 200 pairs of nesting prairie falcons in the conservation area.

A golden eagle rides a warm updraft high above the Snake River Canyon. Pitching and rolling ever so slightly, the bird seems to hang in the cloudless azure sky as if suspended by an invisible string. Suddenly the string snaps—the keen-eyed raptor has spotted a jackrabbit weaving through the low shrubs on the plateau floor below. Plummeting, the eagle seizes the prey in its talons. A heartbeat later the drama is over.

A visit to the Snake River Birds of Prey National Conservation Area is filled with arresting moments like this one. The conservation area is situated along an 81-mile stretch of the Snake River. It is one of the most densely populated nesting grounds for birds of prey in the world. Cliffs, 700 feet high and scarred by cracks and crevices, offer ideal spots for perching and nesting. The raptors take advantage of warm air currents to soar above the canyon floor. Black-tailed jackrabbits and Townsend's ground squirrels—the favorite food of many raptors—hide in sagebrush and winter fat shrubs on the plateau below.

NATURAL AVIARY

From mid-March through June, the sky above the canyon is alive with the sights and sounds of amorous birds, including red-tailed hawks whose swooping courtship rituals involve spectacular aerial acrobatics. Gangly turkey vultures, diminutive saw-whet owls, and low-flying prairie falcons are just some of the 14 species of raptors that nest in this rugged habitat. This section of Idaho is a natural stopover for 10 other species of migrating raptors, including majestic bald eagles, aerodynamic peregrine falcons, and lightning-fast merlins, who track down small songbirds and seize them in swift midair attacks. During late spring the evening stillness is punctuated by the hoots of owls, who rouse themselves to seek out prey. By July most raptor offspring have fledged and moved on.

One of the best ways to explore the natural wonders of the area is to drive along a 56-mile loop that begins in the town of Kuna. Heading south on Swan Falls Road, visitors come to a large lava butte jutting prominently from the plateau. Called Initial Point, this butte was the starting point for the official land survey of Idaho, which began in 1867. A short steep access trail leads visitors up to an observation deck on the summit, which takes in a panoramic view of the desert plain.

Farther down the road, Dedication Point offers a magnificent vista of the gaping Snake River Canyon. In the spring this perch is also the perfect vantage point to watch birds of prey as they court prospective mates or scour the Snake River Plains for food. Prime bird-watching times are in the morning and evening hours when these birds are at their hungriest.

Continuing south along Snake River, visitors will encounter the Swan Falls Dam, built in 1901. The dam harnesses the might of the river and converts it into hydroelectric energy. Initially used to supply power to mining operations in the Owyhee Mountains, the dam now provides electricity to residents of the Snake River Valley.

Making their way north to Celebration Park, visitors can lunch in the well-kept picnic area or set off on excursions from the boat launch. There are also developed launch sites at Grand View and at Walter's Ferry. From Celebration Park, hikers and bikers have their choice of several trails. One nature trail leads past a series of large black boulders etched with enigmatic Native American petroglyphs. Another path takes visitors to Guffey Bridge, built as a railroad span across the Snake River in 1897 and now serving as a pedestrian crossing that provides access to trails on the river's southern bank.

For all its human history, the area is chiefly renowned for its birds. About 20 miles down the road, just outside Boise, the World Center for Birds of Prey offers presentations on the magnificent raptors bird-watchers can observe in the wild. The largest bird of prey breeding and research center in the world, this facility is dedicated to the conservation of these predators. Multimedia exhibits, interactive displays, and live bird presentations explain the center's program, which attempts to breed endangered birds in captivity and prepare them for their reintroduction into the wild.

Outside the center visitors are likely to see the striking silhouettes of kestrels perched atop power poles in the surrounding landscape. Sometimes the birds seem to be as curious about humans as humans are about them.

FOR MORE INFORMATION:
Bureau of Land Management, Lower Snake River District, 3948 Development Ave., Boise, ID 83705; 208-384-3300.

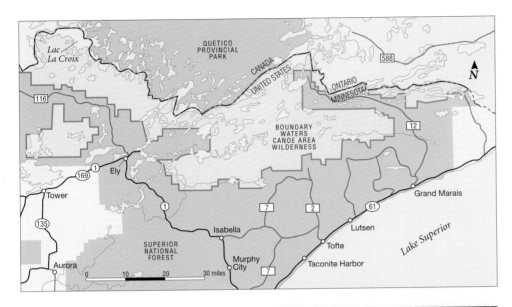

Canoes are the only permitted means of transport on most of the lakes and there are no camping facilities. Visitors must plan their trips with care and foresight. Fortunately, wilderness rangers and local canoe outfitters are available to give novice campers advice on how to enjoy the area while ensuring their safety. Approximately 200,000 visitors a year are advised to obtain current maps and a good compass before venturing into the region. A wilderness travel permit is required for each overnight stay. Visitors are discouraged from making campfires, washing in lakes or streams, and leaving behind any trace of their stay.

Many people come here for some of the country's finest fishing. The most common native game fish are walleye, northern pike, and lake trout. Some lakes have small-mouth bass and others are well stocked with rainbow and brook trout.

More than 150 species of birds flock to the region during the summer months, ranging from tiny ruby-throated humming-birds to great bald eagles. Subarctic vegetation grows in abundance on the forest floor. About 30 native orchid species flourish in the cool climate of the wilderness area.

The silence of the evening is broken by the eerie howl of a timber wolf, answered in turn by a chorus of wolves, their haunting refrain a reminder that these woods form the last refuge for these elusive creatures of the wild. Scientists and dedicated volunteers track the timber wolves through the use of radio collars. Minnesota is the only state outside Alaska with a resident wild timber wolf population. At last estimate there were about 1,200 left in the state.

FOR MORE INFORMATION:
Superior National Forest, P.O. Box 338, Duluth, MN 55801; 218-720-5324.

W ith the first dip of the paddle, a canoe begins to glide across the glassy surface of one of the many crystal clear lakes in Boundary Waters Canoe Area Wilderness. Dense aromatic forests of spruce and pine, balsam fir, and northern white cedar line the shore, broken here and there by huge outcroppings of sun-bleached rocks. An eagle wheels in the bright blue sky overhead. Deep in the forest, a moose lowers its great head to drink from a bubbling stream, while at lake's edge the melancholy cry of a loon ushers in the twilight.

Canoeing in the Boundary Waters Canoe Area Wilderness often brings to mind the exploration of French voyageurs who paddled their canoes through the region 200 years ago. Located about 60 miles north of Duluth in Superior National Forest, this sanctuary is part of the National Wilderness Preservation System. The area is more than 1 million acres in size and extends nearly 150 miles along the border between the United States and Canada from Grand Portage to Rainy Lake.

A solitary canoeist, above, paddles along one of the many lakes within Boundary Waters Canoe Area Wilderness.

CANADIAN SHIELD
The wilderness arises from the Canadian shield—a geological formation of unparalleled beauty. Scattered across the green landscape are 2-billion-year-old rocks polished to hues of rainbow brilliance, their jagged edges softened by mosses and lichens. The region's several thousand lakes are linked by overland trails or portages.

A rainbow arcs above a lake in the area, right, which is fringed with thick boreal forests of spruce and red and white pine trees. The frothing white spume indicates fast-moving water.

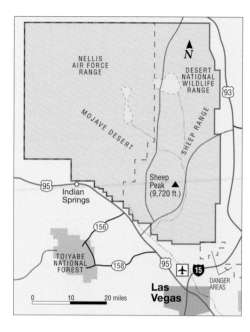

The chief concern of the Desert National Wildlife Range is to protect the bighorn sheep, left, and its habitat.

In the Desert National Wildlife Range, small birds sometimes migrate from one elevation to another instead of flying over long horizontal distances. From the desert floor to the 10,000-foot peaks of six mountain ranges, temperatures in this protected region vary from 120°F to below zero, and vegetation shifts from desert shrubbery to ancient pine forests. The range is one of more than 500 refuges within the National Wildlife Refuge System—and the largest one outside the state of Alaska, covering 1.5 million acres of the Mojave Desert in southern Nevada.

Desert bighorn sheep graze in the craggy refuge, which was created as a sanctuary for the largest existing population of these shy mammals. Other wildlife includes mountain lions, desert tortoises, and golden eagles, all of which find their niches among the range's six elevational life zones. The lower elevations are lined with creosote bush and white bur sage, which give way to yucca, Joshua tree, and piñon-juniper vegetation in the middle zone. Ponderosa pines and white firs thrive at higher elevations, although they thin out at 9,000 feet where the growing season becomes too short for them to survive. Only the bristlecone pines withstand the rarefied conditions of the peaks that reach 10,000 feet.

About two-thirds of the refuge are used as an air force gunnery range, which is off-limits to visitors, but the rest of the region offers excellent opportunities for picnicking and primitive camping. About 150 miles of roads and hiking and backpacking trails crisscross the refuge.

Mormon Well Road, accessible by truck and four-wheel-drive vehicles, passes through the main vegetation zones and leads to historical sites and the habitats of bighorn sheep. The road begins at the main entrance near the Corn Creek Field Station, where stream-fed ponds are home to the endangered Pahrump poolfish. Originally an inhabitant of Pahrump Valley's Manse Spring, this minnow-sized fish has thrived since it was transplanted in 1971 from the spring to these ponds.

DESERT OASIS

Many bird species are drawn to Corn Creek's thriving oasis, where they alight on mulberry trees, elms, cottonwoods, Russian olives, and mesquite. This lush habitat has a varied roster of full-time residents including Gambel's quail, moorhens, blue grosbeaks, phainopeplas, gray flycatchers, and ladder-backed woodpeckers. During spring and autumn migrations, as many as 21 species of warblers and vireos descend on the oasis area. Other seasonal feathered visitors include pygmy nuthatches, lesser nighthawks, poor-wills, and green-tailed towhees. In May, when the mulberry, apple, and apricot trees blossom, bird-watchers have been known to spot as many as 55 species in less than two hours.

As the eastern branch of Mormon Well Road climbs higher, it takes visitors to the bighorn area at the southern end of the Sheep Range. Midmorning is the time to head off on foot and search the terrain for the steep ledges where the sheep feed on scrubby vegetation. Bighorn sheep blend in well with the desert landscape and can be hard to see. Wildlife watchers may spot other animals such as cliff chipmunks, gray foxes, coyotes, and bobcats, as well as a variety of reptiles, including chuckwallas and collared and leopard lizards.

Farther down the road, visitors can examine an agave roasting pit that was once used by aboriginal people to slow-cook meats and vegetables. Food such as agave was buried in a bed of hot coals and covered with earth. The ashes and debris eventually formed small hills that, when excavated, revealed the depressions in the ground where the fires were made. Archeologists learn much about the early Americans from these refuse heaps, also known as midden circles.

Peek-a-Boo Canyon was named for a large hole in the top of its southeastern wall. The bare mountainsides buffed by erosion expose the colorful layers of rock created eons ago when southern Nevada was covered by a shallow sea. A natural cave is located near the mouth of the canyon.

At Mormon Well Corral, a short footpath leads to a spring that served as a stopover during the days of the horse and buggy. Mule deer and other wildlife are often spotted drinking their fill at the water hole. An old horse and cattle corral, situated to the north of the spring, is listed in the National Register of Historic Places.

Rainfall in the desert is sporadic, but in May on a good year the desert blooms in an exotic blend of color as Mojave asters, desert marigolds, and a rich collection of cacti blossom forth. When rainfall is heavy, runoff waters flood through severely eroded lands called washes. Sawmill Wash is a deep alluvial fan created by runoff from Sawmill Canyon, which extends to the crest of the Sheep Range. Early settlers from Moapa Valley logged ponderosa pines at the head of the watershed, hence the canyon's name. Sawmill Canyon is a popular destination with backpackers and horseback riders.

FOR MORE INFORMATION:
Desert National Wildlife Range, 1500 North Decatur Blvd., Las Vegas, NV 89108; 702-646-3401.

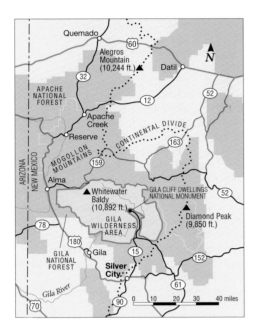

The dappled coat of a young white-tailed deer, above, provides excellent camouflage as it crouches motionless in a rocky haven.

T he celebrated ecologist and forest ranger, Aldo Leopold, recognized that humankind has an ethical responsibility to cherish and respect the land in all its different forms. Due largely to Leopold's farsighted efforts at the beginning of this century, the Gila Wilderness Area of southwestern New Mexico became the world's first designated wilderness area in 1924. Since that time, the Gila has been cared for in keeping with the spirit of Leopold's words: "Harmony with land is like harmony with a friend . . . the land is one organism."

Set within the 3.3 million acres of the Gila National Forest, the 750,000-acre Gila Wilderness Area embraces the Mogollon Mountains and part of the Colorado Plateau. The wide variety of flora and fauna in the area is due to elevations that range from 4,000 to more than 10,000 feet. The diversity of habitats here allows species from the northwestern United States to thrive alongside species that are more common to southern Arizona and Mexico.

Firs, spruce, and aspens grow at higher elevations of Whitewater Baldy and the Mogollon Mountains. At about 8,000 feet, virgin stands of ponderosa pines dominate vast plateaus that are riven by deep narrow rock canyons. In the valleys walnut trees, cottonwoods, willows, and Arizona sycamores predominate, and at 5,000 feet near the eastern approaches to the wilderness area, piñon and juniper trees flourish.

The amount of sun a habitat receives is influenced by whether it faces north or south, and its orientation makes a significant impact on the type of vegetation a habitat can sustain. The south-facing canyon at Gila Cliff Dwellings National Monument near the entrance to the wilderness is scattered with desert plants such as cacti, manzanita, and great oak. Across the canyon, facing north, the terrain at the same level is cloaked in fir trees.

WILDERNESS TRAILS

A network of more than 700 miles of trails in the Gila Wilderness Area offers visitors opportunities for recreation year-round. Cross-country skiing and snowshoeing are popular winter activities, and the cool comfortable temperatures of the summer months make Gila an ideal setting for hiking, horseback riding, and camping. Arrangements can be made for local outfitters to take campers into drop camps by horse or mule and then return to pick them up at a designated time.

This carefully managed preserve provides a habitat for a wide variety of animals. The headwaters of the Gila River are filled with Gila trout—a protected species within the wilderness area. Anglers can fish the waters downstream for rainbow and German brown trout. Elk, wild turkeys, and mule deer are frequently sighted on the plateau. Harder to spot are black bears, mountain lions, and javelinas. Campers should keep an eye out for the western diamond-backed rattlesnake and the rare Gila monster, a lizard that grows up to two feet long. The venomous Gila monster has a sluggish nature, but may strike when disturbed.

The most popular trails in the Gila Wilderness Area are located between the middle fork of the Gila River and the southwestern rim of the Mogollon Mountains. Less-traveled trails generally begin at lower elevations on the southern and western sides of the area, and at higher elevations in the forested regions of Willow Creek-Snow Lake. Towering rock pinnacles are found along the area's network of 1,510 miles of trails, the most popular of which runs between the Middle Fork of the Gila River and the southwestern rim of the Mogollon Mountains. Hikers can revitalize themselves by soaking in the steaming waters at several hidden hot springs.

Visitors must travel on foot or by horseback throughout the wilderness area, since there are no roads. There are also no designated campsites, and visitors are strongly urged to respect the environment. This is a true wilderness where sojourners can go for days without seeing another human face.

FOR MORE INFORMATION:
Gila National Forest, Silver City Ranger District & Supervisor's Office, 3005 East Camino del Bosque, Silver City, NM 88061; 505-388-8201.

Meadows of bright yellow wildflowers, left, spread out invitingly under rolling clouds near the entrance to the Gila Wilderness Area.

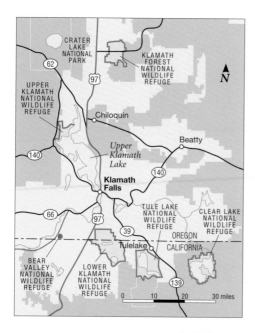

these vital breeding grounds shrank drastically. Then in 1908 a first parcel of land—called the Lower Klamath—was designated as a national wildlife refuge.

Today some 189,000 acres are under federal protection. During the migration, the sky darkens with the arrival of hundreds of thousands of winged travelers. In the shadow of Mount Shasta, huge flocks of snow geese—sometimes numbering as many as 150,000—gracefully alight on the serene lakes and marshes of the Lower Klamath and Tule Lake units. White pelicans, great blue herons, Caspian terns, and up to 80 percent of the world's population of Ross' geese visit the refuges from mid-September to mid-December.

Of the more than 300 types of birds that pass through the area each year, some 180 species rear their young here. In a good year more than 60,000 ducklings and

BIRDS OF PREY

Small animals must also beware of the danger from above. More than 20 types of raptors nest in the refuge, including thousands of northern harriers, golden eagles, and red-tailed hawks. Most impressive of all is the bald eagle. DDT and other pollutants almost wiped out this magnificent bird in the 1960's. Today Bear Valley attracts between 500 and 1,000 roosting bald eagles every year. The basin provides an important wintering location for migrating eagles, primarily from Canada, although some birds fly here from as far afield as the Northwest Territories and Alaska. The birds begin to arrive in November and usually leave by late March or early April. Few sights are as stirring as that of dozens of bald eagles swooping on their massive, seven-foot wingspans through the blood-red sunrise of a January morning.

The main visitor center distributes information on each unit, as well as providing displays on the region's history and wildlife. Breathtaking scenic drives wind through much of the refuge, allowing visitors to cover a lot of ground in a short time. Photographers and bird-watchers can get a more intimate view of the wildlife on foot by following one of the nature trails or by slicing through the waterways aboard a canoe. But no matter what means visitors use to tour the area, they always come away with a feeling of awe.

FOR MORE INFORMATION:
Klamath Basin National Wildlife Refuges, Route 1, Box 74, Tulelake, CA 96134; 916-667-2231.

The clear water of Upper Klamath Lake, above, provides an ideal habitat for one of the few remaining breeding colonies of the American white pelican in the West.

Chief Seattle of the Suquamish tribe was said to have asked, "What is man without the beasts? If all the beasts were gone, men would die from a great loneliness of spirit." These profound words could well serve as the motto for the Klamath Basin National Wildlife Refuges. Straddling the Oregon-California border, this complex of six refuges protects one of the world's richest habitats for waterfowl and other birds. Before the arrival of white settlers, Klamath Basin was composed of almost 350,000 acres of lakes and marshes that attracted some 6 million nesting and migrating birds annually. When much of the wetland was converted into farmland

goslings poke through their shells and take in their first breath of the sweet air. In the early summer visitors delight in watching downy western grebe hatchlings hitch rides on the backs of their parents as they paddle in the pristine water and dive down to hunt for fish. The birds' cousins, the golden-tufted eared grebes, construct unique floating nests that bob in the waterways by the hundreds.

Back on land, pronghorn antelopes bound through the uplands, and mule deer graze peacefully by the marshes. When coyotes patrol the fields in search of prey, yellow-bellied marmots send out piercing whistles to alert others in the colony.

As with all owls, the soft feathers of the northern pygmy owl, above, allow it to swoop in on its prey in total silence

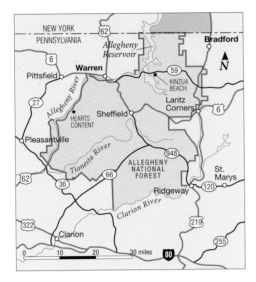

As summer comes to a close, the lush, green canopy of the Allegheny National Forest is set ablaze with the yellows, oranges, and reds of autumn, above.

The view from Rimrock Overlook is only a teaser. From atop the high bedrock bluff, visitors gaze out on stately hardwood forests and knee-high ferns and the wide blue swath of the Allegheny Reservoir. On clear days the sunlight glints off the 27 miles of this man-made lake, creating a sense of peace. But this is just one of the magical places in the Allegheny National Forest, a 513,125-acre wilderness that spans the northwestern corner of Pennsylvania.

Established in 1923, the forest is a haven for old-growth deciduous trees. At the Hearts Content and Tionesta National Scenic Areas, visitors can walk along gently winding trails through some of the oldest tracts of beech, hemlock, and white pine forest in the nation—trees that date back to the 17th century. The rest of the Allegheny plateau supports dense stands of hardwood trees, including oak, yellow poplar, white ash, and red and sugar maple. One hundred years ago many a fortune was made from these trees in the lumber industry. Today about a third of the world's supply of black cherry timber is culled here for use in fine furniture and veneers.

Life abounds under the gracious canopy of Allegheny's trees. The forest floor is carpeted with hay-scented and maidenhair ferns, rhododendrons, trilliums, and wood sorrels. In June mountain laurel bursts into bloom with clusters of pale pink flowers. Although these beautiful blossoms are more commonly found beside roads and in the deep woods, they can sometimes be seen in small, colorful clusters along the powerful Allegheny River.

The scenic river teems with prize walleyes and aggressive northern pikes, and is best viewed on a leisurely drive south on Highway 62. Along the way, the winding road skirts the 23,100-acre Allegheny National Recreation Area, where visitors are likely to see wild turkeys, grouse, white-tailed deer, and black bears foraging for food in the thickets. Another pleasant drive, the Longhouse National Scenic Byway, winds for 29 miles through thick forests inhabited by woodchucks, snowshoe hares, gray foxes, and minks. The road continues past Kinzua Beach to the Rimrock Overlook, where fortunate visitors may catch glimpses of bald eagles soaring high above Kinzua Bay.

BIRD-WATCHING OPPORTUNITIES

During spring and fall, the Allegheny River Islands Wilderness is aflutter with activity. Some 200 species of birds, among them herons, wood ducks, warblers, and woodpeckers, flock here to feed. Canoeists paddle to seven federally protected islands and fish for bass, muskellunge, pickerel, and trout. At the nearby 8,663-acre Hickory Creek Wilderness Area, hikers can loop through the backwoods on an 11-mile trail, and anglers can plumb the depths of the East and Middle Hickory creeks for brook trout. When the sun sets the rustle of flying squirrels and the lonesome hoots of barred owls interrupt the stillness of night.

The avid backpacker will find all kinds of opportunities for exploration. The forest is crisscrossed by an extensive network of hiking trails from the short, picturesque Loleta Trail to the physically demanding North Country National Scenic Trail, which twists and turns for 87 miles through the heart of the woodland. At Buzzard Swamp visitors walking along the 1.7-mile Songbird Sojourn Interpretive Trail will be serenaded by the lyrical calls of northern orioles, rose-breasted grosbeaks, and chipping sparrows. Patient nature enthusiasts may spot menacing snapping turtles or more benign Canada geese and leopard frogs in nearby ponds.

The five interconnected trails that comprise Beaver Meadows Trail offer the careful observer the opportunity to watch families of beaver hard at work in or around several of the area's placid waterways. These web-footed rodents can sometimes be seen chiseling aspen trees and towing branches through the water back to their dams.

Where hikers, boaters, and backpackers traversed under the summer sun, sledders, cross-country skiers, and ice-fishing enthusiasts go in winter. Allegheny National Forest attracts people looking for fun in the great outdoors year-round.

FOR MORE INFORMATION:
Forest Supervisor, Allegheny National Forest, P.O. Box 847, 222 Liberty St., Warren, PA 16365; 814-723-5150.

Water, both fresh and salt, is the lifeblood of the Cape Romain National Wildlife Refuge. Each year thousands of pelicans, wood ducks, storks, and other kindred waterfowl flock to this 22-mile stretch of the spectacular South Carolina coastline and its offshore islands. They come in droves, attracted by shallow bays, brackish ponds, and a lacework of tidal creeks and marshland offering peace and tranquillity. Quiet waterways with names like Muddy Bay, Oyster Bay, and Five Fathom Creek offer tantalizing meals to a multitude of hungry birds.

Muddy waters are a blessing for Cape Romain. In the shallow bays of this 64,000-acre national wildlife refuge, the rich Atlantic tide mingles with the fresh waters of the Romain, Bull, and Harbor rivers, producing nutrient-rich marshlands. The largest barrier islands, including Cape Island, Raccoon Key, and Bull Island, act to protect the delicate salt marshes from the battering surge of the open ocean.

In this sheltered environment, wild creatures of the land, river, and ocean thrive alongside each other. Bottle-nosed dolphins and otters cut through the water, and short-snouted alligators bask on the creek banks.

By day fleet-footed white-tailed deer and marsh rabbits make their way cautiously through the swamps as bold black fox squirrels scramble from tree to tree. At night the silhouetted forms of Brazilian free-tailed bats can be seen flitting overhead. These flourishing creatures help make Cape Romain one of the most pristine wilderness areas left on the East Coast. This spectacular stretch of undeveloped beach is certainly worth preserving—and well worth a visit.

The refuge headquarters lies about 20 miles north of Charleston on Highway 17. The only access to Cape Romain is via a pleasant 20-minute ferry ride that departs at high tide from Moore's Landing and travels across salt marshes alive with egrets, herons, royal terns, and clapper rails. Visitors are dropped off on 5,018-acre Bull Island, the largest of the refuge islands, where they can set out to explore the lush coastal forest.

The two-mile National Recreation Trail plunges into a live oak forest draped with Spanish moss and leads past fragrant magnolias, loblolly pines, and cabbage palmettos. Another 16 miles of island paths take visitors to tranquil ponds where wintering widgeons, canvasbacks, and ring-necked ducks nestle among the banana water lilies. Approximately 277 species of birds have been recorded at the refuge.

Ill suited for saltwater environments, much of Cape Romain's reptile and amphibian population can be found in the vicinity of Moores Landing on the mainland. Skinks, narrow-mouthed toads, and copperhead snakes are just some of the creatures that slink, hop, and slither through the refuge grounds.

ISLAND PARADISES

Rare wildlife sightings are the main allure of Bull Island. Sharp-eyed visitors may be fortunate enough to spot one of the red wolves that was reintroduced to Bull Island in 1987 as part of a unique breeding program. Considered extinct in the wild since 1980, the only red wolves left on the planet are those that have been bred under the watchful eye of what was once its former worst enemy: humankind.

Along the fringes of the island, is a landscape of scrubby salt-spray forest, rolling sand dunes, and gentle beaches. Wildlife watchers can scan the surf for the four-foot-wide loggerhead sea turtles, who wait until nightfall to lay their eggs. More of these giant turtles nest here than anywhere else on South Carolina's coast. On occasion the lucky visitor might see a patch of beach erupt as freshly hatched loggerheads burst through the sand and make their headlong dash to the crashing surf.

The 17 smaller, more remote islands of the refuge—among them Bird Island and White Banks—can be reached only by chartered boat. With an experienced guide at the helm, boats ply unpolluted tidal waters that are rife with channel bass, crabs, and clams. Every November the world's largest wintering population of black-and-white American oystercatchers flocks here. Prying open oysters and mussels with their bladelike beaks, these clamorous birds make short work of their shellfish bounty.

FOR MORE INFORMATION:
Refuge Manager, Cape Romain National Wildlife Refuge, 5801 Hwy. 17 North, Awendaw, SC 29429; 803-928-3368.

An American oystercatcher and its chick, above, feast on crustaceans along the shores of Bull Island. These sturdy shorebirds make their nests in rock crevices or in shallow depressions in the sand.

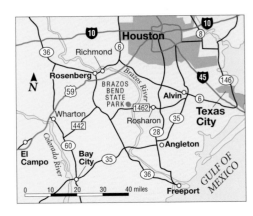

Bursting through tranquil waters, perfect yellow lotus blossoms, above, reach toward the golden sun.

Just west of Houston, where the pinelands begin to thin out, the sky spreads like a powder blue serape over a wide crescent of coastal prairie where rivers and bayous wind leisurely to the Gulf of Mexico. One of the historic towns in the region is Richmond, settled by the first colonists to come to Texas in 1821 and now all but swallowed up by urban sprawl. However, surviving plantation mansions, a log replica of Fort Bend, and restored Civil War–era buildings keep the past alive—as do the oft-told tales of the town's colorful characters. Before she charged on Kansas with her ax, temperance agitator Carry Nation was a hotel-keeper here and a figure of no small reputation. In 1887 during a lengthy drought, she knelt in the streets near her Nation Hotel and prayed for rain. A three-day downpour followed.

Richmond is also the point of departure for an outing to Brazos Bend State Park, a medley of wetlands, prairie, and hardwood forest. The park, located just 45 miles southwest of the steel and concrete of bustling downtown Houston, is a 4,897-acre wilderness. Migratory birds pause here on their pan-American passages, feral hogs root for acorns among the bottomland oaks, and alligators silently patrol the languid waterways as egrets look on.

HISTORIC TERRAIN

Brazos is one of the Lone Star State's newest and largest parks, spreading over the expanse of land where Mexican general Santa Ana camped his troops en route to the decisive defeat that gave Texas its independence. Although much of the park is accessible by car, it is primarily a hushed enclave of nature trails, picnic grounds, and rustic campsites.

Oak, elm, and pecan trees occupy the region's drier bottomlands, and sycamore and cottonwoods thrive along the waterways. The park's diverse habitats attract a wide array of wildlife, including deer, armadillos, bobcats, opossums, gray foxes, coyotes, and Russian boars. But the park's most intriguing denizen is the ubiquitous American alligator. These primeval creatures are so abundant that visitors are given educational pamphlets titled "Alligator Etiquette." Sometimes they can be seen sunning themselves in the middle of a trail.

Outdoor enthusiasts will enjoy top-rated fishing at sites along all of the park's six lakes. Specially constructed docks and platforms supply ideal vantage spots to plumb the depths for crappies, bass, perch, and catfish. Both Forty Acre and Hale lakes have lighted piers for night fishing. Bank fishing is also permitted, but boating is not allowed due to the hungry alligators that cruise the waters. Fishermen shouldn't be surprised if they hook a fish only to have the tasty trophy plucked from their line by a wily alligator.

The abundance of water in Brazos makes the park a natural gathering place for a multitude of waterfowl. For optimal viewing, bird-watchers may want to spend most

The muddied snout of a feral hog, right, attests to the zeal with which the animal roots for food in Brazos Bend State Park.

of their time staked out near the park's two largest bodies of water: Elm and Pliant lakes. Here, white ibis and yellow-crowned night herons wade along the shore on long, spindly legs as mottled ducks and blue-winged teals bob on the gentle waves.

Vultures, hawks, various species of hummingbirds, and the occasional roadrunner have also been sighted within the confines of the park. The wooden observation tower on Forty Acre Lake affords an ideal lookout for sighting some of the more than 200 species of birds that wing their way through the region each year.

With more than 20 miles of hiking and biking trails, Brazos Bend is the perfect destination for anyone looking to commune with nature. Many of the paths follow the winding contours of the Brazos River. The park's other major waterway, Big Creek, runs diagonally through the park and converges with the Brazos in the southeastern corner. Rounding a bend in a trail, visitors will encounter one of the park's picturesque sloughs, lakes, or oxbow basins.

Tucked amid the thickets in this bucolic setting is one of the park's biggest draws—George Observatory—a monument to modern astronomy, installed at a cost of more than $1 million. The 12-ton, 36-inch telescope allows Brazos visitors to peer through the night skies far into the universe for glimpses of nebulas, exploding stars, the rings of Saturn, and other remote regions of outer space.

Whether fixed by the unsettling gaze of an alligator or moved by the mysteries of the heavens, visitors to this park will leave with many stories to tell.

FOR MORE INFORMATION:
Brazos Bend State Park, 21901 FM 762, Needville, TX 77461; 409-553-5101 or 800-792-1112.

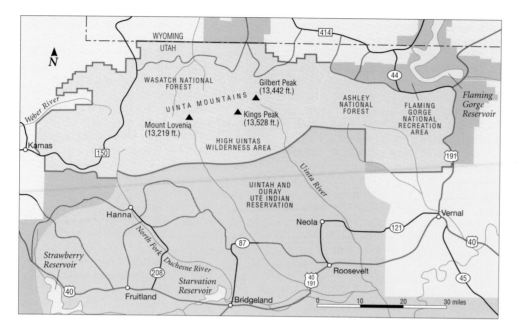

A wary bobcat, above, peers out from the snowy cliffs of Utah's Uinta Mountains.

Buckled and knotted into snow-capped summits, the Uinta Mountains look like the knuckles of a giant's hand. In the valley below, dark blue waters spin out across the land like a fine spider's web. Four of Utah's largest rivers—the Bear, Weber, Provo, and Duchesne—begin here in the northeastern pocket of the state. Their headwaters stem from thousands of lakes and 20 drainage basins fed by melting snow from the massive mountains.

Twenty-six of the Uinta peaks surpass the 13,000-foot mark, and Kings Peak—the highest summit in Utah—juts 13,528 feet above sea level. The most prominent east-west range in the United States, the Uintas rise out of the Wyoming and Uinta basins and extend from the Colorado border almost to Salt Lake City.

Uinta's rocks tell an ancient story. The core of the mountain range is 600 million years old, a belt of Precambrian rock shaped out of quartzite, sandstone, and shale. Ice-Age glaciers carved the majestic, U-shaped canyons that inspire the admiration and awe of visitors today. In this severe, stony wilderness, moose, elk, Rocky Mountain bighorn sheep, and mule deer can be seen walking through the knee-high grasses and wildflowers.

HAPPY TRAILS

Nature steals the show in the High Uintas Wilderness Area, a 460,000-acre region within two national forests—Wasatch and Ashley. An extensive system of trails invites hikers to stroll through thick stands of lodgepole pine, Engelmann spruce, and fir. The popular Highline Trail runs east to Rocky Sea Pass and then to more secluded areas. Another worthwhile hike, the China Meadows Trail, leads to a rewarding view of Red Castle Peak. The Henrys Fork Trail is a more demanding trek, requiring a steep climb to the top of Kings Peak. Along the way, backpackers may spot black bears nibbling on berry bushes, a goshawk soaring overhead, or watch as a lithe bobcat slinks by silently.

Motorists who wish to explore the mountains have plenty of side roads to choose from. The Rock Creek Road runs past Miner's Gulch and sparkling Rock Creek into the vast Uintah and Ouray Ute Indian Reservation. Interesting side loops circle past glacier-carved canyons and valleys where crystal-clear streams are home to rainbow and cutthroat trout and small-mouth bass. The Red Cloud Dry Fork Loop meanders by Brownie Canyon and Sims Peak and enters the quiet seclusion of Kaler Hollow. The Flaming Gorge Uintas Scenic Byway cuts through the Uinta range to the red rocks of Flaming Gorge National Recreation Area.

Paved trails take mountain bikers from the quiet town of Vernal deep into the heart of the Uinta range. The 20-mile Sheep Creek Canyon Loop, considered an advanced run, ventures into the narrow canyon confines to the powerful creek where, in August, bright red kokanee salmon begin their final spawning run. The salmon's heroic battle against the torrent is a fitting counterpoint to the sublime peaks of these magnificent mountains.

FOR MORE INFORMATION:
Ashley National Forest, 355 North Vernal Ave., Vernal, UT 84078; 801-789-1181.

The powerful waters of the Bear River, left, churn through the Uinta Mountains.

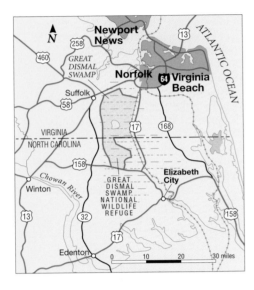

Looking out across the expanse of the Great Dismal Swamp, some people might see nothing more than a vast tract of inhospitable bog. But when George Washington first laid eyes on the swamp in 1763, he called it a "glorious paradise" and set out to purchase the fertile land. Founding the Adventurers for Draining the Great Dismal Swamp company, the future president proceeded with plans to clear the boggy peat soil in order to grow cotton and rice. Despite his painstaking efforts—including digging a five-mile-long drainage ditch—Washington was unable to tame this wild land. Subsequent efforts to cultivate it also failed and the region remains as it has for centuries, a marvel of forested wetlands and brooding, stagnant swamps.

The Great Dismal is the northernmost swamp in a chain of Atlantic Coast swamplands that begins with Florida's Everglades. Its unique habitat was placed under the protection of the federal government in 1974 when a 106,716-acre tract was set aside as the Great Dismal Swamp National Wildlife Refuge. Most of this rich refuge lies in the southeastern corner of Virginia, with a small portion of land spilling into North Carolina.

Visitors who journey to this neck of Virginia step into a wildlife haven that has inspired the imagination of adventurer and author alike. Fanciful sightings of six-foot-long water moccasins and the ghostly figure of a long-dead Indian maiden haunting the swamp have made it the subject of poems by Thomas Moore and Henry Wadsworth Longfellow, and the setting for one of Harriet Beecher Stowe's novels.

At the heart of Dismal Swamp lies 3,100-acre Lake Drummond. The lake's opaque, coffee-colored waters—called juniper water by locals—are stained by seepage from the submerged roots of gum, cypress, maple, and juniper trees. People of the area swear by the sweet taste and healthful qualities of this dark liquid.

The Dismal Swamp fish, a member of the blind cave fish family, swims in this murky lake. Catfish are also commonly found here, sharing their watery kingdom with black crappies, redfin pickerel, and yellow perch. Golden shiners and speckles also glide through the inky waters, along with miniature creatures such as the blue-spotted sunfish—a spined dwarf in glittering iridescent hues. Lurking beneath the water, hungry snapping turtles wait patiently for small fish and amphibians to swim by.

More than 140 miles of trails and roads cut across the landscape, offering intrepid explorers wonderful opportunities to venture deep into the swampy territory. Birdwatchers will enjoy the 4.5-mile hike

along Washington Ditch Road to Lake Drummond. The mile-long elevated Boardwalk Trail looks out on the habitat of more than 200 species of birds. Sightings include yellow-billed cuckoos, kinglets, Carolina wrens, and woodcocks. Male woodcocks can be seen performing their acrobatic courtship flights for prospective mates. Up to 25 million blackbirds alight here in winter. Relatively rare elsewhere, southern Swainson's warblers and black-throated green warblers chatter excitedly under the thick canopy of trees. Visitors who listen carefully may hear Brimley's chorus frogs chiming in with the birds or the rhythmic croaks of the half-inch-long grass frog—the nation's tiniest frog.

ANCIENT CYPRESS TREES

For wildlife enthusiasts, few experiences rival slicing through the misty swamp canals aboard a canoe. These crafts slip silently through the living forest of red maple, Atlantic white cedar, black gum, and loblolly pine, and a thick undergrowth of briars and vines. The log fern, one of the rarest American ferns, grows in abundance here, as well as the rare dwarf trillium and silky camellia. Growing up to 40 feet in height, the malevolent-looking devil's walking stick wards off hungry animals with jagged spines jutting from its 12-foot stem. Black bears, river otters, gray foxes, white-tailed deer, and the native Dismal Swamp short-tailed shrew can occasionally be spotted foraging among blackberry and honeysuckle bushes. Gnarled cypress trees dating back more than 1,500 years dominate the watery pools.

Travelers will thrill at the extraordinary sights and sounds of the swamp. Visitors can sit near spotted turtles basking on logs and feast their eyes on abundant growths of pawpaw, black gum, and wild grapes. Nearby, the heads of snakes break the water's surface like tiny periscopes, and flying squirrels glide through the air above. As they explore this strange and beautiful world, visitors feel thankful that this unique land proved untamable.

FOR MORE INFORMATION:

Refuge Manager, Great Dismal Swamp National Wildlife Refuge, P.O. Box 349, Suffolk, VA 23434-0349; 757-986-3705.

A cluster of bald cypresses, left, is reflected in the still waters of Great Dismal Swamp. Extremely resistant to rot, the wood of this tree is known as the wood eternal.

Gazing out over the shallow, treacherous shoals of Assateague Island and its smaller sister isle, Chincoteague, it's easy to see why this stretch of the Atlantic coast was once dubbed a ship graveyard. Late in the 18th century, the wreckage toll in local waters grew so high that Virginia was forced to appoint a commissioner of wrecks. Soon after, the state of Maryland—which claims a portion of Assateague Island—followed suit and appointed its own wreckmaster. The relentless action of wind and wave on the shifting sands makes the shoreline of these barrier islands hard to traverse even with modern-day high-tech navigational devices.

Early settlers in the region were dumbstruck by the huge numbers of birds living here. By the early 1900's merciless bird hunting and egg collecting threatened to wipe out entire populations of feathered creatures. In 1943 the Virginia section of Assateague Island was designated a national wildlife refuge to protect migrating waterfowl from the wholesale slaughter. The Chincoteague National Wildlife Refuge, a 14,014-acre tract of coastal terrain, is now a prime stop along the Atlantic flyway. Bird-watchers marvel at the spectacle of fall migration, when up to 30,000 snow and Canada geese alight on the marshes to rest. Other birds include snowy egrets, black and pintail ducks, and herons. In the neighboring mudflats, sanderlings, dowitchers, dunlins, and red knots search for food. The brant—a small goose from the Arctic—feeds among the tall grasses that wave softly in the salty breeze. Offshore, graceful terns can be seen diving for fish. In all, some 300 species of birds, including peregrine falcons, tundra swans, and red-tailed hawks, have been sighted within the refuge's protective boundaries.

Leisurely summer boat cruises take travelers for a closer look at the shorebirds.

Originating on Chincoteague Island, the tour circles around the southern tip of Assateague Island. The shallow waters of Chincoteague Bay, sheltered from the ocean surf by this thin slip of an island, are ideal for canoeing. Surf fishing lessons are also given to novice anglers. If visitors prefer to stay on solid ground, they can cycle or hike through the refuge on a variety of designated trails populated by the refuge's four-legged inhabitants.

Along the heavily forested trails, it's common to spot white-tailed deer at rest in poison-ivy thickets and the small, spotted Sika deer from Asia—introduced here in the early 1920's—nibbling on greenbrier. Near the visitor center, the picturesque 3.2-mile Wildlife Loop leads travelers past Snow Goose Pool, mud flats, and stands of loblolly pine, where endangered Delmarva Peninsula fox squirrels leap from branch to branch.

WILD HORSES

Muskrats, eels, mullets, gizzard shads, and tiny nest-building sticklebacks thrive in the islands' freshwater ponds matted with thick algae growths. The Woodland Trail takes hikers across the wetlands to an overlook where they can see the wild ponies of Assateague fame. According to lore, the 150-odd herd descends from horses that swam ashore from a Spanish galleon, which was shipwrecked off the coast in the 18th century. The islands are packed with visitors in late July, who come to watch the famous Wild Pony Round-Up, when some

of these equine beauties are herded together to cross the channel for the annual pony auction on Chincoteague Island. Proceeds from the roundup help support the island's volunteer fire department.

Amusement of a different type awaits visitors to the Toms Cove Nature Trail. Its looping path leads to the shallow waters of Toms Cove, once acclaimed for its thriving clam and oyster beds. During the past century, however, storms and constantly shifting sands dramatically altered the shoreline environment, leading by the mid-1900's to the ruin of the oyster trade. Nature compensated for the loss of one habitat by gradually building up the sand dunes on the refuge's western tip. Known as the Hook, these secluded shores serve as a primary nesting zone for the tiny, endangered piping plovers.

The cove is closed from mid-March to August to ensure the plovers' safety, but 10 miles of undisturbed beach north of the Toms Cove Visitor Center are open at that time of the year. Exploring the unspoiled dunes, a visitor may chance upon a wily red fox—one of those thrilling moments when human and animal come face-to-face in an untamed world.

FOR MORE INFORMATION:

Refuge Manager, Chincoteague National Wildlife Refuge, P.O. Box 62, Chincoteague, VA 23336; 804-336-6122.

Sheltered waters and large beds of sea grass beckon shorebirds to Assateague Island, above, in the Chincoteague National Wildlife Refuge.

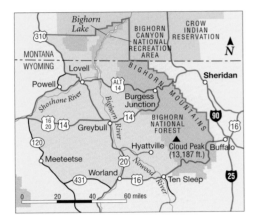

The lofty slopes of the Pryor Mountains afford a spectacular view of Bighorn Canyon National Recreation Area, above. Bighorn sheep are sometimes seen navigating the canyon sides.

S pilling over to southern Montana from Wyoming, Bighorn Basin is a land of mountain ranges, dense forests, grasslands, and red badlands erupting with geysers and hot springs. The area was named Ahsahta or the Bighorns by Native Americans for the bighorn sheep that roamed the region, also once a wintering ground for bison.

Nearly all of the region's mountains lie within the million-acre Bighorn National Forest. Crowning the skyline at 13,167 feet is Cloud Peak, the tallest mountain and the towering centerpiece of the Cloud Peak Wilderness. Cloud Peak encompasses 189,000 acres of land and provides a sanctuary for moose, deer, elk, and bighorn sheep. A network of trails crisscrosses the wilderness, allowing for hiking and horseback riding, as well as for camping, fishing, and hunting. On a clear day, visitors atop Cloud Peak can see west across Bighorn Basin to the Beartooth and Absaroka ranges that loom in the distance. Also discernible on the eastern side of the mountain is a permanent snowfield—the remnant of the glaciers that carved this rugged terrain.

At the delta of the Bighorn and Shoshone rivers, which both pour into Bighorn Lake, the 19,424-acre Yellowtail Wildlife Habitat Management Unit contains a variety of habitats that attract one of the richest concentrations of wildlife in Wyoming. As well as supplying a nesting area for 155 species of birds, Yellowtail's old-growth cottonwood forest is home to mule deer, wild turkeys, and birds of prey.

ELUSIVE WILD MUSTANGS
The nearby Bighorn Canyon National Recreation Area offers gorgeous sightseeing opportunities. Cutting across the sharp escarpment of the Pryor Mountains, Route 37 provides breathtaking vistas of the terracotta-colored canyon. This area is primarily a desert landscape, sustaining yucca and prickly pear cacti. Although arid climate

A yellow-bellied marmot, below, surveys Bighorn Basin from a secure niche in the rock. The marmot warns its colony of approaching predators by emitting a shrill whistle.

and thin vegetation make the canyon's upper reaches inhospitable to many creatures, peregrine falcons find the craggy cliffs ideal for nesting sites.

Adjacent to the recreation area is the 38,000-acre Pryor Mountain Wild Horse Range. The range's mission is to protect wild horses, the "living symbols of the historic and pioneer spirit of the West."

Naturalists are unsure whether these powerful animals are the descendants of the horses brought over by Spanish explorers or are related to the horses set free by bankrupt ranchers during the Depression, but one thing is certain: it is magnificent to see them roam free.

The Pryor Mountain range encompasses steep-walled canyons, isolated grassy plateaus, and rugged foothill slopes. About 120 wild horses live side by side with bighorn sheep, elk, black bears, and a wide variety of birds and reptiles. Mustangs are also often sighted traveling in bands of three to six horses, usually comprising a stallion with his mares and colts.

In the early 1900's oil was discovered in the Bighorn Basin. Although oil production continues, most of the basin remains pristine and undeveloped. The majority of the region has been set aside to protect its unique wildlife and historical significance, and to provide wild country for future generations to enjoy.

FOR MORE INFORMATION:
Bighorn National Forest, 1969 South Sheridan Ave., Sheridan, WY 82801; 307-672-0751. Montana Bureau of Land Management, Billings Resource Area, 810 East Main St., Billings, MT 59105-3395; 406-238-1540.

INDEX

PICTURE CREDITS

Cover photograph by Carr Clifton
2 Laurence Parent
5 Momatiuk/Eastcott/Woodfin Camp & Associates

THE NORTH WOODS
8, 9 Carr Clifton
10 (both) Alan Briere
12 (both) Kevin Shields
13 (upper right) Alan Briere
13 (lower left) Kevin Shields
14 (both) Alan Briere
14, 15 Thomas Mark Szelog
15 Alan Briere
16 Voscar the Maine Photographer
17 (upper) J.A. Kraulis/Masterfile
17 (lower) Voscar the Maine Photographer

BUCK ISLAND REEF
18, 19 Steve Simonsen
20 (upper left) Scott Frier/Uniphoto Picture Agency
20 (lower right) Courtesy of David Nellis
22 Carol Lee
22, 23 Steve Simonsen
23 Carol Lee
24 Carol Lee
25 (upper left) Steve Simonsen
25 (lower right) Gerry Ellis/Ellis Nature Photography
26 Dave G. Houser
27 (upper left) Dave G. Houser
27 (lower right) Carol Lee

ATCHAFALAYA BASIN
28, 29 Greg Guirard
30 (upper left) Konrad Wothe/Ellis Nature Photography
30 (lower right) Michael Durham/Ellis Nature Photography
32 Michael Durham/Ellis Nature Photography
32, 33 Greg Guirard
33 Momatiuk/Eastcott/Woodfin Camp & Associates
34 (upper left) Greg Guirard
34 (lower right) C.C. Lockwood/DDB Stock Photo
35 Greg Guirard
36 Momatiuk/Eastcott/Woodfin Camp & Associates
36, 37 C.C. Lockwood/DDB Stock Photo
37 Momatiuk/Eastcott/Woodfin Camp & Associates
38 D. Donne Bryant/DDB Stock Photo
39 (upper right) Philip Gould
39 (lower left) D. Donne Bryant/DDB Stock Photo

THE SANDHILLS
40, 41 Thomas Mangelsen
42 (upper left) Michael Collier
42 (lower right) Michael Durham/Ellis Nature Photography
44 (upper right) Tom Till
44 (lower left) Michael Collier
45 Tom Till
46 Michael Durham/Ellis Nature Photography
46, 47 Michael Collier
47 Art Wolfe
48 Brian Vanden Brink
49 (upper right) John Elk/Dave G. Houser
49 (lower left) Dave G. Houser

MOUNTAIN OASIS
50, 51 Laurence Parent
52 George H.H. Huey
53 Gerry Ellis/Ellis Nature Photography
54 Laurence Parent
54, 55 Laurence Parent
55 Gerry Ellis/Ellis Nature Photography
56 (left) Gerry Ellis/Ellis Nature Photography
56 (right) Laurence Parent
57 (upper left) Michael Durham/Ellis Nature Photography
57 (lower right) George H.H. Huey
58 (left) Laurence Parent
58 (right) George H.H. Huey
59 Laurence Parent

BOB MARSHALL COUNTRY
60, 61 David Muench
62 (upper left) Art Wolfe
62 (lower right) Chuck Haney
64 (upper left) Chuck Haney
64 (lower right) Gavriel Jecan/Art Wolfe
64, 65 Carr Clifton
65 George Wuerthner
66 (upper left) Art Wolfe
66 (lower right) David Muench
67 Carr Clifton
68 (upper left) Gerry Ellis/Ellis Nature Photography
68 (lower right) Art Wolfe
69 (left) Carr Clifton
69 (right) Art Wolfe
70 Dave G. Houser
71 (upper) Carr Clifton
71 (lower) John Elkins

COCHISE COUNTY
72, 73 Laurence Parent
74 David Muench
75 Gerry Ellis/Ellis Nature Photography
76 (both) George H.H. Huey
77 (upper) Laurence Parent

77 (lower) George H.H. Huey
78 George H.H. Huey
79 (upper) George H.H. Huey
79 (lower) Suzi Moore/Woodfin Camp & Associates
80 George H.H. Huey
81 (upper right) Dave G. Houser
81 (lower left) James P. Rowan

THE MOJAVE DESERT
82, 83 Carr Clifton
84 (left) Tom Bean
84 (right) John Elk
86 Carr Clifton
87 (both) Tom Bean
88 (left) John Elk
88 (right) Tom Bean
89 David Muench
90 Tom Bean
90, 91 Tom Bean
91 Zandria Muench Beraldo
92 James P. Rowan
93 (upper right) Dave G. Houser
93 (lower left) Carr Clifton

THE FAR NORTH
94, 95 Kim Heacox
96 Gerry Ellis/Ellis Nature Photography
97 Art Wolfe
98 (upper) Gerry Ellis/Ellis Nature Photography
98 (lower) Art Wolfe
99 (upper left) Carr Clifton
99 (lower right) Gerry Ellis/Ellis Nature Photography
100 (left) Kim Heacox
100 (right) Art Wolfe
101 (both) Carr Clifton
102 Jeff Foott
102, 103 Carr Clifton
103 Konrad Wothe/Ellis Nature Photography
104 (upper) Gerry Ellis/Ellis Nature Photography
104 (lower) Carr Clifton
104, 105 Kathy Bushue
105 Art Wolfe
106 Lee Foster
107 (both) Carr Clifton

MOLOKAI ISLAND
108, 109 Jeff Gnass
110 Jack Jeffrey/Photo Resource Hawaii
111 Bill Schildge/Pacific Stock
112 David Muench
112, 113 Jon K. Ogata/Photo Resource Hawaii
113 (upper left) Rita Ariyoshi
113 (lower right) Greg Vaughn/Pacific Stock
114 Rita Ariyoshi

114, 115 Richard Alexander Cooke III
115 Bill Schildge/Pacific Stock
116 (left) Marc Schechter/Photo Resource Hawaii
116 (lower right) Rita Ariyoshi
116, 117 Franco Salmoiraghi/Photo Resource Hawaii
118 Dave G. Houser
119 (lower left) Dave G. Houser
119 (upper right) Franco Salmoiraghi/Photo Resource Hawaii

GAZETTEER
120 Ric Ergenbright
121 (both) Gerry Ellis/Ellis Nature Photography
122 Steve Kaufman/Peter Arnold
123 (upper) Art Wolfe
123 (lower) John Elk
124 (lower left) James P. Rowan
124 (upper right) Gerry Ellis/Ellis Nature Photography
125 John Elk
126 (both) Julie Robinson
127 Julie Robinson
128 (upper right) John Elk
128 (lower left) James P. Rowan
129 Steve Bly/Dave G. Houser
130 Art Wolfe
131 (both) Tom Bean
132 Art Wolfe
133 (upper right) Gerry Ellis/Ellis Nature Photography
133 (lower left) Laurence Parent
134 (upper left) Tim Thompson
134 (lower right) Gerry Ellis/Ellis Nature Photography
135 Gerry Ellis/Ellis Nature Photography
136 Gerry Ellis/Ellis Nature Photography
137 (upper left) Laurence Parent
137 (lower right) Gerry Ellis/Ellis Nature Photography
138 (upper right) Kevin Schafer/Peter Arnold
138 (lower left) David Muench
139 Gerry Ellis/Ellis Nature Photography
140 Carr Clifton
141 (upper right) David Muench
141 (lower right) Andy Caulfield/Ellis Nature Photography

Back cover photography by Momatiuk/ Eastcott/Woodfin Camp & Associates

ACKNOWLEDGMENTS

Cartography: Dimension DPR Inc.; map resource base courtesy of the USGS; shaded relief courtesy of the USGS and Mountain High Maps® Copyright © 1993 Digital Wisdom, Inc.

The editors would also like to thank the following: Chantal Bilodeau, Lorraine Doré, Dominique Gagné, Pascale Hueber, and Valery Pigeon.

Edited by Belinda Gallagher
Designed by Oxprint Ltd

My first book of verse

Illustrated by Pamela Storey

Brimax • Newmarket • England

The Owl and the Pussy-cat

The Owl and the Pussy-cat went to sea

In a beautiful pea-green boat,

They took some honey, and plenty of money,

Wrapped up in a five-pound note.

The Owl looked up to the stars above,

And sang to a small guitar,

'O lovely Pussy! O Pussy, my love,

What a beautiful Pussy you are,

You are,

You are!

What a beautiful Pussy you are!'

Pussy said to the Owl, 'You elegant fowl!
How charmingly sweet you sing !
O let us be married! Too long we have tarried:
But what shall we do for a ring ?'
They sailed away, for a year and a day,
To the land where the Bong-tree grows
And there in a wood a Piggy-wig stood
With a ring at the end of his nose
His nose,
His nose,
With a ring at the end of his nose.

'Dear Pig, are you willing to sell for one shilling
Your ring?' Said the Piggy, 'I will.'
So they took it away, and were married next day
By the Turkey who lives on the hill.
They dined on mince, and slices of quince,
Which they ate with a runcible spoon;
And hand in hand, on the edge of the sand
They danced by the light of the moon,
The moon,
The moon,
They danced by the light of the moon.

The Butterfly's Ball

Come take up your hats, and away let us haste,
To the Butterfly's Ball, and the Grasshopper's Feast,
The trumpeter Gadfly has summoned the crew,
And the revels are now only waiting for you.

On the smooth-shaven grass by the side of a wood,
Beneath a broad oak which for ages has stood,
See the children of earth and the tenants of air,
For an evening's amusement together repair.

And there came the Beetle, so blind and so black,

Who carried the Emmet, his friend, on his back.

And there came the Gnat, and the Dragonfly too,

And all their relations, green, orange and blue.

And there came the Moth, with her plumage of down,

And the Hornet, with jacket of yellow and brown;

Who with him the Wasp, his companion, did bring,

But they promised that evening, to lay by their sting.

Then the sly little Dormouse crept out of his hole,
And led to the feast his blind cousin the Mole.
And the Snail, with his horns peeping out of his shell,
Came, fatigued with the distance, the length of an ell.

A mushroom their table, and on it was laid
A water-dock leaf, which a tablecloth made.
The viands were various, to each of their taste,
And the Bee brought the honey to sweeten the feast.

With steps most majestic the Snail did advance,
And he promised the gazers a minuet to dance;
But they all laughed so loud that he drew in his head,
And went in his own little chamber to bed.

Then, as evening gave way to the shadows of night,
Their watchman, the Glow-worm, came out with his light.
So home let us hasten, while yet we can see;
For no watchman is waiting for you and for me.

Little Raindrops

Oh, where do you come from,
You little drops of rain,
Pitter patter, pitter patter,
Down the window pane?

They won't let me walk,
And they won't let me play,
And they won't let me go
Out of doors at all today.

They put away my playthings
Because I broke them all,
And then they locked up all my bricks,
And took away my ball.

Tell me, little raindrops,
Is that the way you play,
Pitter patter, pitter patter,
All the rainy day?

They say I'm very naughty,
But I've nothing else to do
But sit here at the window;
I should like to play with you.

The little raindrops cannot speak,
But 'pitter patter pat'
Means, 'We can play on *this* side,
Why can't you play on *that*?'

Nonsenses

There was an Old Man with a beard,
Who said, 'It is just as I feared! –
Two owls and a hen,
Four larks and a wren,
Have all built their nests in my beard!'

There was an Old Lady of Chertsey,
Who made a remarkable curtsey;
She twirled round and round,
Till she sank underground,
Which distressed all the people of Chertsey.

There was an Old Man in a tree,

Who was horribly bored by a bee;

When they said, 'Does it buzz?'

He replied, 'Yes, it does!

It's a regular brute of a bee!'

There was an Old Man who said, 'How

Shall I flee from this horrible cow?

I will sit on this stile,

And continue to smile,

Which may soften the heart of that cow.'

There is a Young Lady, whose nose
Continually prospers and grows;
When it grew out of sight,
She exclaimed in a fright,
'Oh! Farewell to the end of my nose!'

There was an Old Man of Dumbree,
Who taught little owls to drink tea;
For he said, 'To eat mice,
Is not proper or nice,'
That amiable Man of Dumbree.

There was an Old Man who said, 'Hush!
I perceive a young bird in this bush!'
When they said, 'It is small?'
He replied, 'Not at all!
It is four times as big as the bush!'

There was an Old Person of Gretna,
Who rushed down the crater of Etna;
When they said, 'Is it hot?'
He replied, 'No, it's not!'
That mendacious Old Person of Gretna.

The Rainbow

Boats sail on the rivers,
And ships sail on the seas;
But clouds that sail, across the sky
Are prettier far than these.

There are bridges on the rivers,
As pretty as you please;
But the bow that bridges heaven,
And overtops the trees,
And builds a road from earth to sky,
Is prettier far than these.

The Frog

Be kind and tender to the Frog,
And do not call him names,
As 'Slimy skin', or 'Polly-wog',
Or likewise 'Ugly James',
Or 'Gape-a-grin', or 'Toad-gone-wrong',
Or 'Billy Bandy-knees':
The Frog is justly sensitive
To epithets like these.
No animal will more repay
A treatment kind and fair;
At least so lonely people say
Who keep a frog (and, by the way,
They are extremely rare).

The Land of Counterpane

When I was sick and lay a-bed,
I had two pillows at my head,
And all my toys beside me lay
To keep me happy all the day.

And sometimes for an hour or so
I watched my leaden soldiers go,
With different uniforms and drills,
Among the bedclothes, through the hills;

And sometimes sent my ships in fleets
All up and down among the sheets;
Or brought my trees and houses out,
And planted cities all about.

I was the giant great and still
That sits upon the pillow-hill,
And sees before him, dale and plain,
The pleasant land of counterpane.

The Fieldmouse

Where the acorn tumbles down,
Where the ash tree sheds its berry,
With your fur so soft and brown,
With your eye so round and merry
Scarcely moving the long grass,
Fieldmouse, I can see you pass.

Little thing, in what dark den,
Lie you all the winter sleeping?
Till warm weather comes again,
Then once more I see you peeping
Round about the tall tree roots,
Nibbling at their fallen fruits.

Fieldmouse, fieldmouse, do not go,
Where the farmer stacks his treasure,
Find the nut that falls below,
Eat the acorn at your pleasure,
But you must not steal the grain
He has stacked with so much pain.

Make your hole where mosses spring,
Underneath the tall oak's shadow,
Pretty, quiet, harmless thing,
Play about the sunny meadow.
Keep away from corn and house,
None will harm you, little mouse.

Minnie and Winnie

Minnie and Winnie
Slept in a shell.
Sleep, little ladies!
And they slept well.

Pink was the shell within,
Silver without;
Sounds of the great sea
Wandered about.

Sleep, little ladies,
Wake not soon!
Echo on echo
Dies to the moon.

Two bright stars
Peeped into the shell.
'What are they dreaming of?
Who can tell?'

Started a green linnet
Out of the croft;
Wake, little ladies,
The sun is aloft!

Measles in the Ark

The night it was horribly dark,

The measles broke out in the Ark;

Little Japheth, and Shem, and all the young Hams,

Were screaming at once for potatoes and clams.

And 'What shall I do,' said poor Mrs Noah,

'All alone by myself in this terrible shower?

I know what I'll do: I'll step down in the hold,

And wake up a lioness grim and old,

And tie her close to the children's door,

And give her a ginger-cake to roar

At the top of her voice for an hour or more;

And I'll tell the children to cease their din,

Or I'll let that grim old party in,

To stop their squeazles and likewise their measles.

She practised this with the greatest success:

She was everyone's grandmother, I guess.

Pleasant Changes

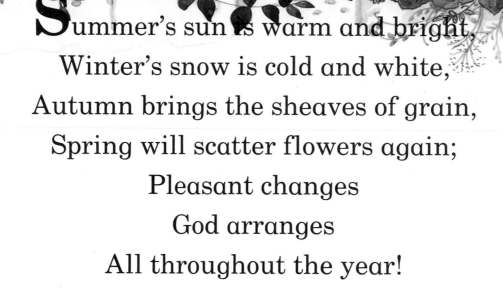

Summer's sun is warm and bright,
Winter's snow is cold and white,
Autumn brings the sheaves of grain,
Spring will scatter flowers again;
Pleasant changes
God arranges
All throughout the year!

First there's darkness then there's light,
First we've day and then we've night,
First we're hot and then we're cold,
First we're young and then we're old;
Are we knowing
Where we're going,
What we're doing here?

The Cow

The friendly cow, all red and white,
I love with all my heart:
She gives me cream with all her might,
To eat with apple tart.

She wanders lowing here and there,
And yet she cannot stray,
All in the pleasant open air,
The pleasant light of day;

And blown by all the winds that pass
And wet with all the showers,
She walks among the meadow grass
And eats the meadow flowers.

Two Little Kittens

Two little kittens, one stormy night,
Began to quarrel, and then to fight;
One had a mouse, the other had none,
And that's the way the quarrel begun.

'I'll have that mouse,' said the biggest cat;
'You'll have that mouse? We'll see about that!'
'I *will* have that mouse,' said the eldest son;
'You *shan't* have the mouse,' said the little one.

I told you before 'twas a stormy night
When these two little kittens began to fight;
The old woman seized her sweeping broom,
And swept the two kittens right out of the room.

The ground was covered with frost and snow,
And the two little kittens had nowhere to go;
So they laid them down on the mat at the door,
While the old woman finished sweeping the floor.

Then they crept in, as quiet as mice,
All wet with the snow, and as cold as ice,
For they found it was better, that stormy night,
To lie down and sleep than to quarrel and fight.

The Star

Twinkle, twinkle, little star,
How I wonder what you are!
Up above the world so high,
Like a diamond in the sky.

When the blazing sun has gone,
When he nothing shines upon,
Then you show your little light,
Twinkle, twinkle, all the night.

Then the traveller in the dark,
Thanks you for your tiny spark,
He could not see which way to go,
If you did not twinkle so.

In the dark blue sky you keep,
And often through my curtains peep,
For you never shut your eye,
Till the sun is in the sky.

As your bright and tiny spark,
Lights the traveller in the dark –
Though I know not what you are,
Twinkle, twinkle, little star.

Tumbling

In jumping and tumbling
We spend the whole day,
Till night by arriving
Has finished our play.

What then? One and all,
There's no more to be said,
As we tumble all day,
So we tumble to bed.